Beethoven

Beethoven

A Political Artist in Revolutionary Times

WILLIAM KINDERMAN

THE UNIVERSITY OF CHICAGO PRESS / CHICAGO AND LONDON

The University of Chicago Press, Chicago 60637
The University of Chicago Press, Ltd., London
© 2020 by The University of Chicago
All rights reserved. No part of this book may be used or reproduced
in any manner whatsoever without written permission, except
in the case of brief quotations in critical articles and reviews. For
more information, contact the University of Chicago Press,
1427 E. 60th St., Chicago, IL 60637.
Published 2020
Printed in the United States of America

29 28 27 26 25 24 23 22 21 20   1 2 3 4 5

ISBN-13: 978-0-226-66905-2 (cloth)
ISBN-13: 978-0-226-66919-9 (e-book)
DOI: https://doi.org/10.7208/chicago/9780226669199.001.0001

Library of Congress Cataloging-in-Publication Data

Names: Kinderman, William, author.
Title: Beethoven : a political artist in revolutionary times /
    William Kinderman.
Description: Chicago : The University of Chicago Press, 2020. |
    Includes bibliographical references and index.
Identifiers: LCCN 2020032956 | ISBN 9780226669052 (cloth) |
    ISBN 9780226669199 (e-book)
Subjects: LCSH: Beethoven, Ludwig van, 1770—1827—Criticism
    and interpretation. | Beethoven, Ludwig van, 1770—1827—
    Political and social views.
Classification: LCC ML410.B42 K606 2020 | DDC 780.92 [B]—dc23
LC record available at https://lccn.loc.gov/2020032956

This paper meets the requirements of ANSI/NISO Z39.48–1992
(Permanence of Paper).

For Daniel and Laura,
Anna and Marie

Contents

Preface

Beethoven has long been regarded as among the greatest of composers, but it has been overlooked that he was also among the most political of artists. He lived through some of the most turbulent events in European history: the French Revolution, the Reign of Terror, the rise and fall of Napoleon Bonaparte, the battles of Wagram and Leipzig, the Congress of Vienna, and the ensuing era of political repression. He depended on the generous support of aristocratic sponsors, yet smashed the bust of Prince Lichnowsky in 1806 and kept a chilly distance from the Austrian emperor Franz. Beethoven was never reconciled with the absolutist politics of the Napoleonic period or its aftermath in the Metternich regime that held power in Austria until after the composer's death in 1827.

Two centuries later, Beethoven's musical legacy retains an astonishing cultural presence. While we mark and move beyond the composer's anniversary year 2020, a fresh investigation of the political importance of Beethoven's artistic legacy seems timely. The political narratives that sustain his art contribute to its remarkable resilience. The background has to do with events much bigger than any individual. Coming of age in the progressive environment in Bonn, Beethoven enrolled in the recently founded Bonn University in 1789, just as revolution broke out in nearby France. Pursuing his musical career from 1792 in Vienna, he encountered an artistically rich yet politically reactionary situation. His risky enthusiasm for Napoleon as First Consul of the French Republic soon cooled, yet Beethoven remained fascinated by Bonaparte, and saw himself as a competitor in the cultural sphere, a "Generalissimo" in the realm of tones. In later years, as his access to acoustic sounds was silenced through deafness, Beethoven achieved his most enduring impact through works like the Ninth Symphony, whose origins reach back to the period of the composer's youth at Bonn.

Like Mozart, Beethoven was a skilled improviser, for whom capricious spontaneity, dramatic surprise, and aesthetic risk-taking were important. Beethoven aimed to communicate teeming emotions in the here and now. The fervor of the moment, the snapshot of intense human feeling, shows every sign of being eternal. When the heroine Leonore hurls the words "First kill his wife!" at villainous Pizarro, or the baritone calms symphonic turbulence in the Ninth Symphony by uttering "Not these tones," these gestures carry a conviction pointing beyond their immediate context, a meaning rich in implications.

How could a composer imagine "effigies of the ideal" (in Friedrich Schiller's words) that model freedoms and social reforms, goals unlikely to be achieved in the real world, whether in the autocratic German states or the chaotic French Republic of Beethoven's time, or under current conditions today? How could the Fifth Symphony help galvanize resistance to fascism, and the Sixth become a recent focus for the environmental movement?

The globalization of the world is bringing fresh recognition to this music. Much has changed since Adrian Leverkühn, the Faustian fictional protagonist of Thomas Mann's *Doktor Faustus*, sought to revoke the promise of Beethoven's Ninth. Writing in California in exile from Hitler's tyranny, Mann set his despairing message against the luminous legacy of Beethoven's last symphony. As we shall see, Beethoven already anticipated this dystopian shadow as part of his project of fashioning affirmative symbols, of which the *Ode of Joy* is the most celebrated of all. Since then, the dream of the Ninth has encircled the globe, from massive ritual enactments in Japan to a flash mob from Sabadell, Catalonia, which has so far captured more than 90 million YouTube viewings. This exciting open-ended trajectory is an outcome of our tale, a very human story touched by pain and sacrifice, fortitude and courage.

Beethoven

A Tale of Two Cities: Bonn to Vienna

"Something revolutionary lurks in the music!"

This response to Beethoven allegedly stems from the Austrian monarch who reigned during the entire period of the composer's residence at Vienna from 1792 until 1827. Emperor Franz sensed something in Beethoven's music that he found suspicious and that aroused his distrust. The original German formulation, "Es steckt was revolutionäres in der Musik!," points to a quality lodged in the music that disquieted him.

The emperor was alert to such resonances. Emperor Franz was the nephew of Marie Antoinette, an Austrian archduchess before she became queen of France as the spouse of King Louis XVI. By 1793, four years after the outbreak of the French Revolution and soon after Beethoven's arrival in Vienna, Louis XVI and Marie Antoinette had been imprisoned and then decapitated by guillotine at Paris. Following these events, the utmost priority for Emperor Franz during his reign was to prevent any such revolution in Austria.

With stubborn tenacity, Franz eventually outlasted his more brilliant French political rival, Napoleon Bonaparte. Unlike the hereditary Austrian emperors, Bonaparte came from modest circumstances and rose through the ranks during the decade of upheaval following the French Revolution in 1789. Achieving prominence through his remarkable success as a military commander, Napoleon became First Consul of the French Republic in 1799.

At that time, Beethoven fervently hoped that the French leader would exert a positive political and cultural influence. No such sanguine expectations were realistic in Austria. Unlike his predecessor Emperor Joseph II during the 1780s, Emperor Franz was not a progressive leader, and he felt threatened by Napoleon's social and political reforms. It has been observed that by 1794, "Franz's dread of 'democracy' became pathological, and so did his animosity to change of any sort." Another historian described how the emperor "detected conspiracy everywhere" as his anxieties about revolution turned into "institutionalized paranoia."

This political background sets the scene for our exploration of the political convictions of Ludwig van Beethoven. The young composer imbibed the spirit of enlightened movements of the 1780s—Immanuel Kant's critiques, liberal reforms, cultural activism—but experienced the shocks and polarization that followed the outbreak of the French Revolution in 1789. It is remarkable that the legacy of a musician should retain so much potency in 2020, a quarter millennium after his birth. This is explained partly from the universality of the musical language, enabling for instance the "Joy" theme of the Ninth Symphony to become anthem of the European Union while Friedrich Schiller's words were never officially adopted. Another factor is the increased polarization of politics in the twenty-first century. Strange parallels link Beethoven's age with our own. Many who had welcomed the French Revolution soon became disillusioned, just as the collapse of the Soviet empire beginning in 1989 encouraged false optimism about an imminent age of democracy.

To explore Beethoven's world is to confront tensions and contradictions: the largely unsuccessful reforms of enlightened despotism under Joseph II in Austria and the precarious allure of Revolutionary France; the patchwork German governments Beethoven knew as a youth and the autocratic Habsburg Monarchy; the Franco-German boundary region on the Rhine and the capital of the sprawling polyglot empire on the Danube. Out of the bewildering complexity of historical conditions, the artist shapes visions of the imagination. It is exciting to come to grips with a composer's effort to respond to the rich disorder of a turbulent period. Whereas Napoleon Bonaparte's rise and fall on the world stage has sunk into historical consciousness, Beethoven's resonant legacy endures undiminished, even as its potential remains untapped. An understanding and appreciation benefits from an awareness of context. As we shall see, the contrast-laden narratives of Beethoven's works convey much more than a neutral play of sounds.

What was it like for Beethoven as a sixteen-year-old court musician to travel from Bonn to Vienna for three months in 1787? What were his experiences when enrolled as a student at the University of Bonn in the revolutionary year 1789? How did his upbringing in the Rhineland at a pivotal time shape his attitudes toward aesthetics and politics? What roles did his musical predecessors Wolfgang Amadeus Mozart and Joseph Haydn play in his evolving artistic path?

The reign of Emperor Joseph II during the 1780s brought a wave of rationalistic reforms imposed from above, a "white revolution" of enlightened despotism. Joseph claimed that the French revolutionaries in 1789 were attempting what he had already tried to bring about. He declared in 1783 that he had "weakened . . . prejudices and deep-rooted habits by means of Enlightenment, and combated them with arguments." He curbed the clergy's power, promoted religious toleration, asserted human equality, and abolished personal serfdom and many privileges of nobles, courts, clergy, guilds, and towns. Joseph granted personal audiences to untold thousands of petitioners. As ruler, he endorsed Kant's principle of Enlightenment as "man's release from his self-imposed tutelage." He improved elementary education, built hospitals, and sought to counter obscurantism and religious superstitions.

Such a social revolution proved vulnerable, stemming as it did from a hereditary ruler surrounded by ministers who were hereditary aristocrats. The virtues and pitfalls of Joseph's approach are illustrated by his support of Mozart's opera *The Marriage of Figaro*. The emperor was knowledgeable about music, and had already supported Mozart's German opera *The Abduction from the Seraglio* in 1782. Four years later, Mozart's collaboration with librettist Lorenzo da Ponte adapted as an Italian opera the second play of Pierre-Augustin Caron de Beaumarchais's trilogy, which had caused a sensation in Paris when performed in 1784, since it was seen as assaulting noble rights and social inequality. In 1785, Joseph himself denied permission for performance of the play in Vienna. A critic in the *Realzeitung* began his review of Mozart's *Figaro* by writing that "nowadays what is not allowed to be spoken is sung." Da Ponte removed some of Beaumarchais's revolutionary cheek, but added more of his own. Although the enlightened emperor enabled the opera, the fallout from the aristocratic community damaged Mozart's prospects. The subscription list for his instrumental concerts supported by nobility of the first rank—princes, counts, and barons—eroded swiftly in response to the performances of *Figaro* based on Beaumarchais's banned play critiquing the aristocracy. There is a parallel between Mozart's difficulties beginning in 1786 and the political problems that beset the increasingly isolated emperor, many of whose reforms were reversed after his death in 1790. Yet this exceptional decade, when power sought to serve the populace, was soon to see another Mozart opera with three levels of society put on stage, each with its own musical accompaniment, joined in the same ballroom at the invitation of an aristocratic host, who greets them all in the name of freedom.

Beethoven visited Vienna for the first time from January to April 1787. When he arrived, Mozart was being feted in Prague, where *Figaro* was immensely successful, leading to the commission for *Don Giovanni*, which would be premiered there in October 1787. Mozart was then residing in handsome lodgings in Vienna, but would soon move out of the city center because of financial pressures. The several weeks from Mozart's return on 12 February until Beethoven's departure provided ample occasion for a meeting of the two composers, facilitated by the aristocratic connections that had enabled the young musician's visit. Beethoven reportedly heard Mozart play; anecdotal reports of Beethoven's improvising for Mozart are plausible if unconfirmed. Beethoven's engagement with *Don Giovanni* is reflected in various works from the *Moonlight* Sonata to the *Diabelli* Variations, and this opera preoccupied Mozart at the time they would have met.

Haydn, on the other hand, still resided at that time in Eisenstadt in isolated servitude to the Esterházy court. Only after the death of his patron Prince Nikolaus in 1790 did he achieve personal freedom and considerable wealth through his sojourns in England. In 1785, a London newspaper suggested that Haydn, a "Shakespeare of music," be kidnapped and taken to England in the cause of freedom: "Would it not be an achievement equal to a pilgrimage, for some aspiring youths to rescue him from his fortune and transplant him to Great Britain, the country for which his music seems to be made?" The Habsburg Monarchy then possessed far-flung territorial holdings and areas of influence, some geographically remote from Vienna. Since Bonn lay on his route of travel, Joseph Haydn stopped there on his way from Vienna to London in December 1790 and again on his return trip from Britain. During that return journey in July 1792, the young Beethoven met Haydn and evidently showed him his single most impressive composition to date: his homage to the recently deceased Austrian monarch, the *Cantata on the Death of Joseph II*.

If the lives of the celebrated musical triumvirate Haydn-Mozart-Beethoven neatly straddle the French Revolution, the cataclysmic impact of that political event impacted most strongly on the works of the youngest of these composers. The youthful Beethoven imbibed the spirit of the Enlightenment. His teachers and mentors at Bonn included persons closely associated with activist organizations of the era: the Freemasons, the Illuminists, and the *Lesegesellschaft* (Literary Society). Soon after the revolutionary outbreak in France, Beethoven's move to Vienna brought him into a culturally rich environment whose politics were then undergoing a reactionary shift. The city where Mozart settled in 1781 and Haydn in 1790 became Beethoven's adopted home in 1792, as conflict escalated and war ensued between Revolutionary France and the absolutist states like Austria that viewed the developments in France with trepidation. The young composer's diary records how during his journey to Austria he paid a tip to the carriage driver who sped through the converging lines of Hessian troops marching toward the French positions.

This eventful historical background is essential to understanding the turbulent political world Beethoven knew, and the ways his music embodies cultural values. The hopes and unfulfilled promises of the French Revolution loom large over Beethoven's creative project. Beethoven's skepticism about Emperor Franz and his ambivalence toward Napoleon reflected his response to far-reaching issues. The composer's unwavering enthusiasm for the principles of the French Revolution coexisted with a disdain for repressive absolutist rule. Key aspects of his aesthetic attitudes and the content of his music are inseparable from this context. Artworks need not mirror external conditions, but can embody a competing set of values. As we shall see, the portrayal of heroism in the *Eroica* Symphony draws on a mythic context that exposes Bonaparte's *failure* to achieve heroic stature. The idea of the transformative work of art as promoted by fellow artists including Friedrich Schiller, Johann Wolfgang von Goethe, and Jean Paul Richter exerted deep influence on Beethoven's creativity.

Documents from Beethoven's last years record his continued reflections about political issues and his frequent disappointment with public leaders. In September 1825 the deaf composer spoke with his Paris publisher Moritz Schlesinger, who wrote comments into a conversation notebook. Schlesinger states that "If Napoleon had remained First Consul instead of becoming an insatiable world conqueror, he would have been one of the greatest of living men." Beethoven's answer is unrecorded, but Schlesinger's reply, "Der Ehrgeiz" ("ambition"), surely identifies the character flaw that in Beethoven's view disqualified Napoleon from true heroism. In the continuation of the conversation, Schlesinger quips about the Austrian emperor Franz that "the Emperor, however, is a stupid beast. He says: I don't need learned people, I just want good citizens."

Another source reflecting Beethoven's conflicted attitude toward Napoleon stems from Johann Doležalek from February

1827, when the composer was on his deathbed. After complaining about the hereditary French royal house of the Bourbons, Beethoven said about Napoleon that "in dem Scheisskerl habe ich mich geirrt" ("with the shithead I was mistaken").

Beethoven's confession of having invested false hopes in Napoleon is consistent with various sources that collectively cast his career and artistic achievements in a fresh light. The composer was far from indifferent to politics. His attraction to Friedrich Schiller's works and ideas about the affirmative artwork embodying resistance or an "effigy of the ideal" hold outstanding importance. Beethoven's choice of a gritty real-life drama from the Reign of Terror in France as the subject of his opera *Fidelio* is a political theme of striking relevance for us today. Extraordinary is the worldwide impact of Beethoven's last symphony with its choral setting of Schiller's "Ode to Joy," a long-standing preoccupation of the composer about which he nevertheless entertained some doubts, as his manuscripts reveal.

To be sure, some recent commentators have been inclined to develop more skeptical, alternative views about Beethoven's cultural and political stature. One approach involves rehabilitating the composer's most propagandistic pieces, such as the ceremonial cantata *The Glorious Moment* written for the Congress of Vienna. Another revisionist strategy associates the evolution of Beethoven's later musical style with the reactionary trend in Austrian politics during the era of Metternich. A more radical approach doubts the value of freedom itself, purporting to unmask autonomy as void or as disguised authority. Reductionistic views may offer the allure of novelty or appearance of cleverness at the cost of aesthetic substance and historical accuracy. More promising is to enlarge our horizon of engagement as we seek a creative potential that goes beyond conventional modes of understanding.

During the Congress of Vienna period around 1814, when Beethoven garnered the most public attention and richest financial rewards he was ever to receive, the composer declared that rather than monarchs and monarchies, he much preferred "the empire of the mind, and regard[ed] it as the highest of all spiri-

tual and worldly monarchies." The essay that follows explores this
artistic "empire of the mind or spirit" against the colorful counterpoint of Beethoven's life.

During Beethoven's formative youth, the Rhineland was a far from
placid setting. The political winds blowing at Bonn differed radically from the environment he was to encounter in Austria. As
a young court musician, Beethoven benefited from a lucky con-
fluence of stimulating developments. Since the Catholic Elector,
or *Kurfürst*, at Bonn from 1784 was Maximilian Franz, youngest
brother of Emperor Joseph II, close links connected the small city
on the Rhine with the distant capital on the Danube, ten times
its size. Max Franz continued the reforms pursued by his predecessor, the Elector Maximilian Friedrich, reforms that paralleled
those of his brother Joseph II in Vienna. The clerics were curbed;
musical, literary, and theatrical institutions were reorganized and
supported. In 1785 the Bonn Academy was elevated to the rank of
a university. Johannes Neeb was engaged to teach Kantian philosophy, and men like the later revolutionary Eulogius Schneider
and Friedrich Schiller's friend Bartholomäus Ludwig Fischenich
lectured on Greek literature, aesthetics, ethics, and law.

During the 1780s Bonn became a center of the Enlightenment,
that fragile yet immensely productive movement whose liberal
reforms were imposed from above, not in response to revolutionary strivings of the suppressed classes. Bonn might have become
another Weimar except for the upheavals brought about through
the French occupation, which was to sweep away the government
of Max Franz in 1794, less than two years after Beethoven's departure. But no one could have anticipated these events a few years
earlier.

As the eldest surviving son of an alcoholic father and a beloved
mother who had died already in 1787, the young Beethoven sought
a psychological path toward compensation and overachievement.
The tyrannical, abusive behavior of Beethoven's father presumably
hardened his son's capacity for resistance. Beethoven's troubled
relationship with his father and early loss of his mother opened

a void that was filled by friends and role models, art and ideas. By 1784, through his intimate friend Franz Gerhard Wegeler, Beethoven came into the orbit of the cultured von Breuning family. Through the von Breunings, he became acquainted with German literature and poetry. During the summers, he presumably spent time at the von Breuning estate at Kerpen, west of Cologne. The widow Helena von Breuning assumed a protective, motherly attitude toward Beethoven. Franz Wegeler pursued medical studies in Vienna during the 1780s, and helped pave the way for Beethoven's resettlement in the Austrian capital. Years later, when plagued by his incurable symptoms of deafness, Beethoven confided his dilemma to Wegeler.

An important role model was the composer and court organist Christian Gottlob Neefe, a Protestant from Saxony who had studied in Leipzig. Neefe was an avid admirer of J. S. Bach eager to pass on the legacy. Beethoven's early acquaintance with the music of C. P. E. Bach, Haydn, and Mozart also owed much to Neefe. Among Neefe's own larger compositions were twelve imposing settings of odes by Friedrich Gottlieb Klopstock. In 1782, Neefe set another Klopstock ode, *Dem Unendlichen* (*To the Infinite One*), for four choral voices and orchestra. This piece forms part of the context out of which was to emerge Beethoven's weighty *Cantata on the Death of Joseph II* written eight years later, in 1790.

Neefe was a freemason who later assumed a role in the *Orden der Illuminaten* and still later in the *Lesegesellschaft* (Literary Society), organizations closely tied to the Enlightenment. Once the Freemasons' Lodge founded at Bonn in 1776 disappeared in response to Empress Maria Theresia's suppression of the order, its role was largely filled during the 1780s by the two aforementioned societies. The Bonn chapter of the *Orden der Illuminaten*, founded in 1781, included among its members many who stood close to Beethoven, including the horn player (later a publisher) Nikolaus Simrock, and Franz Ries, violinist and father of Beethoven's student and friend Ferdinand Ries. Neefe was a leader of the group. When in 1785 the *Orden der Illuminaten* was suppressed, the Bonn circle continued their activities in the *Lesegesellschaft*. Many key players surrounding Beethoven during his last years in Bonn were members, including Count Ferdinand Waldstein, who facilitated crucial contacts for Beethoven in Vienna and who wrote in the young composer's album that "with the help of assiduous labor you shall receive *Mozart's spirit from Haydn's hands...*" One measure of its importance for Beethoven is the fact that it commissioned the *Joseph* Cantata.

Another crucial yet underestimated figure in Beethoven's formative education was the "secular priest" Eulogius Schneider. Schneider took to heart the principle of *Volksaufklärung*—the idea that the tenets of the Enlightenment required public promotion, thereby advancing freedom of thought, human rights, the overcoming of an aristocratic class, and rejection of religious authority. Schneider vigorously embraced the ideals of the French Revolution—*liberté, égalité, fraternité*—and sought to put these into practice. However, at each station of his career, Schneider's passionate advocacy of Enlightenment principles caused him to transgress the limits of convention and authority in ways that caused conflict.

In 1789, on the eve of the Revolution, Schneider was appointed as professor of aesthetics and fine arts at the University of Bonn. Concurrently, Schiller assumed a professorship in history at the University of Jena. This year of revolution was when Beethoven, a generation younger than these men, enrolled as a student at the University of Bonn. The timing served to impress on the young composer how ideas could exert real impact on human destiny. Of all his instructors, Schneider was the one whose career soon displayed most vividly the potential but also the perils of political action.

Schneider collected many of his writings into a volume entitled *Gedichte* (*Poems*) published in 1790; the court musician (*Hofmusikus*) "Bethoven" appears in the list of subscribers (figs. 1 and 2). Ample evidence testifies to Schneider's importance to Beethoven at this time. As a member of the *Lesegesellschaft*, it was Schneider who proposed that the death of Emperor Joseph II be commemorated by a musical work, the initiative that enabled the *Joseph* Cantata. Schneider himself wrote a poetic elegy on the death of Joseph II, which was printed in his *Gedichte*. Some parts of the cantata's text reflect Schneider's influence, such as the phrase "Ungeheuer des Fanatismus" ("monster of fanaticism"). His interest in contemporary poets such as Klopstock and Christian Fürchtegott Gellert corresponded to Beethoven's. Schneider was a gifted speaker, whose passionate rhetorical flair surely left its mark on the youthful composer. Most influential, perhaps, would have been Schneider's sharp critique of Catholic ritual and orthodoxy in association with his deistic or pantheistic convictions.

Schneider's poem "To Theology" ("an die Theologie") is as follows (rendered in free rhyme):

Farewell Theology!
You have long tormented me,
with old wives' tales that deceived
and that you thought I believed
Feed whomever you wish with fluff
Set yourself forth as a fake bluff
Farewell! From you I'm freed
through a rift as wide as eternity.

Lebe wohl Theologie!
Lange hast du mich gequälet,
Weibermärchen mir erzählet,
Und gedacht, ich glaubte sie.
Speise, wen du willst, mit Luft,
Hülle dich in falschen Schimmer:
Lebe wohl! Uns trennt auf immer
Eine himmelweite Kluft.

whereas Schneider writes about nature as follows:

Sacred Mother Nature!
Do you serve as stepmother to the
Catholic German lands? No! Whoever claims

GEDICHTE

VON

EULOGIUS SCHNEIDER.

Mit dem Portrait des Verfaffers.

FRANKFURT,
in Commiffion der Andräifchen Buchhandlung,
1790.

1.1 *Gedichte (Poems)* by Eulogius Schneider, title page. Private collection of Luigi Bellofatto.

this is ungrateful, bringing offense to you . . .
Sacred Mother Nature!

Heilige Mutter Natur!
Bist du den stiefmütterlich mit

14

Bingen. Hr D. Gentil, Stadtpf.
Blumenthal. Hr Hofmann, Amtsverwalter.
Bonn. Hr Aleff, Stud.— Hr Amecke, Stud.
Hr Angelbis.—Hr Anſchel,Stud.—Hr Arnds,
Hofr.— Hr Averdonk, Canon. in Ehrenſtein.
Hr Bacciochi — Hr Sim. Baruch.— Hr Baſch,
Bürgerm.— Hr Becker, Prof.— Hr de Berg-
hes, Refer.— Hr von Bersword, kurköln.
geh.Rath.— Hr van Bethoven, Hofmuſ.— Hr
Engelb. Biegeleben. — Hr von Blum, Rath.
Hr Boosfeld, Hofkammerr.— Hr von Brau-
mann, Stud.— Hr von Breuning, kurk. geh.
Rath.— Hr von Breuning, geiſtl. Rath.— Hr
von Breuning, Stud. — Hr Caramé, Stud.
Hr Chriſt. Stud.—Frau von Coels.— Hr Cor-

1.2 Page of the *Gedichte* showing Beethoven as subscriber
(Mr. van Be[e]thoven, Court Musician). Private collection of Luigi Bellofatto.

dem katholischen Deutschlande umgegangen? Nein! Wer dies
behauptet, der
ist ein Undankbarer, ein Lästerer wider dich . . .
Heilige Mutter Natur!

Beethoven's disinclination to embrace dogma or attend church
services and his passionate nature-worship are well documented.
He frequently moved from Vienna to rural villages during the summer months, a conspicuous pattern beginning with his six-month
stay at Heiligenstadt in 1802. The landscape near Heiligenstadt
likely reminded him of the Rhineland. The position of Bonn in
relation to the Rhine and the Seven Hills (*Siebengebirge*) is parallel
to that of Vienna on the Danube with its Kahlenberg and Leopoldberg, even if Bonn lies on the opposite side down the river from
these imposing hills.

Due to his outspoken views and sharp attacks on Catholicism,
Eulogius Schneider was dismissed from his professorship in Bonn
in 1791 but found a new base in nearby Strasbourg, France, where

1.3 Eulogius Schneider, portrait, from his *Gedichte*.
Private collection of Luigi Bellofatto.

he rapidly assumed prominence in the revolutionary regime. Schneider led a radical overthrow of the mayor, Philippe Friedrich Dietrich, and was the first to translate the *Marseillaise* for the predominantly German-speaking Alsatian populace in 1792. Around the same time, a keyboard instrument maker in Paris, Tobias Schmidt, devised a prototype of the beheading machine soon to be put into action; his patent for the guillotine became far more profitable than was his sale of musical instruments. Ironically, although Schneider was instrumental in depicting Joseph II as a slayer of the "monster of fanaticism" in Beethoven's *Joseph Cantata*, his own fierce political passions led him to transgres-

1.4 Execution of Schneider on the guillotine on 1 April 1794.
Historical Museum, Strasbourg, France. Wikimedia Commons.

sions in his role as *accusateur public* during the Reign of Terror in 1793, when he sent thirty persons to the guillotine. Soon thereafter, Schneider himself was arrested under the regime of Maximilien Robespierre, and he was beheaded at Paris in April 1794 (figs. 1.3 and 1.4). Beethoven did not forget Schneider in later years, as a conversation-book entry from 1819 shows.

During these post-Revolutionary years in the Rhineland, careers and lives could rest on a knife's edge. Another such example is Georg Forster, the noted naturalist, ethnologist, and travel author who accompanied his father Johann Forster on James Cook's second voyage around the world. His book, which appeared in German as *Reise um die Welt* in 1780, made him famous, and influenced Goethe, Johann Gottfried von Herder, and Alexander von Humboldt. In a diary he kept starting in 1812, Beethoven copied extracts from Forster's German translation of the play *Shakuntala* by the fifth-century Sanskrit dramatist Kālidāsa as well as other ancient Indian sources. The same translation of *Shakuntala* had captivated Schiller in the 1790s, who wrote that "In the whole world of Greek antiquity there is no poetical representation of beautiful love that approaches it even from a distance." Forster was a prominent Freemason and possibly an Illuminist, and became university librarian at Mainz in 1788, preceding the outbreak of the revolution and the French control of this part of the Rhineland in 1792. Embracing the French Revolutionary ideals of *liberté, égalité, fraternité*, Forster joined those eager to establish a German republic on the French model, becoming a delegate to Paris for the Mainz Republic in 1793. The French National Convention granted the accession of this Rhenish-German Free State to France on 30 March, one year before Eulogius Schneider was guillotined. Unfortunately for Forster, Austrian and Prussian coalition forces soon reconquered the territory of the Mainz Republic. Declared a traitor, Forster died in isolation in Paris in early 1794.

In their collaborative collection of satirical epigrams from 1797 entitled *Xenien*, Goethe and Schiller took aim at both Schneider and Forster. No. 337, titled "Unhappy Haste," parodying Odysseus's luckless companion Elpenor, critiques Schneider's relentless ambition and precipitous downfall:

Oh, how they screamed freedom
and I wanted equality to come swiftly
and since I thought the steps too long
I leapt from the roof.

Ach, wie die Freiheit schrien
und Gleichheit,
geschwind wollt' ich folgen,

und weil die Trepp'
mir zu lang däuhte,
so sprang ich vom Dach.

Yet another illustration of the precarious post-Revolutionary conditions stems from Beethoven's close friend Franz Wegeler. When, in his role as rector of the University of Bonn and as a trained physician, Wegeler prohibited contact of the students with infected French soldiers to prevent the spread of contagious disease during the French occupation, an article in the Paris newspaper *Moniteur* accused him of being a fanatical enemy of the French Republic. As Wegeler himself put it, "at that time the following of Robespierre was hardly less poisonous than his own head had been, and it was imperative to save my own," so he prudently followed Beethoven to Vienna in October 1794.

How can the creative artist inspired by political ideals find a way forward amid polarized ideologies and the strife of recurrent warfare? For Beethoven, no artist reflected persuasive political convictions tempered by prudence as much as did Friedrich Schiller. Schiller's ideas about aesthetic education—affirming freedom through artistic creativity—exerted a profound influence. A review of Schiller's impact on Beethoven at Bonn alerts us to the ways contemporary drama and literature shaped the young composer's beliefs and aroused his desire to collaborate, as he responded in his own musical works to contemporary writers and thinkers.

Schiller did not express a strong affirmation of the revolution in France. Nevertheless, the French National Assembly of 1792, responding to the revolutionary reputation of his early drama *Die Räuber* (*The Robbers*) from 1781, made Schiller ("Monsieur Gille") an honorary citizen of the republic. This was ironic, inasmuch as *The Robbers* is a ruthless exposition of the logic of possessive individualism; the idealist Karl Moor, head of the robbers, does not share power but indulges in violent criminal acts following the principle that the end justifies the means; Schiller once described him as a monster ("Ungeheuer"). *The Robbers* is not a drama of rebellion as such but criticizes the ethos of the rebels and over-weening ambition of Karl Moor.

Schiller's *Don Carlos*, completed by 1787 before his move to Jena and later Weimar, conveys how individual cultivation of the self should take precedence over revolutionary idealism. This work surfaces conspicuously in entries in the album Beethoven kept at Bonn and in other sources, including two quotations that Beethoven cited to friends during the 1790s:

> I am not wicked—Hot blood is my fault—my crime is that I am young. I am not wicked, truly not wicked. Even though wildly surging emotions may betray my heart, yet my heart is good. [act 2, scene 2]

> Truth exists for the wise,
> Beauty for the feeling heart.
> They belong to each other. [act 4, scene 21]

The first quotation stems from the distraught Carlos, whose beloved has married his father, King Philipp. The second citation, from the Marquis de Posa directed to Queen Elisabeth of Valois, advocates a union of thought and feeling, head and heart, a conviction endorsed by Schiller and Beethoven alike. Yet another entry in Beethoven's farewell album is drawn from the same scene, capturing a thought from Posa spoken shortly before his self-willed sacrificial death, a thought directed to Carlos and to posterity:

> Tell him, in manhood, he must still revere
> the dreams of early youth, not expose the heart
> of heaven's all-tender flower to canker-worms
> of boasted reason,—nor be led astray
> when, by the wisdom of the dust, he hears
> enthusiasm, heavenly-born, blasphemed.

In January 1793, a few weeks after Beethoven's arrival in Vienna, Schiller's friend Bartholomäus Ludwig Fischenich reported from

Bonn to Schiller's wife that the young composer intended a composition based on another well-known work of the poet, an ode from the time when *Don Carlos* was written. Fischenich described Beethoven as "a young man of this place whose musical talents are universally praised and whom the Elector has sent to Haydn in Vienna," and continued that

> He proposes also to compose Schiller's "Freude," and indeed strophe by strophe. I expect something perfect, for as far as I know him he is wholly devoted to the great and the sublime.

Beethoven's youthful goal of setting Schiller's "An die Freude" ("To Joy") was fulfilled in the Ninth Symphony only decades later. Its eventual completion shows that he indeed "continued to revere the dreams of early youth" while seeking "the great and the sublime" and was not "led astray" when hearing "enthusiasm, heavenly-born, blasphemed." Schiller himself, in a letter from 1800 to his friend and patron Christian Gottfried Körner, had distanced himself from "An die Freude," describing it as "detached from reality" and "of value perhaps for us two, but not for the world, nor for the art of poetry." How astonished he would have been to realize that through Beethoven's music, his poem encircled the world, embracing millions in unprecedented ways!

Beethoven's youthful engagement with literature from his time is also reflected in his surviving sketch for a musical setting of Mephistopheles's "Flohlied" ("Song of the Flea"), a key episode of the action in the Auerbach's Cellar scene of Goethe's *Faust*. It is striking that the young composer had gained access to Goethe's *Faust, ein Fragment*, soon after its publication in 1790 and responded to it musically, although a definitive completion of his setting waited until 1809. Auerbach's Cellar is at once a real place in Leipzig and a setting for fictional events, blending life and art. It corresponds to the *Zehrgarten* locale on the Markplatz at Bonn that was a favorite social meeting place during Beethoven's youth as well as to those inns and wine cellars where the composer consorted with friends during later years in Vienna. Goethe frequented Auerbach's Cellar during 1765–1768 when he was a student, which lends an autobiographical resonance to this highly political song with its sharp critique of favoritism and nepotism.

In *Faust*, Mephisto's "Flea Song" is one of a handful of bawdy drinking songs in Auerbach's Cellar. Mephisto's song begins "There was once a king who had a big flea" and uses an emphatic shouting chorus to reinforce the last lines aimed at the annoying parasite(s):

But we snap and smother
At once, if someone bites.

Wir knicken und ersticken
Doch gleich, wenn einer sticht.

The closing couplet—sung by the whole group of revelers—encapsulates the political meaning. For the worthless flea is the king's special favorite, who is dressed up and accorded undeserved honors. The flea rises to the rank of minister, whereupon all his flea relations become courtiers, rich and great, immune from all critique. From the protected distance of Auerbach's Cellar, however, the drinkers need not conceal their disdain. We shall return in chapter six to this song, which had gained contextual meaning by the time it appeared in print in 1810 and remains relevant to the degraded politics of our present day.

Choral singing of a loftier kind is found in Beethoven's setting of "Der freier Mann" ("The Free Man"), a song dating from his last years at Bonn that was later used by the Freemasons, as Wegeler attested. The text, by the blind French-German poet Gottlieb Konrad Pfeffel, appeared in the *Hamburger Musenalmanach* of 1792. For Masonic ceremonies, the opening phrase was adapted to the words "Was ist des Maurers Ziel?" ("What is the Mason's goal?") by Wegeler. The phrase "Ein freier Mann" had wide currency. As we shall see, it appears at the end of Eulogius Schneider's ode to the French Revolution as "Ein freier Mann ist der Franzos!" ("A Freeman Is the Frenchman!").

First sketch, Der Freie Mann ('Wer ist ein freier Mann?'),
WoO 117 (Hess 146) ("Kafka" Sketchbook, fol. 153v)

Vier männliche Stimmen
[Four male voices]

Wer	wer	ist____	ein	Frei	-	er	mann
[Who	who	is____	a	man		made	free]

Fifth Symphony, op. 67, finale

Allegro

ff

1.5 Comparison of sketch for "A Free Man" with the Fifth Symphony, finale.

The opening of Beethoven's first draft for "A Free Man" is to be sung by four male voices in a setting in duple time in C major (fig. 1.5). Its first six notes—outlining the melodic pattern of a rising triadic chord of C major and descent by step, while prolonging the third and shortening the fourth notes—resemble the opening of the last movement of the Fifth Symphony, a work completed almost twenty years later (fig. 1.5). This thematic parallel—encompassing motive, rhythm, key, and character—is too close to be coincidental, showing once more how a musical kernel from Beethoven's youth found pride of place in one of his most celebrated compositions. Nor is this idea confined to "A Free Man" and the finale of the *Fifth*. Another parallel passage is the stirring episode in the Funeral March of the *Eroica* Symphony, when the oboe emerges, shifting the key from C minor to C *major*, and thereby sounding the rising pattern C–E–G, with the sustained fifth G yielding to an expressive stepwise descent. The first stanza of "A Free Man" is as follows:

Who is a free man?
Who is a free man?
He who from neither birth nor title,
neither velvet jacket nor smock
can conceal the brother,
He is a free man!

The references to "velvet jacket" and "smock" target the attire of aristocrats and clerics, whose status should not be elevated above their fellow citizens. The narratives of Beethoven's music strongly reinforce Pfeffel's egalitarian message, that a free human being not be subordinated to arbitrary rule. The core notion of fraternity or community, as reflected in the choral setting, is glorified in a movement like the finale of the Fifth Symphony, in which the full orchestra is brought emphatically to bear, augmented by additional instruments like the trombones and piccolo.

A tonal vocabulary with rhetorical associations connected to ideas of liberation extends to the biggest single compositional achievement of Beethoven's Bonn years: his *Joseph* Cantata from 1790. Only in 1884, almost a century after Beethoven left Bonn, did the score of the cantata come to light. Even now, the piece remains unfamiliar to the general public. It never reached performance in 1790, possibly because its technical challenges overtaxed the performers. Beethoven could have been justly proud of the piece, the most prophetic single composition of his Bonn period. After the cantata's discovery, Johannes Brahms commented glowingly that "Even if there were no name on the title page none other could be conjectured—it is Beethoven through and through!"

A glance at the score suggests why Beethoven did not publish the cantata in later years, since two of the most extraordinary passages in his opera *Fidelio* were mined from its material. Comparison of the cantata with the opera—which first reached the stage fifteen years later, in 1805—alerts us to an overarching quality of Beethoven's art, a communicative power of gigantic simplicity that is already present in the best music from his Bonn period.

The *Joseph* Cantata displays a symmetrical design of seven numbers. The opening and closing choral pieces lament the emperor's passing: "Tot! Tot! Tot, stöhnt es durch die öde Nacht, die öde Nacht" ("Dead! Dead! Dead, it groans through the bleak night, the bleak night"). These choral laments in C minor frame a chain of recitatives and arias, at the center of which is lodged a soprano aria to the text "Da stiegen die Menschen ans Licht" ("Then the people ascended to the light"). This aspirational music conveys the positive value of Enlightenment that was identified with the deceased emperor.

Darkness and the void of death are set here against light and hope. The musical symbolism is so arresting that Beethoven could later absorb the motives and orchestration intact into his opera. *Fidelio* similarly concerns a confrontation with impending death: Florestan's dungeon aria begins with the utterance "Gott! Welch Dunkel hier!" ("God! What darkness here!"), and continues "Öd' ist es um mich her, nichts, nichts lebet äusser mir" ("bleak it is around me here, nothing, nothing lives apart from me"). The tenor's piercing high G at "God!" yields to the lower, resigned figure at "What darkness here!" as the duality of hope and despair is folded into a single compressed utterance of the prisoner.

In the cantata, the choral laments are set in C minor, but for the dungeon scene of his opera Beethoven chooses a tonality a fifth lower: F minor. This allows the luminous shift to F major for Florestan's delirious vision of Leonore in his aria to match tonally to the later *Sostenuto assai* passage in this same key heard when the assembled populace and liberated prisoners witness Leonore's unchaining of Florestan. A piercing cry portends an inner vision, which foreshadows a redemptive scene of collective liberation from tyranny—such narratives lend psychological depth to the music.

An association of C minor with pathos encompasses a long through line in Beethoven, starting with the Nine Variations on Ernst Dressler's march that the twelve-year-old composed by 1783. The *Joseph* Cantata is stationed on this path, which extends to the *Sonate pathétique* and the Funeral March of the *Eroica*, the Fifth Symphony, and the final sonata op. 111. A glimpse ahead to Beethoven's opera illustrates the bond between aesthetics and ethics that guided much of his work. Despite a difference in key, the dark rhetoric of the *Joseph* Cantata haunts the orchestral music of Pizarro's dungeon. Low soft octaves on F alternate with high penetrating chords in the upper registers featuring woodwinds and horns. The two initial high chords ascend from C to D♭, a figure soon inverted in the strings to become animated sighing gestures laden with human suffering. With awareness of the cantata, we can perceive these two opening *forte* chords as meaningfully shaped by their prehistory. Beethoven surely heard these stark sonorities as echoing the sentiment "Dead, dead," as in the framing choruses of his cantata.

The last act of *Fidelio* embraces a rising tonal polarity from F minor to C major in association with the idea of liberation. Beethoven's choice of F minor—a perfect fifth under C—helps convey in this context the notion of depth. A compression of time and space focuses the action in *Fidelio*; the drama unfolds within a single day and is confined to a single place. Pizarro's prison shadows the abode of the jailor Rocco with his daughter Marzelline. Their lives display a narrow self-interest and ambivalent behavior due to the morally compromised environment of the political prison. Of all those incarcerated, it is Florestan who is concealed on the lowest level in the dungeon, literally buried alive, directly beneath the dwelling place of Rocco and Marzelline.

Leonore's odyssey—her descent into the dungeon followed by an ascent into a light that stands for Enlightenment—is distinctly prefigured in those symbolic musical elements that Beethoven extracted from his *Joseph* Cantata. The failure of Joseph's reforms, like the betrayal of the French Revolution or Napoleon's regression to tyranny, belongs to an ongoing tensional process that continues to the present. As a political process, the ascent of people to the light may always remain problematic, but the negative examples of history—despotism and oppressive misuse of power—remind us of the indispensable need to curb cynicism and keep ethical standards in view.

The hymnlike aspirational resonance of the soprano aria of his early cantata reminds us of the enduring persistence of a humanistic spirit in Beethoven's art. "Da stiegen die Menschen ans Licht" ("Then the people ascended to the light") is set to rising fourths that embody an emblematic shape comparable to later themes in his instrumental and vocal works. Such a pattern of rising fourths pitted against music of strife or pathos is found not only in *Fidelio* but in the *Adagio cantabile* of the *Sonate pathétique*, the fugue of the penultimate Piano Sonata in A♭, op. 110, and the "Dona nobis pacem" of the *Missa solemnis*. Each of these themes is distinctive, and the pliable rhythm of rising fourths followed by the stepwise *dolce* descent embracing a larger continuity of tones in the cantata stands for the fulfillment of a renewed community.

The shared political meaning of *Fidelio* and the *Joseph* Cantata is linked through the idea of a humanistic legacy threatened and suppressed by authoritarian force: an entombed freedom that is rescued and rehabilitated. Schiller's Marquis de Posa dies after urging the political liberation of the Netherlands in terms of progressive liberal thought of the 1780s; the enlightened Emperor Joseph was interred in 1790 as many reforms were reversed; the imprisoned freedom fighter of Beethoven's opera was modeled on a reformer become victim during the Reign of Terror. Having spoken truth to power, Florestan finds himself buried alive in the depths of Pizarro's prison.

Pizarro embodies a despotic "monster of fanaticism" in the language of Beethoven's early cantata. The prison governor is obsessed with personal honor, egocentric in his performance of official duties, vain, unprincipled, corrupt, and corrupting. He thereby perverts the state into an instrument of personal force. He rages over Florestan's effort to expose his abuses. Recalling that "Once I was nearly humbled," Pizarro responds by tormenting and attempting annihilation of his critic while indulging in a cover-up. Pizarro's soldiers dread his temper; the prisoners fear his spies. Pizarro tries to bribe Rocco to commit murder. Were he to have achieved his aim, both Rocco and Fidelio would have become accomplices.

When the assembled chorus of prisoners and townspeople greets the arrival of the minister Don Fernando at the opera's conclusion, he responds to their servile petition for justice with words radiant with the revolutionary principles of liberty, equality, and fraternity:

Kneel no longer slavishly,
Harsh tyranny is far from my mind.

I come as a brother to my brothers,
and help gladly if I can.

Fernando had thought Florestan dead: he was a missing person who disappeared, was tortured and marked for murder at Pizarro's hands. Florestan's unchaining stands metaphorically for a broader liberation of other prisoners, for Leonore's compassionate gaze is open to their suffering. To the music extracted from the *Joseph* Cantata heard as Leonore removes the chains, we contemplate a moment of exemplary civic virtue recognized by Fernando in his role as representative of an enlightened monarchy or a properly constituted revolutionary state.

Pizarro and Fernando are not intended as fully rounded individuals. These figures stand for opposing principles: despotic terror pitted against humanistic compassion and civic virtue. This dualistic framework, together with the original transposition of the drama's action from France to Spain, promotes the applicability of the opera to actual political contexts. In 1945, Thomas Mann wrote about the opera during the Third Reich: "How could it happen that Beethoven's *Fidelio* . . . was not forbidden in the Germany of the last twelve years? . . . For what utter stupidity was required to be able to listen to *Fidelio* in Himmler's Germany without covering one's face and rushing out of the hall."

The political relevance of Beethoven's music remains tangible. What is the symbolic import of Pizarro's citadel? A fortified castle from the time whose inmates are collectively liberated inevitably recalls the storming of the Bastille on 14 July 1789. Eulogius Schneider, ever ready in response to contemporary events, interrupted his university lecture to recite a poem he devised as soon as the news of the fall of the Bastille reached him:

The chains of despotism have fallen away,
fortunate people! from your hands:
from the throne of princes to your place of freedom
from the realm of kings to the fatherland
No royal edict, no: this is our will,

from now on it shall shape the citizen's destiny.
There lies, in ruins, the Bastille,
a free man is the French man!

The medieval Bastille with its eight towers, long used as a state prison and place of detention, had become a symbol of dictatorial oppression. As such, the demolishing of the Bastille by 1790, like the execution of King Louis XVI in 1793 or the adoption of a new revolutionary calendar, could be regarded as landmarks of permanent historical change. But no such actions in themselves restrain the forces of political oppression. Mob rule is prone to replace unjust conditions by equally defective or even worse developments.

For Beethoven's opera, the original historical point of reference was not the storming of the Bastille in 1789 but the liberation of political prisoners in an episode from the Reign of Terror during 1793–1794. Rooted in an actual incident connected to post-Revolutionary excesses, but sustaining multiple points of reference, *Fidelio* cannot be adequately described as either revolutionary or reactionary. Instead, it vigorously promotes a progressive political position through aesthetic means, becoming a moral force, or in Schiller's terms an "effigy of the ideal." In the ninth of his *Aesthetic Letters* of 1796, Schiller recommended that "the artist endeavor to give birth to the ideal by uniting the possible and the necessary. Let him stamp illusion and truth with the effigy of this ideal; let him apply it to the play of his imagination and to his most serious actions, in short, to all sensuous and spiritual forms; then let him quietly set forth his work into infinite time."

As Ernst Bloch put it, "every future storm of the Bastille is intended in *Fidelio*." The most striking stage music in the opera is the twofold trumpet fanfare played offstage, from a prison tower. The sentry sounds the trumpet under strict orders from Pizarro, signaling to the governor a warning of the imminent arrival of the minister of state. Through an ironic dramatic reversal—a kind of Promethean theft—this gesture is stolen from Pizarro to convey an opposing message. Apart from its role as a signaling instrument associated with military authority and royalty, the trumpet holds biblical associations. Seven trumpets are sounded in the Book of Revelation; a trumpet blown from the holy rock in Jerusalem announces the Day of Resurrection. Proclamations are delivered by the sound of trumpet. Trumpets often appeared in French Revolutionary ceremonies, with a pair of trumpets played from a tower during Robespierre's Festival of the Supreme Being in 1794.

The uncanny timing of the trumpet interrupting the breathless vocal quartet in the dungeon—as Leonore holds Pizarro in check—gives us pause. Instead of serving Pizarro, the trumpet is repurposed to confirm Leonore's positive intervention as an act of virtue breaking the chain of events that otherwise would have taken their expected tragic course. The moments of contemplation opened by the trumpet fanfares—of time frozen—arrest the swift unfolding action, lifting the artistic discourse to another, more distanced level, thereby encouraging us to weigh the broader meaning for ourselves.

Now, two centuries after Beethoven, the megalomania and trumpet-and-drums swagger of Pizarro are widely ascendant. James Madison's conviction from 1788 about the "great republican principle, that the people will have virtue and intelligence to select men of virtue and wisdom," seems naïve at a time of heightened propaganda and inept dishonest leadership. How to respond when a towering demagogue builds a tower of lies, applauded by a crowd of cronies?

In his remarkable novella *Tonio Kröger*, Thomas Mann depicts his protagonist as deeply moved by Schiller's *Don Carlos*, and as with Beethoven, it is the interpersonal relationships centered on the humanist Marquis de Posa in act 4 that haunt him. Tonio refers to "places . . . so lovely they make you jump . . . as though it were an explosion—" and he continues:

For instance, the place where the king has been crying because the marquis betrayed him . . . but the marquis did it only out of love for the prince, you see, he sacrifices himself for his sake. And the word comes out of the cabinet into the antechamber that the king has been weeping. "Weeping? The king been weeping?" All the courtiers are fearfully upset, it goes through and through you, for the king has always been so frightfully stiff and stern. But it is so easy to understand why he cried, and I feel sorrier for him than for the prince and the marquis put together. He is always so alone, nobody loves him, and then he thinks he has found one man, and then *he* betrays him . . .

In Schiller, the isolated king is himself a spiritual prisoner, made a victim of his own system, as is made clear in his chilling closing encounter with the Grand Inquisitor. However, Posa's earlier audience with the king had opened a brief moment when the monarch might have accomplished good through political intervention. Posa's idealistic argument for political progress—liberation of the Netherlands—rests on his conviction about a world changing for the better:

The century is unripe for my ideal. I live
As a citizen of ages yet to come.

Das Jahrhundert ist meinem Ideal nicht reif. Ich lebe
Ein Bürger derer, welche kommen werden.

An attitude diametrically opposed to the Grand Inquisitor's reprimand to the king:

To what purpose human beings? Humans are
for you just numbers, nothing more.

Wozu Menschen? Menschen sind
Für Sie nur Zahlen, weiter nichts.

asserting absolutism over change, death over life.

For Beethoven, it is Posa's vision of a brighter future that carries weight, like "Joy . . . daughter from Elysium," the poem written by Schiller around the same time. The original version of "An die Freude" from 1785 offers a glimpse of a transformed political realm: "Beggars become the brothers of princes / where your gentle wing rests" is even more explicit than the later version Beethoven set: "All human beings become siblings" ("Alle Menschen werden Brüder"). Beethoven seized his chance to return to Posa's vision of liberation in 1810 when he wrote music to Goethe's play based on overlapping historical material: *Egmont*. The thrilling apotheosis of the *Victory Symphony* in *Egmont* is yet another example of a work of a political character whose roots reach back to Beethoven's formative years at Bonn.

The Sublime
and Inverted Sublime

On 2 August 1794, soon after the fall of Robespierre and the end of the Reign of Terror in France, Beethoven slipped a few heated comments into the middle of a letter to his friend Nikolaus Simrock, a hornist and music publisher in Bonn, and a Francophile:

> It's very hot here; the Viennese fear that it will soon be impossible for them to find frozen refreshments; since the winter was mild, ice is scarce. Various persons of importance have been arrested here; one says a *revolution* was breaking out—but I believe that as long as an Austrian has his brown beer and sausages he will not revolt. The gates to the suburbs are ordered to be locked at ten o'clock at night. The soldiers have loaded guns. One dare not speak too loudly here, otherwise the police will lock you up.

Those "various persons *of importance*" included the Freemason Franz Hebenstreit, a passionate democrat and so-called Jacobinist supportive of the French Revolution who was charged with treason and publicly hanged at Vienna in January 1795. Responding to the repressive turn in Habsburg politics in 1792, Hebenstreit had designed a *Kriegsmachine* or combat chariot that he hoped might assist the French against the Austrian cavalry. In his letter, Beethoven refers ironically to "cavalier talk" in "our democratic times," presumably alluding to Hebenstreit, who had served in the cavalry. Hebenstreit was associated with Andreas Riedel, who described his colleague as a "communist." Riedel promoted adoption of a constitution in 1791 and enjoyed support from Emperor Leopold II, but resisted the reactionary turn under Emperor Franz, which led to his arrest and long imprisonment until he was freed by Napoleon in 1809. While mentioning the political crackdown, Beethoven wryly surmised that a revolt would fail in Austria so long as brown beer and sausages remained, even if ice cream was in short supply. As Beethoven well knew, the recipient of his letter was sympathetic toward the revolution. Nikolaus Simrock prospered and grew wealthy during the years of French domination.

Like Eulogius Schneider, Franz Hebenstreit gave expression to his longings for reform and social utopia through verse, as in his widely disseminated revolutionary song in Austrian dialect, the "Eipeldau Song," which begins with these lines:

Was denkts enk den, dass gar so schreit
Und alles auf d' Franzsosen?
Den Louis haben's köpft—, Ja nun mich freuts
Er war schlecht bis in d'Hosen.

What d'ya think then, about that shrill whine
And everything mean said about the French?
They've cut off Louis's head—, for me that's fine
He was bad as could be and raised a stench.

The continuation includes the following:

'S ist, ja das Volk kein Arschpapier
Und darf auf sich wohl denken,
Wer halt nicht lernen will Manie,
Den Lümmel muss man henken.
Drum fort mit ihm zur Guillotin
Denn Blut für Blut muss fließen
Hätt man nur a hier so an maschin,
Müsst's mancher Großkopf büßen.

The people are really not toilet paper

And should think of themselves well,
Whoever doesn't learn to show us some favor
That lout we must kill.
Then take him forth to the guillotine
Since blood for blood must flow
If only we had here such a machine
Many big heads would fall down low.

Beethoven rightly sensed that such efforts were not enough to arouse the general population to revolt and bring about the collapse of the monarchy. Hebenstreit and Riedel had not mobilized the kind of mass movement necessary for a revolution. Their punishment followed a show trial calculated to discourage other political activists. After his public execution, Hebenstreit's decapitated head was placed on display as an object of curiosity for more than two centuries, and was removed from Vienna's Criminal Museum in response to protests only in 2012.

Once he settled in Vienna in 1792, Beethoven encountered a tense and reactionary political environment. At the same time, he was aware that conditions in some other countries were more repressive. A recently discovered letter from 1795 to his friend from Bonn, Heinrich von Struve, reflects Beethoven's political attitudes. Struve had entered diplomatic service in Russia. After stopping in Vienna earlier that year, Beethoven's friend had traveled to Kiev, Moscow, and Saint Petersburg. Beethoven writes that

You are now in the Cold Land, where humanity is treated very much beneath its dignity, [and] I am sure that you will witness many things that go against your way of thinking, your heart, and all together against your entire sensibility. When will the time come when there is just humanity? We will probably experience the approach of this happy outcome only in a few places, but in general we won't see that, even as centuries come to pass.

During the reign of Catherine the Great, the status of the rural peasants had declined, which helps explain Beethoven's reference to Russia as a "Cold Land." Three years earlier, Struve had entered humanistic sentiments into Beethoven's farewell album, citing the Enlightenment philosopher Moses Mendelssohn. In the shared spirit of the "Zehrgarten" circle at Bonn, to which both men had belonged, Beethoven wrote in 1793 the following lines into the album of another friend, Theodora Johanna Vocke:

Do good, where one can,
Freedom above all is to be loved,
Truth never (not even
before the throne) to be denied.

A tensional gap between lofty ethical principles and harsh political realities is conveyed in these sources, whose predictive power retains potency.

How in this context could an artist mark out new paths and show his independence? How could musical performance assume social or political significance? Let us consider in this regard Beethoven's works for the instrument that dominates his first Vienna decade: the piano. Keyboard instruments were then handcrafted by a variety of makers; they were lighter in construction and more individual than most instruments familiar since the mid-nineteenth century. Beethoven's style as a keyboard virtuoso was differentiated and energetic. He demanded much from the piano in conveying a musical language that was rhetorically nuanced and dynamically shaped. He was an orator in tones, or a tone poet (*Tondichter*), as he liked to describe himself, a musician devoted to the "great and sublime," as Fischenich claimed in his letter to Schiller's wife in 1793.

A link between the artistic and political spheres—and a personal connection between Beethoven and Friedrich Schiller—was embodied in the musician and later instrument maker from Stuttgart, Johann Andreas Streicher. Streicher first met the young composer during 1787, probably at Munich or Augsburg, during Beethoven's return journey from Vienna to Bonn. Five years earlier, Streicher had aided and accompanied Friedrich Schiller when the young playwright fled Württemberg after being arrested and briefly imprisoned following the spectacular premiere at Mannheim of his controversial political drama *The Robbers*. Under cover of night Streicher and Schiller fled together as "Doctor Ritter" and "Doctor Wolf"; Streicher sacrificed his plans to study with Carl Philipp Emanuel Bach in Hamburg in order to lend support to Schiller at his time of crisis and uncertainty. Years later, Streicher moved to Vienna with his wife Nannette Streicher, herself an accomplished instrument maker and daughter of Johann Andreas Stein, one of the foremost piano builders of the time. Their piano factory eventually included an important performance space. One of Beethoven's most enduring friendships was with Andreas and Nannette Streicher.

Schiller's dramas posed challenges to the Habsburg regime. Performances of many of the plays were banned for fifteen years, from 1793 to 1808; the censors rejected *The Robbers* as "immoral" and "dangerous." However, Schiller's influence was disseminated not simply from staged performances but through the printed texts. After it was published in 1787, around the time the young composer first met Streicher, *Don Carlos* became something like required reading in the circle of Beethoven's friends at Bonn. Beethoven's early interest in Schiller's ode "To Joy" may also have been linked to Streicher.

Streicher recognized the pathbreaking qualities in Beethoven's music. In 1803 he stated that "Beethoven will certainly bring about a revolution in music as did Mozart. With great speed he hurries toward this goal." It is instructive to regard Beethoven's works of his first Vienna decade in light of the new ideas circulating during the post–French Revolutionary years. Schiller wrote various essays during an extended interruption in his composition of dramatic works during the 1790s. His concepts fit well to Beethoven's music, supporting Fischenich's observation about the composer's devotion to "the great and the sublime." While lecturing at Jena starting in 1790, Schiller wrote on topics such as "On the Reason for Enjoyment of Tragic Subjects," "On Tragic Art," "On Pathos," and "On the Sublime." The subject of the sublime took an honored place in his aesthetic theory. These treatises were followed by Schiller's essay on "Naïve and Sentimental Poetry" and his biggest single contribution in this vein: the *Aesthetic Letters* of 1796.

Schiller urges the artist engaging with tragic themes to bring a sense of moral purpose vividly to the consciousness of his audience. How can this be achieved? For Schiller, ethical purpose can be conveyed through tensional opposition, such as between the appalling oppression of a despot and steadfast determination of an innocent victim resisting exploitation. The relevance of this example to Beethoven's *Fidelio* is readily apparent, but how could such dramatic content be embedded in instrumental music without text? Like spoken theater, music is a temporal art, often involving a series of character-states shaped into a whole larger than the sum of its parts. In this context, Schiller's observations show a range of applicability that lends itself readily to the non-verbal sphere of instrumental music.

Schiller's treatise on tragic art, *Über das Pathetische*, likely helped inspire Beethoven's celebrated *Sonate pathétique* in C Minor, op. 13, published in 1799. Schiller argues that tragedy is not confined to a depiction of melancholy, but involves an embodiment of moral resistance. In resistance—a refusal to accept tragic conditions as final—the artist posits a dissenting voice, opening an expressive space that projects dynamic alternatives, envisioning utopian strivings or "effigies of the ideal." In his essay "On the Sublime," Schiller describes how individuals as moral agents should shield their will and creative potential against arbitrary power and oppression. He urges emphatically that a *"relationship*, which is disadvantageous . . . *be completely and utterly nullified*, and the power . . . *be destroyed in concept."* For Schiller, the sublime differs from the beautiful in that the latter is confined to the world of sensibility. The sublime, by contrast, reaches beyond sensuous immediacy to evoke mixed or competing emotions of fascination, delight, astonishment, fear, or terror, and involves a manifestation of spiritual freedom. The sublime destabilizes the predictable world of conventional expectations. As such, the sublime can even promote an inversion of meaning, enabling a comic or ironic dimension.

Such tension is illustrated in a humorous French caricature from 1930 (fig. 2.1). In this picture, the *Sonate Pathétique* is a recognizable score that has occupied the gracious young woman at the piano, who is drawn into the Beethovenian maelstrom. The caption "Sous L'Oeil du Maitre," "under the eye of the master," refers to the composer's face on the wall, peering through Franz Klein's life mask from 1812 (fig. 2.2). The life mask is alive. Beethoven's gaze is ironic but sympathetic, critical but compassionate. The engrossing spell of the music is reflected through the pianist's forward-thrusting position, with piano bench tilted and hands ready to pounce; the wind blowing from the instrument engulfs her gauzy capelet. Her wide-eyed countenance with mouth agape conveys the spell cast by the music.

The living mask and uncanny wind depart from a realistic, naturalistic representation. Transcending these limits, they evoke the sublime, in this instance with comic effect. From our perspective, more than two centuries after Klein made his cast, the animated gaze and instrument annul time, becoming more real than the young lady, whose affluent attire in the art nouveau drawing room points to her amateur status. A level of irony arises if we compare her privileged appearance with the depiction of suffering in the *Sonate pathétique*. In Schiller's words, such "suffering, bound up with sensibility and with the consciousness of our inner moral freedom, is *tragic sublimity*."

The revolutionary aura of the *Sonate pathétique* immediately excited young artists of the day like the pianist Ignaz Moscheles, who secretly copied it, against the wishes of his teacher. Moscheles related that

> The novelty of its style was so attractive to me, and I became so enthusiastic in my admiration of it, that I forgot myself so far as to mention my new acquisition to my teacher, who reminded me of his injunction, and warned me not to play or study any eccentric productions until I had based my style upon more solid models.

2.1 Humorous vignette "Beethoven": "Sous L'Oeil du Maitre" ("under the eye of the master") by Georges Paul Gaston Léonnec, from "La Vie Parisienne," 1930. Biblioteca Beethoveniana, Carrino Collection, Muggia (Trieste).

Without, however, minding his injunctions, I seized upon the pianoforte works of Beethoven as they successively appeared, and in them found a solace and a delight such as no other composer afforded me.

In the *Pathétique*, a character of resistance is invested in a prom-

2.2 Beethoven, life mask, Franz Klein, 1812. Biblioteca Beethoveniana, Carrino Collection, Muggia (Trieste).

inent quality of the robust first movement: its use of contrast-ing music in split tempi: *Grave* and *Allegro di molto e con brio*. The gloomy meditative slow introduction seems reminiscent of a Shakespearean soliloquy, such as Hamlet's probing "To be, or not to be," a passage Beethoven's nephew Karl tried to master many years later, much to his uncle's delight. Leaden dissonant chords underpin the reflective phrases of the *Grave*. Striving upward, the music struggles against ominous thick dissonances in lower regis-ters. As it does so, it becomes increasingly plaintive and recitative-like, a searching soliloquy in tones. The final phrases of the *Grave* ascend to an airy height, with the melody poised as high as was possible on keyboard instruments of the 1790s.

The ensuing connection to the lower pitch registers—to earthly concerns—is invested with brilliance through a rapid chromatic scale falling close to the original sonorous position—the same tonic pitches on C—of the initial chord of the *Grave*. To convey a character of resistance, Beethoven then reshapes in the open-ing theme of the *Allegro di molto e con brio* the ascending contour and harmonic colors that had unfolded far more gradually from the outset of the *Grave*. The brooding opening soliloquy is supplanted by dramatic action, by a dynamic thrust of active resistance, with hints of the brighter major mode built into the rising opening theme of the *Allegro di molto e con brio*, which lifts the musical discourse above the gloomy accents of the *Grave*. The brilliant dialogue passages that ensue provide further evidence of energetic struggle.

This dualism of melancholy meditation and rapid dramatic music—contemplation leading to action—had precedents in earlier music, such as Haydn's slow introductions to the swift opening movements of his London symphonies. Yet Beethoven carries this idea further in psychological terms. In the *Sonate pathétique* opening movement, the *Grave* returns at the outset of the development section, then again in the coda. Searching melancholy repeatedly triggers action: in the development, a somber motive from the *Grave* invades the *Allegro*, linking these contrasting states of mind in a psychological progression. What was contemplated in the slow introduction breaks through into the sphere of dramatic fulfillment in the development of the *Allegro*. This music is invested with experiential meaning, signaling an attitude of confrontation or defiance.

Such experiential meaning is often reflected in Beethoven's music through his handling of the character of keys, which is somewhat comparable to the treatment of plots in literature. The dark turbulence of C minor, with its tragic associations, can be counterpoised to the lyric fulfillment of A♭ major or to a shift to C major, whose brighter radiant quality can signal an overcoming of strife. The acoustic structure of music enables a network of sonorous relationships, promoting an expressive narrative. Whereas in literature a telltale motive may foreshadow later events, a single chord in music can be later expanded into a tonal area, while a variety of expressive meanings can emerge through dramatic juxtaposition.

Beethoven's use of such transformational patterns had deep roots reaching back to his years at Bonn. The first such instance is his youthful Sonata in F Minor, the second of the three *Electoral* Sonatas, composed in 1783 when he was just twelve years old. This

2.3a *Electoral* Sonata in F Minor, WoO 47, no. 2, beginning.
2.3b *Electoral* Sonata in F Minor, WoO 47, no. 2, *Allegro assai.*

piece begins with a slow *Larghetto maestoso* excerpt (fig. 2.3a). An imposing F-minor chord is set on the downbeat, joined to a dotted rhythmic figure as part of a *forte* gesture; the second measure offers a balancing continuation in continuous eighth notes over a sustained tonic F in the bass, played *piano*. It is remarkable how the faster music of the main body of the movement, marked *Allegro assai*, audibly transforms the initial music (fig. 2.3b). The drop of an octave from F in the *Larghetto maestoso* becomes an energetic falling scale in the *Allegro assai*, as the gap is filled with vigorous motion. The lower half of the descending gesture is reinforced by the left hand, whereupon the sustained F in the bass is transformed into a throbbing repetitive rhythm. The rising thirds from the start of measure 2 of the *Larghetto maestoso* are developed in an ascending texture that resembles the rising theme heard over a pedal point that launches the *Allegro di molto e con brio* in the *Pathétique.*

Sensitive performance can convey this transformative process. Beethoven underscores its importance by recalling the *Larghetto maestoso* passage in the second half of the movement. This sonata by the adolescent Beethoven already shows his fascination with contrasts of tempi bridged through a psychological process. The "solace and delight" described by Moscheles and discovered by countless listeners in the *Pathétique* and other Beethovenian works stems in part from a vivid dynamic quality, which is not merely eccentric and goes beyond solidity. The hints of this process contained in some pieces from Beethoven's adolescence are richly developed in the works of his Vienna years.

With the *Pathétique*, familiarity easily blunts sensibility; the encompassing design of the work as a whole is easily overlooked. Its three movements need to be grasped in relation to one another. Expressive motivic connections impose a larger narrative; the master's gaze and a cosmic wind haunt the music. Beethoven meaningfully excludes lyrical warmth from the first movement in order to concentrate that quality in the slow middle movement, the *Adagio cantabile*. The middle C that served as initial melodic pitch in the *Grave* and *Allegro* of the first movement is absorbed into A♭ major in the initial chord of the *Adagio cantabile*; the change of key infuses subjectivity with heartfelt feeling. This lyrical Adagio is associated with utopian strivings, but its second internal episode, with darker harmonies and rhythmic agitation, signals the tension of the outer movements. In the finale, on the other hand, Beethoven recaptures a rising four-note upbeat motive from the opening *Allegro*. Once that figure has made its mark in the dramatic dialogue sections of the *Allegro di molto e con brio*, the listener will recognize its return at the outset of the closing rondo.

This main theme of the finale unfolds generously, as a well-rounded rondo subject. Against it are arrayed a colorful collection of subsidiary ideas, culminating in a brilliant pianistic gesture—a loud downward sweep across the keyboard from high F, the highest pitch of the keyboard in 1798. This rhetorical signpost prefaces the repetitions of the rondo theme, though not its final return.

Beethoven recalls the *Adagio cantabile* in two crucial passages of his finale. The central episode revisits A♭ major and those notes in the middle of the keyboard associated with the beautiful lyrical theme. Contrapuntal variations of this musical idea rise in pitch while becoming rhythmically animated; the reflective character gradually changes into turbulent agitation. As this process unfolds, it reaches a turning point: the key of A♭ major collapses onto the dominant of C minor, reaching the brilliantly sweeping downward scale and the next return of the obsessive rondo theme. The musical progression signals a psychological transition from reflection to action, from meditation to determined resistance.

Most provocative of all is Beethoven's integration of these soul-states in the coda to the finale. The last return of the rondo subject leads into a passage racked with syncopated rhythmic tension, building toward the climactic close. At this juncture—at one minute to midnight in the life-story of the artwork—Beethoven jolts the listener with a sudden modulation, as the sweeping downward scale figure returns yet again, now bringing a sudden change of key to the dominant of A♭ major! What can ensue at such a late stage in this drama in tones, just as the curtain is about to close?

Beethoven strips away the three-note upbeat figure from his rondo theme, revealing a placid variant of the rondo subject in A♭ major, a gesture conspicuously resembling the opening of the gentle *Adagio cantabile*. This is a vision of the slow movement glimpsed through the veil of the rondo theme. The rondo subject, itself derived from the spirited dialogue passages of the first movement, is reshaped to accommodate the subjective inwardness embodied in the slow movement. This moment of active reinterpretation leads to two short questioning phrases, setting up a final surprise for the listener. In the *Pathétique*, the luminous sphere of A♭ major stands in a dependent relation to C minor, just as human aspirations often remain unfulfilled, constrained by the conditions of external reality. Beethoven's final gambit reasserts the dive-bomb scale that was withheld from the previous statement of the rondo theme. This last return comes with a vengeance. Here, for the first time, the falling scale is rammed into the tonic chord of C minor, bringing a decisive resolution.

Beethoven thereby embeds in sound a Schillerian conviction about tragedy: how determined resistance symbolically bridges the gulf between human goals and the barriers to their realization. A tensional simplicity hovers over the import of the *Pathétique*. In the outer movements, the downward scalar cascades signaling resistance seem locked into a cyclic pattern, while the tender lyricism of the *Adagio cantabile* is set apart, remote from action. A glimpse toward transcendence of this experiential dilemma is lodged in the last moments, as utopian desire confronts reality.

In 1799, the *Sonate pathétique* was published by Franz Anton Hoffmeister, himself a composer who had been a friend of Mozart and a fellow Freemason. Since Hoffmeister moved to Leipzig in 1800 and continued publishing Beethovenian works, letters survive, including one that sheds light on Beethoven's attitude about the financial aspects of artistic production. The composer wrote in January 1801 regarding the negotiation of prices that "Well, that tiresome business has now been settled. I call it so because I wish things were different in the world. There just ought to be in the world a marketplace for art [*Magazin der Kunst*] to which the artist would only bring his artworks in order to take what he needed; as it is one must be half businessman, and how can one be reconciled to that!" The principle Beethoven espouses involves an exchange of creative work for livelihoods guaranteed by society. In June 1801, in a letter to Wegeler, Beethoven professes a wish "to practice his art solely for the benefit of the poor." Anti-materialist socialist sentiments rose in the second half of the 1790s, especially in France in connection with figures like Gracchus Babeuf and Sylvain Maréchal. Babeuf's political convictions led to vain attempts to incite revolt and to his execution on the guillotine in 1797. While likely agreeing with Maréchal's critique of equality in his *Manifesto of the Equals* as being just a "beautiful and sterile legal fiction" and with its warning to the rich and powerful that "it is now your turn to listen," Beethoven certainly would not have endorsed Maréchal's culturally leveling recommendation to "Let the arts perish, if need be, as long as real equality remains."

Beethoven's works in a tragic mode sometimes relate to the celebrated dramatist once dismissed as an "upstart crow, beautified by feathers": William Shakespeare. The musical essays in this vein include his slow movements from his Piano Sonata in D Major, op. 10, no. 3, and the String Quartet, op. 18, no. 1. Both movements are in D minor—a key associated with Mozartian tragic pathos as in

Don Giovanni—but a tangible poetic connection exists to the tomb scene at the end of Shakespeare's *Romeo and Juliet*. Beethoven associated the *Adagio* of the quartet with Shakespeare's closing scene, and the link to the death of the lovers is confirmed by entries in one of the composer's sketchbooks. The composer surely knew Friedrich Schlegel's German translation from 1796, but a revealing musical sketch carries the composer's inscription "les derniers soupirs" ("the last sighs"), drawn from a French translation of the play. In its musical content, the sketch relates as closely to the *Largo e mesto* of op. 10, no. 3, as it does to the quartet.

Both of these musical pieces display a rapport of sound with silence—a cessation carrying the implication of death. An impressive feature of the *Largo e mesto* resides in the contrast between its somber opening theme and a recitative-like rhetoric that emerges in the high registers. This dramatization of low and high regions of pitch mirrors human sensibility and aspiration. In Shakespeare's tomb scene, the amorous feelings and heartfelt outreach of the protagonists are overpowered by a fateful reality. In Beethoven's slow movement, as well, the expressive content is shaped by an existential struggle. Thick, leaden chords signal the depressive *mesto* quality. A gradual ascent of the theme through an octave to an accented dissonant chord recedes quietly to the original position, before delicate dreamlike inflections yield to somber resignation. Accented dissonances trigger gentle figuration in the upper registers, fragile gestures like fleeting thoughts. These gestures dissipate into silences, leading to a darkened restatement of the melancholy beginning of the movement.

Beethoven's association of musical figuration with Shakespeare's "last sighs" is not merely a literal illustration of the play. The Shakespearean inspiration contributed to his shaping of an intrinsically musical narrative. The melancholy *Largo* in the sonata belongs to the larger span of the four-movement work; it displays points of connection to what precedes and follows it. The motivic kernel of the *Largo* consists of the half-step C♯–D and the third, F, the notes that serve as a focus of obsessive rumination from the outset of the *Largo*. Variants of this motive in the brighter

2.4 Sonata in D Major, op. 10, no. 3, *Largo e mesto*, end of coda.

major mode dominate the outer movements—the expansive opening *Presto* and the humorous, quixotic rondo finale. In the context of the whole sonata, the pattern C♯–D–F in the *Largo e mesto* can be heard as a melancholy transformation of elements present in the brilliant, expansive first movement, whereas the three-note figure F♯–G–B—posed like a question to launch the finale—is a provocatively witty answer to the tragic slow movement.

"The last sighs" hang like a motto over the entire *Largo e mesto*, but nowhere so movingly as in the last measures (fig. 2.4). The theme shows signs of disintegration, as notes drift into the void. The lingering inflections toward the end retain a hold on the higher registers. These melancholy gestures signal the "last sighs" as the two-note figures C♯–D are answered by low Ds, a bleak substratum of sound. Following this conclusion of the *Largo e mesto*, the exquisite *dolce* opening of the minuet seems like a return to life.

The character of Beethoven's rondo finale, on the other hand, reflects a brighter side of his art, a dimension bearing a kinship to another writer and thinker of the day: Jean Paul Richter. On account of their humoristic and ironic qualities, Haydn and Beethoven were compared at various times to the authors Laurence Sterne and Jean Paul. Critics dubbed Beethoven as "our musical Jean Paul," and found that the "strange and Romantic" qualities of a work like the *Eroica* Symphony bore an "unmistakable affinity with the humor" of the celebrated author of *Tristram Shandy*. Gottfried Weber referred to "Beethovenian bizarrerie" and to "Jean Paul's cloven hoof," alluding thereby to a satyr, the satiric role Jean Paul envisioned for himself. Other sources describe Beethoven's ironic sense of humor, his mischievous love of jokes and wordplay. Nannette Streicher attested that "All Beethoven's character was of . . . [an] energetic forcible cast—his laugh was like no other person—so loud and boisterous." Carl Czerny related that after moving his listeners to tears through his meditative playing, Beethoven would sometimes scold them for their sentimentality, telling them "You are fools!"

In Jean Paul's formulation, humor is the inverted sublime, the sublime in reverse. The author's aesthetic ideas are richly evident in his novels from the 1790s, but received definitive expression in his treatise *Vorschule der Ästhetik* (*Introduction to Aesthetics*) of 1804, in which he writes that

> Humor, understood as the inverted sublime, annihilates not an individual entity, but the appearance of its self-contained existence through its contrast with an idea. There is in this sense no isolated folly and no fools, but only foolishness and a mad world; humor lifts up—unlike a single joker with his pranks—not a single act of foolishness, but it lowers the sublime, while—unlike parody—raising up the trivial, and—unlike irony—sets the trivial beside the sublime and so annihilates both, since in relation to the infinite everything is the same and nothing.

Jean Paul employed the overriding concepts of the "Great" and the "Small," corresponding to the sublime or infinite, on the one hand, and the commonplace or trivial, on the other. In his view, the Great is the critique of the Small, and the Small the critique of the Great. In so placing the sublime in relationship to everyday experience, Jean Paul encouraged the artist to seek tensional perspectives engaging with the broad range of life's challenges.

A variant of this idea of contrasting affinities was advanced even earlier by the British-American author and political activist Thomas Paine, who wrote in *The Age of Reason* in 1794 that

> The sublime and the ridiculous are often so nearly related, that it is difficult to class them separately. One step above the sublime, makes the ridiculous; and one step above the ridiculous, makes the sublime again.

Beethoven's keyboard works of the 1790s include various pieces manifesting what Jean Paul described as the "annihilating or infinite idea of humor" in Haydn's music, whereby "whole rows of tones are negated through others and in which an alternation storms through, between Pianissimo and Fortissimo, Presto and Andante." Beethoven sometimes extends Haydn's tricks, as in the *Andante* variation movement of his Sonata in G Major, op. 14, no. 2, in which the trademark *fortissimo* from Haydn's "Surprise" Symphony No. 94 is shifted from the opening theme to the very last chord. Another example worthy of comparison with some of the funniest passages in Sterne's *Tristram Shandy* is the scherzo of Beethoven's Sonata in C Major, op. 2, no. 3. This high-spirited piece begins with a lively turn-figure and polyphonic voices in an atmosphere of gaiety and musical laughter. The higher perspective, or "annihilating" or "negating" idea of humor, surfaces in the middle section and again in the coda, in which the turn-figure is altered to become a repetitive ostinato motive, stuck or imprisoned in the darker sphere of the minor mode. The mock bluster of the first episode becomes an exercise in comic paradox in the coda, when the droll turn-figure in minor in the depths of the bass clashes against chords in the major mode in the right hand. Beethoven thereby utilizes the two variants of his turn-figure like a large-scale pun analogous to the word "whereabouts" in the hilarious episode in *Tristram Shandy* in which the widow Wadman vainly seeks to discover the precise location of Uncle Toby's war wound in his groin.

In Beethoven's concluding rondo of his Sonata op. 10, no. 3, unpredictability contributes to the comic character. Dynamic stops and starts become a game of hide-and-seek for the main theme. Indeed, is the theme ever found? The rondo seems to suggest a process of seeking, doubting, and evasion. The prominent deceptive cadence on B minor (m. 7) is later developed in an entire central episode built upon a more jarring deceptive cadence on B♭. This episode, in turn, leads to a false recapitulation in that key. The final episode is like a quest for a more substantial but unattainable goal, and its sequences rise ecstatically into the highest register of the piano before falling back in a short cadenza. In a peculiar way, we seem not to have left the original ground: the opening motive returns yet again, now assuming the minor mode and reminding us briefly of the tragic slow movement. A series of chords based on the rhythm of the initial motive follows, and the sonata ends quietly with repetitions of that figure in the bass, heard beneath chromatic scales and arpeggios in the right hand. The sonata has an open, dissolving conclusion, as befits its commitment to ongoing development, as well as the deft circumspection of its wit.

The finales of the two other sonatas of op. 10 are also musical essays rich in humor. The *Prestissimo* finale of the C-minor Sonata, op. 10, no. 1, exploits motives such as the figure C–B, which in the first movement conveyed grim pathos, but reappears here in a mischievous vein. Still more surprising is the way the motive is absorbed, with comic effect, into the second subject group of this movement in sonata form. Riotous humor bursts forth in the closing theme: after drastic contrasts of dynamics and register and hammering rhythms, Beethoven wickedly inserts a "wrong" chord, played *fortissimo*, just before the cadence. Both outer movements of the second sonata of op. 10 in F major revel in the unexpected, the incongruous, and the grotesque. While the middle movement—an *Allegretto* in F minor—serves as the focus of gravity in this otherwise lighthearted work, the beginning of the *Presto* finale reshapes the registral ascent from the *Allegretto*, transforming its structural aspects in an atmosphere of unbuttoned wit and musical laughter. In all these instances, earlier passages "are negated through others," to recall Jean Paul's formulation.

The aesthetics of Beethoven's devotion "to the great and the sublime" are well illustrated by his contributions to a genre closely associated with Mozart: the piano concerto. Beethoven knew the Mozartian legacy intimately, and remembered his predecessor's works when shaping his own. His Concerto in C Major, op. 15, first performed in 1795, recalls aspects of Mozart's concerto in this key, K. 503. His Concerto in C Minor, op. 37, from a few years later, invites comparison to Mozart's masterpiece in the same key, K. 491. Beethoven's admiration for Mozart was profound. He reportedly exclaimed to fellow pianist and composer Johann Baptist Cramer in 1799 about Mozart's K. 491: "Cramer, Cramer, we'll never be able to do anything like that!"

How then did he respond to these works in his own, building on the opportunities for collaborative exchange but also the spectacle of dramatic tensions between individual and society that are reflected between the soloist and the large communal group, the orchestra? By 1793, one commentator compared the concerto to Greek tragedy, whereby the orchestra was seen in the role of the chorus. In this view, the concerto showed "a passionate conversation of the soloist with the accompanying orchestra; he conveys his impression, [and] the latter signals to him through short interspersed statements its approval, soon affirming his very expression; or it seeks in the Allegro to further arouse his sublime feelings; soon it laments, then consoles him in the Adagio." In his concertos, Mozart brought the genre to new heights, drawing on the resources of comic opera, whereby the music embodies psychological qualities and changing dramatic events in its rhetoric and structure. Beethoven tests the balance between personal and social ideals in his piano concertos, in which, like Mozart, he originally acted not only as the composer, but as the soloist and improviser, risking spontaneous decisions in the act of performance.

The opening gestures of the Concerto in C Major, op. 15, resemble a magic trick: an important motive is produced out of nothing, like a rabbit drawn from an empty hat. Quiet C-major chords with a long-short-short rhythm are played, with a change in pitch from middle C to the C an octave higher. The leap is then filled as a rising C-major scale spans the gap (fig. 2.5). This simple resource has extraordinary consequences in the concerto, in which Beethoven as pianist took full technical advantage of the keyboard's white keys in C major, which enables brilliant and rapid scalar motion.

Scalar gestures assume prominence in the "passionate conversation" of soloist and orchestra. Following a robust conclusion of the opening orchestra ritornello, Beethoven takes a cue from Mozart's K. 503 in having the soloist enter somewhat shyly and obliquely, with understated accents. Yet, after a few moments,

Allegro con brio

2.5 Piano Concerto in C Major, op. 15, beginning.

scalar embellishment elaborates the solo passage, leading into the *fortissimo* response of the *tutti*. The later solo passages elaborate scalar patterns in various ways. Striking is Beethoven's handling of the end of the development section. A soft passage brings a dialogue between the solo piano and the horns, once more reducing the music to the long-short-short rhythmic pattern. A static pedal point on G sustained by the two horns yields a sense of suspended motion. Yet the soft mystery of the passage sets a trap for the listener: all at once the piano is given a loud double *glissando* descending across the entire keyboard, while an accented note is added in the deep bass. On modern instruments, this passage is virtually unplayable as written, since it would require three hands!

Beethoven makes witty allusion to this passage later, at the end of the solo cadenza he devised for the piece in 1809. His cadenza is an extravagant romp, the most extended improvisatory cadenza he ever published, vividly preserving his inspired style of extemporization. Arresting is his treatment of that most conventional of musical gestures: the cadence. Nothing in the classical music language seems more predictable than the anticipated resolution of a pre-cadential trill on the harmony of the dominant-seventh chord, which in the context of a concerto signals the end of a solo cadenza and reentry of the orchestra. In the face of such conventions, Beethoven's bad behavior is provocative. As the cadenza is extended to a generous length, he indeed indulges in such trills, while failing to complete the cadenza. As it continues, he cites another theme, a marchlike subject in G major. Virtuosic textures ensue, now with an extended double trill, then a triple trill, a specialty of Beethoven's piano playing. Despite all such delays and pyrotechnical displays, the cadenza still does not reach its expected outcome, while the orchestra is obliged to wait. An extended series of rising scales on the dominant seventh finally breaks free from the lower pitch registers, stretching with a *crescendo* across the entire keyboard.

If it seems nothing more should remain to be heard from the indulgent soloist, this too proves deceptive. Another surprise remains: a soft arpeggiated chord recalling the soft broken chords from the end of the development. The understated chord triggers at last the long-delayed event, with orchestra and soloist pouncing together on the tonic chord with a bang. The earlier surprise from the end of the development is recaptured, in accordance with a principle of humorous unpredictability.

Beethoven's ironic treatment of such performance conventions was typical. A similar situation reportedly arose during one of his performances of the Quintet for Piano and Woodwinds, op. 16, with Friedrich Ramm as oboe soloist:

> In the last Allegro there are several holds [or pauses] before the theme is resumed. At one of these Beethoven suddenly began to improvise, took the Rondo for a theme and entertained himself and the others for a considerable time, but not the other players. They were displeased and Ramm even very angry. It was really very comical to see them, momentarily expecting the performance to be resumed, put their instruments to their mouths, only to put them down again. At length Beethoven was satisfied and dropped into the Rondo. The whole company was transported with delight.

Such returns of the rondo theme are given subtle treatment by the soloist in the finale of Beethoven's C-major Concerto. The first two passages make the approach from F minor and G minor, respectively; the last such passage from B major, with a soft magically visionary effect, is followed by a rousing *fortissimo* statement of the main theme from the orchestra. The soloist takes the lead in seeking alternative versions, imaginative projects of shared conventional material. The rondo theme has the character of a contredance, a dance type of special political importance in the 1790s because of its exchange of partners and consequent association with the erosion of class distinctions after the French Revolution. Beethoven was highly focused on the genre of the contredance, employing it prominently in his *Creatures of Prometheus* ballet and in the finale of the *Eroica* Symphony. The joyous swing of this contredance preserves the long-short-short rhythm present in all three movements of the concerto. The accented first half of each measure receives rhythmic emphasis, with the characteristic upbeat figure carried over into the main subsidiary themes.

The contredance absorbs the scalar motion from the first movement, both descending and ascending. The initial motive falls a third from an accented E to C and from C to G, then reverses direction to traverse the same tonal space. At the end of the theme, this idea is elaborated in faster notes, becoming a sweeping octave scale. The vivacious tune displays a regularity of structure in accordance with its dance character, but measures 15–18 feature the scale figure in gestures recalling those in the opening *Allegro con brio*. Without this interpolation, a simpler but impoverished version of the theme would result.

The main secondary theme employs offbeat accents and then a humorous dialogue technique with a crossing of the left hand over the right. It is as if two comic figures engaged in debate, while the accompaniment continues unbroken in the middle of the keyboard. With orchestral wind instruments reinforcing the harmonies, a kind of "three-hand" technique ensues. The middle episode, on the other hand, is even more obviously humorous: a *staccato* bass with wide skips supports rhythms suggestive of a samba.

The *tour de force* is withheld until the coda, after an emphatic *fortissimo* statement of the contredance by the orchestra. The soloist and woodwinds square off in exchanging the two key motives: the rising scale familiar from the first movement and tail of the main rondo theme, on the one hand, and the falling-third idea from the head of the contredance, on the other. The piano takes up the scalar figures in octaves, while the orchestra recites the head motive from the rondo subject. This contrapuntal motivic combination crowns the work, with celebratory effect, while the closing gestures center on the cadential figure E–D–C, first in the piano and then in a short *Adagio* for the oboe. This passage harbors a distant premonition of later works: the poignant oboe in the Fifth Symphony, and the evocative "Le-be-wohl" motive of the "Farewell" Sonata.

Even more direct engagement with the Mozartian legacy is felt in Beethoven's next concerto, the work in C minor, op. 37. Here again, one senses the importance of Beethoven's abilities of an improviser, an orator in tones. As early as 1796, he notated a seminal idea for this concerto: "in the concerto in C minor, timpani at the cadenza." Mozart's Concerto in C minor, K. 491, looms in the formative background of this concerto. Mozart's first notes—C–Eb–Ab—surface as a counterpoint in Beethoven's opening theme (mm. 9–10). Both concertos exploit a pervasive G–Ab conflict as an expressive focus.

The comparison of Beethoven's concerto with Mozart reveals its more idealistic character. Mozart's work evokes an expressive atmosphere of elegiac resignation or grim passion. Commentators have written of "a passion, even a kind of terror, that is central to the work," and found it to be perhaps "Mozart's most personal work," surpassing even the D-minor Concerto or G-minor Symphony in its "abysmal depth and tragic quality." Beethoven's concerto lacks such abysmal or tragic qualities; the range of character extends from a military quality reflected in the dotted rhythmic figures first heard in measure 3 of the opening *Allegro con brio*, to the jubilant atmosphere of the coda of the rondo finale. Beethoven's original inspiration of using the timpani at the cadenza is borne out in his fascinating close of that passage, as a series of trills alight on an ambiguous harmony, whereupon the dotted figure from the main theme is played in the timpani. This mysterious gesture precedes the cadence and reentry of the orchestra, and draws the drums into the sphere of the solo cadenza.

Beethoven sets his meditative slow movement in the remote key of E major, while melodically emphasizing G♯, the third of that key. Enharmonically equivalent to Ab, G♯ is a stable consonance in E major. The initial serene chord in the piano embodies this new key as a tonal environment for reflection; the *Largo*'s closing chord in the orchestra serves as transitional springboard to the rondo finale. As the pianist launches the rondo, the telltale G♯ reverts to C minor as part of the upbeat motive G–A♭. This dissonant semitone figure sticks out, as A♭ becomes the problematic "sore" note of the tune. The rondo theme is yet another contredance, with the upbeat in 2/4 meter. In accordance with its political character, in a spirit of liberation from constraints, the "sore" note of A♭ is tested and ultimately overcome. In two *tutti* passages (mm. 42–43; 168–169), a brave oboist dares to replace A♭ by G♯, venturing into C major, but the orchestra, in a display of angry bluster, insists on the minor. This disagreement is dispelled at the conclusion. A solo cadenza reshapes the semitone motive definitively as G♯–A, whereupon the whole ensemble celebrates C major in a witty coda in *opera buffa* style.

As in the *Pathétique*, Beethoven opens a window onto the soundscape of his slow movement in the midst of the finale. After a robust orchestral fugato passage, the pianist plays octaves on A♭, which are transformed into G♯ blended with E, a sonority veiled in pedal with a *decrescendo* to *pianissimo*. This mysterious passage presents a poetic reminiscence of the initial sonority of the *Largo*, whose uncanny spell enables an exquisite soft statement of the contredance melody in the piano's high register, resonating above *pianissimo* chords in the strings. With this ethereal transposition of the rondo tune into E major, Beethoven gazes back at the *Largo*, while anticipating the resolving coda of the rondo in C major. Seldom is this episode performed with the nuance it deserves. Beethoven ends the passage with quiet repeated notes echoing the last inflections from the piano's dissipating phrases, as this vision of the key of the *Largo* glimpsed through the melody of the rondo recedes into inaudibility. This episode enlarges the E-major chord from the *Largo* into a passage fourteen measures long, an imaginative vision of special poignancy.

Such visions, bending the temporality of experience, are compatible with Schiller's conviction about artistic representations of the ideal. Schiller writes how "divined instinct, and creative force, much too ardent to follow a placid path, often throws itself immediately on the present, on active life, and strives to transform the shapeless matter of the moral world," and he continues that "a pure, moral motive has for its end the absolute; time does not exist for it, and the future becomes the present to it directly; by a necessary development it has to issue from the present." In Beethoven's music, such creative intervention transcends linear time, harnessing the power of memory and the productive imagination. The ethereal E-major vision in his concerto retrieves the atmosphere of the contemplative slow movement while prefiguring the positive resolution of tensions that will cap the entire work. Annulling time, this music rejects a conventional "placid path"; through its anticipatory quality, it takes flight as "the future becomes the present." In his C-minor Concerto, Beethoven's response to Mozart's "abysmal depth" generates a more optimistic narrative spanning the whole work and sustained by a "pure, moral motive" that integrates the heart and the head, the sensuous and rational sides of human nature. This dimension of Beethoven's art has been explored recently by Robert Hatten, who employs the notion of virtual agency, of "spiritual freedom involved in the capacity to transcend incompleteness and discover greater meaning."

In contrast to the resourceful audacity of his artistic works, Beethoven's overt response to the political events and atmosphere of repression of the later 1790s was guarded and ambivalent. With Austria and France in conflict, he faced a delicate balancing act. Unlike Haydn, he did not make important contributions to music written in support of the Habsburg cause against the French. Haydn's hymnlike tune "Gott erhalte Franz den Kaiser" ("God preserve Franz the emperor") achieved extraordinary dissemination in the empire at the time of its composition in February 1797. Modeled in part on "God Save the King," shaped as a patriotic anthem and first performed on the birthday of the monarch, Haydn's "Emperor's Hymn" was conceived while Austria was under threat and patriotic feelings ran high.

Franz Josef von Saurau, the same official who had led the actions against Hebelstreit and Riedel in 1794, and became a trusted advisor to Emperor Franz, was a key figure promoting Haydn's anthem. As Saurau explained, "I had a text fashioned by the worthy poet [Lorenz Leopold] Haschka; and to have it set to music, I turned to our immortal compatriot Haydn, who, I felt, was the only man capable of creating something that could be placed at the side of 'God Save the King.'"

By contrast, Beethoven's patriotic "Farewell Song to the Citizens of Vienna" and his "War Song of the Austrians," written around this time to texts by Joseph Friedelberg, seem slight and perfunctory. As the century neared its end, and the vicissitudes of the French Revolution were supplanted by Napoleon's meteoric rise to power, Beethoven's political allegiance was tested. To have openly endorsed the French cause would have endangered his career. Suspicions have been raised of his having expressed support for Bonaparte obliquely, under a deliberately ambiguous veil, in the case of his Twelve Variations on a Theme from Handel's oratorio *Judas Maccabaeus* for piano and cello, WoO 45, published in late 1797. The text drawn from the oratorio is "See, the conqu'ring hero comes." Defeated Austria lacked heroic candidates; but, as John Clubb suggests, the timing of Beethoven's publication suggests a connection to another conquering hero, Napoleon, who had then returned to Paris following his conquests in northern Italy.

A real-life Marquis de Posa—a historical model for Schiller's fictional character who would have attracted Beethoven's attention at this time—was the celebrated hero of the American Revolution then held in Austrian captivity, the French Marquis de Lafayette. After a failed escape attempt in 1795, Lafayette was thrown into solitary confinement at the fortress in Olmütz, with hardly enough sustenance to keep him alive. An appeal from George Washington to Emperor Franz in May 1796 failed to obtain his release. However, diplomatic interventions enabled his wife Adrienne and their two daughters to share his imprisonment, keeping him alive until 1797, when after the treaty of Campo Formio and through Bonaparte's insistence they were freed. Lafayette's ordeal and the intervention of his determined wife likely formed part of the context of Beethoven's interest in the French opera that became the basis for his *Fidelio*. In this instance, the imprisoned freedom fighter was a victim of the Austrian monarchy who was liberated through actions of Napoleon.

Shortly thereafter, in 1798, Beethoven associated with Marshal Jean-Baptiste Bernadotte, one of Napoleon's generals during the Italian campaigns, who was appointed French ambassador to Austria in the wake of the treaty of Campo Formio. From February until April, Bernadotte resided in Vienna. Strongly interested in music, he brought with him the violinist Rodolphe Kreuzer, who later received the dedication of Beethoven's Violin Sonata in A Major, op. 47, the "Kreuzer" Sonata. In Beethoven's First Symphony, the main theme of the opening *Allegro con brio* displays a kinship with Kreutzer's *Ouverture de la journée de Marathon, ou, Le triomphe de la liberté*. This suggestive allusive context blends associations of heroic resistance from Greek antiquity with Revolutionary France of the 1790s.

Bernadotte's remarkable career was promoted by personal connections. His wife, Désirée Clary, had been Napoleon's fiancée after her sister Julie married his older brother Joseph Bonaparte; after Napoleon canceled their engagement, she married Jean-Baptiste Bernadotte in 1798. Bernadotte's upward path withstood tensions with Napoleon, who once described him as "a serpent whom I was nourishing in my bosom." In 1805 Bernadotte became the prince of Ponte-Corvo in Italy; in 1810 he was elected crown prince of Sweden, enabling him to ascend the Swedish throne in 1818. At the great Battle of the Nations at Leipzig in 1813, Bernadotte shrewdly switched sides, fighting with the allies against his former benefactor.

When writing to the Swedish king in 1823 to solicit Bernadotte's subscription to the *Missa solemnis*, Beethoven recalled their shared time in Vienna a quarter century earlier. It is questionable whether Bernadotte played a role in the connection of the *Eroica* Symphony with Napoleon, as has been claimed. Beethoven's association to Bernadotte and Kreuzer forms part of the context of the composer's admiration for Bonaparte as First Consul of the French

Republic, a position he assumed in December 1799, a decade after the outbreak of the revolution. The abrupt end of Bernadotte's brief tenure as French ambassador in Vienna in April 1798 speaks volumes about the political tensions at this time. During Easter week, many young people were involved with a ceremony honoring Austrian volunteers who one year earlier had defended Vienna against the French military advance in Italy. When Bernadotte on 13 April brazenly hoisted a large French tricolor flag with the inscription "Liberty, equality, fraternity" over the balcony of his hotel, his action was seen as a provocative incentive to revolution. A crowd gathered; menacing voices were heard. After Bernadotte refused to remove the flag and threatened to defend it by force, a riot broke out, his flag was burned, and probably only the intervention of military assigned for his protection saved his life.

Beethoven
in Heiligenstadt

Only after Beethoven's death in 1827 was vivid light shed on crises that racked his life but helped shape his creative development. Foremost in importance are two documents that came to light when friends of the deceased composer rummaged through his belongings and desk, seeking the bank shares that Beethoven bequeathed in his will to his nephew Karl. Both manuscripts were apparently lodged in a concealed inner drawer of his desk. One of these is his famous letter to the "Eternal Beloved" from 1812, to which we will return. The other is the *Heiligenstadt Testament*, a remarkable confession of despair and personal resolution from October 1802.

In the *Heiligenstadt Testament*, Beethoven describes how he was loath to admit that he was becoming deaf. The document offers a passionate rhetorical explanation of his withdrawal from society, behavior he describes as widely misunderstood. The testament begins as follows: "Oh you who regard or proclaim me to be malevolent, obdurate, or misanthropic, you do me a grave injustice, for you know nothing of the secret cause that makes me appear this way to you." For a performing virtuoso and composer in a competitive cultural environment, the hearing loss triggered intense anxiety. Beethoven mourns "an impairment in that very faculty that ought by rights to be more highly developed in me than in other men, a faculty that I once possessed to the highest degree of perfection, a perfection such as few in my profession enjoy or ever have enjoyed." Apart from its dire implications for his performing career and negative impact on his social life, Beethoven surely also feared a curtailment of his musical creativity. This touches on an issue that has long stimulated discussion: did Beethoven's deafness, which became virtually complete by 1818, harm his compositional work, or actually render it richer?

Beethoven moved to Heiligenstadt by May 1802. His stay there lasted a half year, until after he penned the testament in October. His summer refuge was then a rural village of 400 inhabitants. His choice of Heiligenstadt, rather than a larger, more fashionable spa destination near Vienna such as Baden, signaled a desire for seclusion in nature close to vineyards, hills, forest, and streams. From the higher ground around Heiligenstadt, Beethoven could gaze toward a pair of summits, the Kahlenberg and Leopoldberg, that dominate the northern side of the city near the Danube River. This is a picturesque landscape steeped in history, the vantage point from which the cavalry of the Christian relief army had swept down to break the Turkish siege of Vienna in 1683. Within walking distance of Heiligenstadt is the *Schreiberbach*, the stream that helped inspire the second movement of the *Pastoral* Symphony. Vienna, then ringed by walled fortifications, lies to the south. The hilly countryside around the village offered panoramic views of the old city.

The name "Heiligenstadt" means "holy city," the German form of the old Latin name *Sanctum Locum* that appears in medieval documents. The locality has traces of Roman presence; the first record of a settlement from 1120 refers to the village as St. Michael, and the Archangel Michael is shown on Heiligenstadt's coat of arms. Although Heiligenstadt was devastated and its residents massacred in 1683, it was a prospering small village a century later. Beethoven repeatedly came during the summers to Heiligenstadt. He returned in 1808, when he lived in the same house as the young Franz Grillparzer, who became Austria's leading playwright and who in 1827 penned Beethoven's funeral oration. During another summer stay in 1817, the composer resided partly in Heiligenstadt and partly in nearby Nußdorf.

A few weeks into his summer stay of 1802, in mid-July,

Beethoven wrote to publishers in Leipzig that "I'm in the country-side, and live somewhat lazily, but in order thereafter again to live more actively." The idyllic locality of Heiligenstadt offered him a refuge, yet conflicts remained. The unexpected, faulty publication by the Artaria firm of Beethoven's String Quintet op. 29 around this time triggered bitter accusations of piracy from the composer and led to a messy lawsuit. To Beethoven, Artaria & Co. were "ras-cals," guilty of the "*biggest swindle* in the world"; yet Artaria was exonerated by the court, which requested in vain a retraction of the composer's accusations. Just after his return to Vienna in November 1802, Beethoven viewed himself as having fallen vic-tim to the "arch scoundrel *Artaria* during the time [he] spent in the countryside on account of his health."

What occupied Beethoven artistically during that summer? The fervently desired improvement in his hearing did not hap-pen, as he acknowledged by the fall, when he wrote the *Heiligen-stadt Testament* on the sixth and tenth of October. Older biogra-phies of Beethoven relied on guesswork in seeking to reconstruct the creative events of 1802. The standard approach is to juxta-pose the despairing *Heiligenstadt Testament* with the ebullient Second Symphony, depicting the symphony as Beethoven's bal-ancing artistic compensation to his troubled inner state. This interpretation is mistaken: the sources show that the symphony was completed before Beethoven moved to Heiligenstadt that spring.

The hints contained in letters and in personal accounts of a few witnesses, especially Beethoven's students Ferdinand Ries and Carl Czerny, are valuable, but the main source of reliable fresh insight is his surviving musical manuscripts, mainly his sketch-books. The first proper catalogue of these sources was published only in the 1980s. Despite Beethoven's chaotic lifestyle, and his restless wandering from one apartment to another in Vienna, with summer quarters often spent in the country, the composer took special care of his growing legacy of musical sketchbooks. These preserve a detailed record of his creativity. For the Heiligenstadt sojourn of 1802, the relevant sources are now available in trustworthy editions, and enable insights that are noteworthy and sometimes even revelatory.

Although Beethoven claimed to be living "somewhat lazily" at Heiligenstadt, he used no fewer than three large-sized sketchbooks during his half year there. These manuscripts now bear names derived from subsequent owners or from prominent Beethovenian works contained in their pages. The first sketchbook is known as the *Kessler* Sketchbook, and was largely filled with entries when Beethoven took it with him to Heiligenstadt; a second book, known as the *Wielhorsky* Sketchbook, was used together with *Kessler*, as Beethoven kept these manuscripts side-by-side at his workplace. Ordinarily, a single such sketchbook would suffice for several months of compositional work. Beethoven would also work out ideas on the piano he brought with him to Heiligenstadt; he did not need to commit everything to written form. In any event, the sources indicate that a third sketchbook—the *Eroica* Sketchbook that reached publication only in 2013—was also in use in Heiligenstadt by the fall of 1802. This new evidence underscores the pivotal role of Beethoven's Heiligenstadt summer in his creative development.

The inner drama of Beethoven's creativity is exposed with full force in his process of composing at Heiligenstadt one of his powerful piano sonatas, the Sonata in D Minor, op. 31, no. 2. A character of passionate tragic drama characterizes this unique sonata in three movements. The piece later became associated with the title *Tempest* owing to a report from an untrustworthy witness, Beethoven's nineteenth-century biographer Anton Schindler. To be sure, Beethoven knew Shakespeare's play; many years later, he capriciously fancied himself as the magician Prospero while habitually dubbing as Ariel the young son Gerhard of his old friend Stephan von Breuning. Could Beethoven have imagined himself in his Heiligenstadt village retreat as a kind of exiled sorcerer? Whether his fascination with Prospero dates from this period is hard to say. However, there is something thought-provokingly enigmatic about the opening motto of the *Tempest* rising out of an improvisatory broken chord, hanging in the air as a subject for meditation and later triggering a recitative soliloquy at the reprise. A single musical thought is invested here with an almost magical transformational potential, as is manifested as well in the probing *Adagio* and the *perpetuum mobile* finale.

In view of the aesthetic and even political implications of this D-minor Sonata, we should note Beethoven's vehement rejection at this time of the suggestion of his writing a programmatic sonata with a narrative reflective of the French Revolution. That proposal came forth in April 1802—immediately before his move to Heiligenstadt—from a certain Countess Kielmansegge from Dessau and was communicated to the composer through his publishers Hoffmeister & Kühnel in Leipzig. Beethoven's dismissive reply is as follows:

> Gentlemen, are you then all possessed of the devil, to propose to me *such a sonata*? At the time of the Revolution fever that would have been all very well, but now, as everything is seeking to return to the old rut—and the Concordat drawn up between Buonaparte and the Pope—a sonata of this kind? If only it were a *Missa pro Sancta Maria a tre voci*, or a *Vesper*, etc., then I would at once take pencil in hand, and with great pound notes [*Pfundnoten*] write down a *Credo in unum*, but, good heavens, such a sonata in these newly commencing Christian times—hoho—leave me out of it, nothing will come of it.

Beethoven disdains the idea of illustrative music for the Revolution, and did not regard Napoleon optimistically: "everything is seeking to return to the old rut" while the time for *"such a sonata"* was long past. Napoleon's *Concordat* with Pope Pius VII dates from July 1801, and took effect at Easter 1802, bringing reconciliation between Bonaparte's regime and the Catholic Church. Beethoven did not greet this news positively with a *"Credo in unum,"* as his sarcasm shows. The sonata as a secular genre was hardly the medium to celebrate such an exalted but pragmatic marriage of convenience. Contemporary depictions displayed Napoleon's beatific ascension, as in *Allegory of the Concordat of 1801*, by Pierre

Joseph Célestin François. Significantly, Beethoven's letter dates from two years before completion of the *Eroica* Symphony. His fascination with Bonaparte long coexisted with skepticism. The D-minor Sonata—a sonata he *did* indeed write at precisely this time—embodies an aesthetic perspective that neither depicts nor endorses such political realities.

As we have seen, Beethoven was attracted to the potential of employing contrasting musical sections within a larger continuity, as in the opening movement of the *Sonate pathétique*. In the first movement of the *Tempest* Sonata, Beethoven compresses this idea of a split tempo, while exploiting its formal and psychological possibilities. This was not his original idea, as entries in the *Kessler* Sketchbook show. While at Heiligenstadt, Beethoven turned his attention to a Sonata in D Minor when just a few unwritten pages remained in the sketchbook. A revealing series of sketches preserve his initial conception for this sonata in three movements, and he then flipped back in the nearly filled book to search for room to continue his work. Twenty-five pages earlier, Beethoven found enough remaining space to enter a revised draft of the first movement, one in which an affinity to the finished work is readily apparent. There is no question about this sequence of events, since Beethoven made folds marking the placement of the important second draft in the middle of the book. That the significance of these sketches has been largely overlooked is due in part to their irregular positioning in the original manuscript.

Although the traces preserved in *Kessler* are an incomplete record, we can discern four compositional stages. Beethoven's first sketches were surely preceded by improvisation at the keyboard, presumably on the Anton Walter fortepiano that Czerny described having seen around this time in the composer's lodgings. The sketches at the end of *Kessler* diverge from the finished work, but are bound to it through a genetic process; study of these sketches in relation to the subsequent draft and completed version reveals the creative imagination in action. Beethoven's second draft depicts the first movement in a synoptic form, compressed onto a single page. Much is left out, but the notated musical content corresponds roughly to the sonata as we know it. The fourth and final stage in this reconstruction is embodied in the completed piece, and further insights about the compositional process would surely have been preserved in Beethoven's autograph score, which unfortunately has not survived. The first sound examples accessible on the publisher's website (press.uchicago.edu/sites/kinderman/) include my recordings of both of Beethoven's drafts for the opening movement of the *Tempest* Sonata, together with a recording of all three movements of the completed work.

Beethoven's original draft is shown in figure 3.1. Not just the opening motive but the key, texture, and character are arresting. The passionate, almost operatic character of the theme in D minor is underscored by its *tremolo* accompaniment figuration in the bass, which sounds an open fifth, D–A, omitting the third of the harmony. The mysterious tension of this idea invites comparison not only to passages of the finished sonata starting in measure 21, but to the beginning of the Ninth Symphony. An intertextual affinity is not limited to Beethoven's *oeuvre*; the character of a turbulent D-minor idiom touched by the uncanny or demonic reaches back to Mozart's *Don Giovanni* and Requiem and forward to Brahms's D-minor Concerto.

To open a musical work with a rising broken chord is a familiar enough idea. The Mannheim symphonic school had trademarked that technique by the 1740s; such "Mannheim rocket" themes surface in the finale of Mozart's G-minor Symphony and the opening of Beethoven's own first Piano Sonata in F Minor, op. 2, no. 1. Beethoven's D-minor sketch, however, blends this wellworn motivic idea with other elements, creating an impressive synthesis. The *tremolo* on the open fifth D–A yields to a chromatically descending continuation in the bass while the upper melody leads into an intensely expressive falling contour; a second phrase restates the rising broken-chord figure on an unstable dissonance, before this parallel gesture resolves firmly in D minor. Beethoven specifies no tempo and dynamics, but the implied character is sharply etched, presumably *Allegro* and *forte*.

The rest of Beethoven's movement plan shows him mapping

Keßlersches Skizzenbuch/Kessler Sketchbook, fol. 90v (Gesellschaft der Musikfreunde Wien)

3.1 Draft of *Tempest* Sonata/I, *Kessler* Sketchbook, fol. 90v
(Gesellschaft der Musikfreunde, Vienna). Transcribed by William Kinderman.
Numbers in italics refer to the stave numbers in the original manuscript.

out the defining junctures of the musical form. The designation
m. g. stands for "Mittel-Gedanke" or "second subject"; this lyrical idea in the contrasting key of B♭ major is based on descending
steps of the scale. Beethoven then skips forward to the cadence of
the first part—the end of the exposition—extending this motive of
repeated chords in turn to lead into the development section. He
next envisions the end of the development section. Over a dominant pedal point in the bass, Beethoven ventures a rhythmically

intensified version of the rising broken-chord motive, played against an inverted form of the same figure in the bass. A variant of the repeated chord then returns, whereupon the music takes a surprising new turn: a *dolce* phrase in triple meter, in D major. This gesture marks the crucial place where Beethoven later incorporates passages of recitative bathed mysteriously in the sounds generated by the sustaining pedal, music arising from strings with raised dampers, *senza sordino*. The only remaining notated section in this sketch belongs to the coda, where a swift 6/8 transformation of the opening theme leads into a dissolving close in the low register.

The next draft of this movement written in the middle of *Kessler* resembles the finished work in that the slow-fast tempo duality has become the main focus; a plan for the beginning of the exposition and much of the development is laid out. One of many divergences from the completed version is the first chord: the sonority is notated in exactly the same position, but the opening arpeggiation or broken chord is missing. Here, as elsewhere, Beethoven develops a sonority—the initial A-major chord played with pedal—not by thinking forward but by imagining what should precede—in this case, an unfolding of pitches rising from the low C♯ so that a defined rhythm takes shape only from the A, an octave and a sixth higher. The tentative, enigmatic atmosphere of the opening owes much to this device.

What about the other two movements of the sonata? Both movements have strong genre and rhythmic associations. At the time he wrote his concentrated draft in the middle of the sketchbook, Beethoven's second movement had evolved into an "alla menuetto" in B♭ major, a piece focused on paired contrasting phrases: a figure based on a variant of the rising broken chord from the first movement balanced by a stepwise descending motive resembling the "m. g." second-subject entry in the initial draft for that opening movement (fig. 3.2). At the same time, he excluded B♭ major as the contrasting key in the first movement, confining that movement almost entirely to the sphere of minor tonalities. The consequent darkening of its character went beyond the synoptic draft,

3.2 *Kessler* Sketchbook, fol. 66r, sketch for an "alla menuetto."

3.3 *Tempest* Sonata in D Minor, op. 31, no. 2/II, beginning.

in which the movement was to have ended in D major instead of D minor.

Remarkable is how Beethoven adapts the "alla menuetto" idea in the completed slow movement, marked *Adagio*. The finished piece remained in 3/4 meter and B♭ major, while the primary theme employs broken chords pitted against concise double-dotted figures poised in a higher register (fig. 3.3). The character of the finished movement hardly suggests a minuet. Beethoven used this minuet sketch as a springboard, extracting motivic elements while changing his initial blueprint. In this stylistic setting, the minuet idiom held strong genre expectations with social connotations. Beethoven had already subverted the minuet form in other works, as in the First Symphony, transforming it to resemble a livelier, swifter dance type: the scherzo. In the second movement of the *Tempest* Sonata, he does the opposite: the rhythmic swing of the minuet is supplanted by a searching concentration on terse motivic figures in contrasting registers marked by silences, in a slow tempo.

What Beethoven achieves in this movement resembles what literary critics close to our time have deemed *deconstruction*, an interrogation of a model such that its genre expectations are dissected and transformed. Such deconstruction involves not destruction but rather an ironic, critical reassessment of fixed assumptions or established norms. This kind of probing attitude is also reflected in other pieces Beethoven wrote during his summer at Heiligenstadt, such as the delicious parody of Italian opera idioms embodied in the *Adagio grazioso* of the preceding Piano Sonata in G Major, op. 31, no. 1.

Although Beethoven's *Adagio* in the *Tempest* Sonata is in a major key and evolved in relation to minuet style, it evokes a reflective, somewhat ominous atmosphere. The main theme is meditative, its continuity impeded by a play of registral contrasts; the principal three-note figure generates striking harmonic dissonances. The main theme is characterized by empty spaces: gaps in register, gaps in sound. Might this music perhaps be linked to Beethoven's experience of his hearing loss? The transitional zones between themes are punctuated by terse rhythmic interjections, strange gestures evocative of drumbeats. In Beethoven, such drum rolls can be disquieting owing to their association with the strife of warfare. A later example is contained in the Agnus Dei of the *Missa solemnis*, whose terrifying intrusions of bellicose music threaten the plea for peace, and cast shadows over the conclusion of the Mass.

In the *Heiligenstadt Testament*, Beethoven laments his loneliness ("I am utterly alone") and his being "forced . . . to become a philosopher"; in the addendum of the document, he bids farewell, alluding to his "withered and blighted" hope of attaining a cure for his deafness. The text ends with a fervent prayer:

Of Providence, grant me but one day of unalloyed joy. It has been so long since I have felt the intimate reverberations of true joy. When, oh when, Divine One, shall I feel them again in the temple of Nature and Mankind. Never? No, that would be too cruel!

This passage offers a key to understanding Beethoven's *Adagio*. The sonata contains one bright oasis, a melody that might well be regarded as a moment of "unalloyed" or "true joy": the second subject of the slow movement. This theme stands out for its sensitive

3.4 *Tempest* Sonata in D Minor, op. 31, no. 2/II, second theme.

textures and shaping. The melody is marked *dolce* and exhibits
a flowing accompaniment and gentle rhythmic swing. Only here
does the otherwise suppressed minuet character of the music
receive gracious heartfelt expression (fig. 3.4). The lyric potential of double-dotted figures and ornamental flourishes from the
opening theme comes to fruition. Despite its slow tempo marking,
this melodic subject invites comparison to decorated minuets in
Beethoven's piano music, such as the *Tempo di menuetto, moderato*
that closes the Diabelli Variations, op. 120.

Beethoven frames this exquisite theme by transitions bearing
the ominous drum-roll figures, whereas the absence of a development section in the musical design further emphasizes the gracious slow minuet. Even writers hesitant to indulge in descriptive commentary have been touched by the melodic inspiration
of this theme. In his rather formalistic analysis dismissive of the
alleged Shakespearean connection to *The Tempest*, Donald Fran-
cis Tovey writes about this theme that "it will do you no harm to
think of Miranda," Prospero's compassionate young daughter.
Shakespeare's Miranda, gazing at shipwrecked passengers on the
island, marvels, "How beauteous mankind is!" The utopian thrust
and purity of her character are at one with Beethoven's "intimate
reverberations of true joy" in his *Adagio*. His choice of words in the
Heiligenstadt Testament—"so lange schon ist der wahren Freude
inniger widerhall mir fremd"—"It has been so long since I have felt
the intimate reverberations of true joy"—stresses an acoustical or
musical embodiment of joy, a sublime echo heard in response to
yearning.

Beethoven's secluded stay at Heiligenstadt that summer offered
a very different inspiration for the sonata's finale. According to

Czerny, a reliable witness, Beethoven said this movement reflected his observation of a rider on horseback visible from a window in his lodgings. The movement is a *perpetuum mobile* whose rhythm and character are compatible with this report, though of course the music would not be directly descriptive of such an event, but instead would have drawn on such observation as an impetus to artistic creation. A horse's gallop generates a swinging triple meter with unbroken movement, a kind of sweeping inevitability. The ascending broken chords familiar from the earlier movements surface here in the accompaniment, which forms with the main motive an exciting rhythmic counterpoint analogous to the motion of a galloping horse's legs, with their fascinating point of levitation, that moment when all four hooves are off the ground.

As in the first movement, the end of Beethoven's finale fades away mysteriously, but much power is lodged in transitional and developmental passages. At the transition to A minor, Beethoven six times resolves the half step F–E downward to a consonance, before that accented dissonance asserts itself as primary. A fateful, inexorable quality emerges through the driving momentum of the whole. At the heart of this finale is a false recapitulation on B♭ minor. Here and elsewhere, ethereal quiet passages are juxtaposed with emphatic reassertion of a forceful trajectory that seems beyond human control.

Remarkable about the *Tempest* Sonata in relation to Beethoven's political attitudes are the recitatives at the outset of the recapitulation of the first movement, passages already foregrounded in his synoptic blueprint scrawled in the midst of the *Kessler* Sketchbook. The first recitative closely parallels the baritone recitative at the threshold to the finale of the Ninth Symphony, composed twenty years later. The connection between these works is conveyed through their common key of D minor, and the affinity of the *tremolo* textures in their opening movements, a character that Beethoven associated with "Verweiflung" or despair. "Oh friends, not these tones, let us sing more joyful": this message is bound up with an aesthetic attitude of confrontation, reflecting concerns similar to the *Heiligenstadt Testament*. We shall return to these issues in connection with the genesis and import of the Ninth Symphony.

This interruption of the tragic musical discourse by inflections of recitative that in the Ninth Symphony bear the message "friends, not these tones," provokes thought. Time freezes at this juncture, as another perspective, a poignant utterance, emerges to deepen the effect of the initial mysterious *Largo* with its mysterious rising broken chord. The last five notes of the first recitative in the sonata match to the five syllables "nicht diese Töne!" in the symphony. The thematic similarity amounts almost to quotation, as the sonata anticipates the expressive turning point to Beethoven's own words in the Ninth. Beethoven seized on this moment of internalization and reflection as embodied in the recitative in the sonata to provide a gateway to the utopian plane of the *Ode to Joy* in the choral finale. Already in the sonata, he breaks the flow of the artistic discourse in the service of a higher goal. The recitatives in the *Tempest* Sonata seem incomprehensible—*unverständlich*—in the positive sense articulated by Friedrich Schlegel at the time, since they challenge the listener to seek implied meanings that are not immediately obvious. The artist assumes in this context an oracular role, synthetic rather than analytic in the Kantian sense, urging the listener to become a more active participant in the quest for meaning. Latent political implications can be recognized here, through the provocative protest of the embedded recitatives. Venturing another analogy to Shakespeare's *Tempest*, we might say that as Prospero becomes aware of politics, emerging from the self-imposed isolation symbolized by his books, so did Beethoven emerge from self-absorption in his musical sketchbooks, seeking "thereafter again to live more actively."

What else did Beethoven compose at Heiligenstadt? Next to his sketches for the *Tempest* Sonata is his work on a pair of innovative variation sets for piano on themes of his own invention: the Variations in F Major, op. 34, and the larger set of Variations in E♭ Major, op. 35. Along with his op. 31 piano sonatas, these variation sets embody his self-declared "neuer Weg" or "new path," the threshold to what is known as his "second period" or "heroic style."

The notion of a "new path" should be regarded cautiously, but these pieces are pathbreaking, and the Variations in E♭ assume outstanding significance as Beethoven's springboard to the *Eroica* Symphony.

The through line to the *Eroica* begins with a contredance composed at latest around 1800. Beethoven's choice of a contredance held political significance. As a line dance involving exchange of partners, the contredance (*Kontratanz*) was associated with a crossing of class lines and with social mobility. In the post-Revolutionary period, an erosion of class distinctions, to which the contredance responded, had become ubiquitous, even in conservative Austria.

Yet with this breakdown of social distinctions, the display of identity remained important, and the dance maintained an aesthetic of civilized sociality that made its performance appealing as a marker of social standing. The contredance in question was used four times by Beethoven: as the seventh of his Twelve Contredances for orchestra, WoO 14; in the ballet music for *The Creatures of Prometheus*, op. 43; as basis for the aforementioned Variations for Piano in E♭ Major, op. 35; and in the *Eroica*.

A beginning before a beginning: Beethoven's preoccupation with origins and creative process finds exemplary illustration through his treatment of the contredance in these interlinked pieces. When the *Prometheus* Variations were about to be published in the spring of 1803, he wrote with urgency to Breitkopf & Härtel as follows:

> . . . with the larger variations [op. 35] it has been forgotten that the *theme* of the set stems from an *allegorical* ballet written by me, namely Prometheus or in *Italian Prometeo*, which should have been placed on the title page and if it's possible, I request that in case it's not yet appeared, the title page be changed, which can be done at my expense . . .

Beethoven wanted these allegorical associations indicated, but his wish remained unfulfilled. His Contredance in E♭ is heard as stage music in the ballet finale at the closing apotheosis or glorification of Prometheus, but an impressive enactment of the Promethean creative principle in music first took place in the Piano Variations op. 35 and then in the *Eroica*. A key aspect of Beethoven's approach consists once more in *deconstruction* of a model. Like a minuet, a contredance displays well-defined stylistic features. Beethoven's contredances are concise dances in 2/4 meter with an upbeat, cast in a binary form. While building up a musical edifice from his contredance, Beethoven did not merely elaborate the theme; he first stripped it down, exposing incomplete, fragmentary elements.

This aesthetic strategy motivated Beethoven's special treatment of what he called the *Basso del tema*, or bass of the theme, in op. 35. A *fortissimo* E♭ chord serves as preface, corresponding roughly to the pair of *forte* chords that begin the *Eroica*. The work then unfolds not with the complete preexisting theme, but instead with a vision of bare bones. This elemental aspect is most obvious in the second half of the thematic structure, with its grotesque humor of loud octaves and silences. The wit of Beethoven's treatment is reflected in the dynamics: the *Basso del tema* is presented at first on tiptoes, in *pianissimo* octaves in the first half of the theme and later at the close; surprise is generated through the three *fortissimo* interjections set off by pauses. This presentation of the bass alone then serves as the basis for three variations successively adding more voices, designated "A due," "A tre," and "A quattro." The unfolding progression gradually enlivens the rhythm and expands the musical textures, filling up the registral spaces as the *Basso del tema* rises in pitch in these initial variations.

Consequently, the original *Kontratanz* as such is no longer the starting point. When he wrote op. 35, Beethoven was so experienced as a composer and improviser of keyboard variations—having written sixteen such works—that he did not normally need to make extensive sketches. The *Prometheus* Variations were different: Beethoven wrote sketches in the *Kessler* Sketchbook, but then used the *Wielhorsky* Sketchbook for more extensive entries, including revised versions of much thematic material found in

Kessler; in some instances, his most advanced entries for variations are found in the first of these two interrelated sources. In
composing these variations, Beethoven used the two sketchbooks
simultaneously side-by-side. As these sketches show, it was only
gradually that he recognized the value of withholding the contredance melody from the outset of his work, while preparatory hints
of the *Kontratanz* soon to emerge could be implanted in the evolving contrapuntal voices joined to the *Basso del tema*.

This progression was certainly inspired by the first section of
the *Prometheus* ballet, in which the proto-human protagonists initially resemble statues or figures of clay before being instilled with
animation and awareness, life and movement, by their benefactor. The awkwardness of the figures, and their blank emotionless
state, are reflected musically in the *Poco Adagio* (no. 1), following the tempestuous orchestral introduction conveying the flight
of Prometheus following his theft of fire. Like the contredance
and the *Basso del tema* sections in the op. 35 variations and *Eroica* finale, this *Poco Adagio* is in 2/4 meter. Short soft notes are
heard in lower registers in the strings alone, separated by pauses,
with more silence than sound. This *Poco Adagio* then alternates
with passionate full-bodied *Allegro con brio* passages associated
with Prometheus, who expresses his "divine and fatherly love" for
the emotionless children, who "shake their heads, are completely
indifferent, and stand there, groping in all directions." These comments are found among others in the sketchbook Beethoven used
in composing the music. The connection between the *Poco Adagio* in the ballet and the skeletal reduction to the *Basso del tema*
in op. 35 and op. 55 is tangible and direct, and there can be no
doubt about the presence of similar symbolic implications in these
works. Beethoven enhances the effect in the *Eroica* finale by having the strings play the bass of the contredance in a quiet *pizzicato*.
We shall return below to other aspects of the ballet music and its
symbolic meanings.

As an elemental musical trajectory leads gradually to the contredance in the *Prometheus* Variations, the music stages its own
kind of creation scenario. The vision of the artwork undergoing a

dynamic genesis took strong hold of Beethoven at Heiligenstadt, as is manifested in several compositions. At the outset of the *Tempest* Sonata, the mysterious rising motive seems introductory yet also embodies the main subject, as is confirmed through the moving recitatives at the recapitulation. Powerful incarnation of that motive on D minor becomes a goal of the ensuing *Allegro* passage, but also the springboard for a developmental process, and Beethoven uses a variant of that same passage as the core of the development section. The functions of introduction, exposition, and development are elided. Similarly, in the op. 35 Variations, Beethoven's dissection and reassembly of the contredance opens a tensional space manifesting originality.

Beethoven referred around this time to seeking a "new path" and pursuing a "new manner" of composition specifically in relation to the *Prometheus* Variations and its companion work op. 34, another piece whose sketches exist near those for op. 35 and the *Tempest* Sonata. The scope of the F-major Variations op. 34 is enriched through an artistic strategy of shifting keys and meter in successive variations, with some formal divisions blurred in favor of the individuality of the whole. Beethoven could no longer specify precisely how many variations these works contained, since some sections—including the opening treatment of the *Basso del tema* in op. 35—did not contain the entire main theme.

Beethoven's concern with the allegorical meaning of Prometheus is noteworthy, and rewards closer attention. As we have observed, it is closely bound up with his now-obscure ballet music to *Die Geschöpfe des Prometheus* (*The Creatures of Prometheus*), op. 43. This work was written in 1801 in collaboration with the dance master Salvatore Viganò, who also danced one of the main roles. The *Prometheus* music was Beethoven's first major work for the stage and one of his earliest public successes, with twenty-eight performances given at Vienna during 1801 and 1802, immediately before his summer at Heiligenstadt. The *Prometheus* ballet centers on a creation myth, but what Beethoven produced in his op. 43 is illustrative, programmatic music that follows a scenario imposed from without, even if in its gestural explicitness

it would not have satisfied the expectations for the Revolutionary Sonata that Countess Kielmansegge wanted to commission.
It is not the ballet music but the *Prometheus* Variations and *Eroica* Symphony that embody achievements of Promethean stature,
works eminently worthy of being regarded as "creations." Nevertheless, these pieces owe far more to the earlier work than has been
recognized.

Here again Beethoven's sketchbooks are revealing. Although
the choreography of the original ballet was lost, the coordination
of music with stage action and the related symbolism of the ballet
can be largely reconstructed from Beethoven's surviving sketches.
Subtitled "ballo serio," this work combines aspects of allegorical
pantomime, heroic ballet, and a novel kind of "musique parlante"
that continues to be expressive in the absence of words. A contemporary reviewer for the *Zeitung für die elegante Welt* described the
theme of the ballet as follows: "Prometheus lifts the people of his
time out of their ignorance, makes them more refined through
learning and art, and gives them manners." The ballet is decisively
altered from the ancient myths in some ways: Prometheus is at
one point put to death and subsequently restored to life. Nevertheless, the ballet's action is launched along classical lines: the titan
is pursued by the thundering wrath of heaven, which gives rise
to a turbulent musical prelude, entitled "La tempesta." The ensuing section depicts efforts by Prometheus to animate his proto-
human "creatures," as we have seen. A later tempestuous "Danza
eroica" (no. 8) displays points of rhetorical affinity with the first
movement of the *Eroica*, while its middle section emphasizes D
minor, the key of the *Tempest* Sonata. Especially revealing in relation to the *Eroica* are the parallels of the following two pieces of
the ballet, the "Tragica scena" (no. 9) and "Giuocosa scena" (no.
10, in which the dead Prometheus is revived), to the progression
from the *Marcia funebre* to the scherzo in the symphony. Tangible
affinities connect the ballet to the *Tempest* Sonata as well as to the
Prometheus Variations and the *Eroica* Symphony.

The version of the Prometheus myth that Beethoven and Viganò
tackled reinterprets the ancient saga of the champion of humanity

in the spirit of the Enlightenment. Prometheus ennobled humankind through his gifts of knowledge and art fashioned from fire that he stole from the gods. In all versions of the myth, Prometheus is severely punished on account of his actions on behalf of humanity. Variants of the legend exist in the ancient Greek sources, but all agree that the titan refuses to yield or compromise. In the world of myth, there is no more telling symbol of resistance to the arbitrary exercise of authority.

A crucial change in the version Beethoven set to music consists in the role of the two "creatures," the *Urmenschen,* or archetypal man and woman. In the Greek sources the struggle of Prometheus occurs even before the creation of woman, whereas in the ballet the story is revised to embrace all humanity as potential beneficiaries of the Promethean sacrifice. Prometheus's long trials and agonies in the old myths are replaced here by a progression of death and rebirth, since Prometheus is subsequently restored to life. The ballet concludes with the apotheosis of Prometheus as he is celebrated by his two creatures, who at last begin to display understanding of the significance of his heroic deed.

This version of the myth thus shifts the dramatic focus from the defiant martyr to the reception by humankind of the Promethean gift of culture. Since in the ballet the cultural gifts of the titan are not initially understood or appreciated by his two "creatures," Prometheus's agony thereby comes to resemble the plight of the misunderstood artist. Ultimately, reconciliation is achieved in that final section of the ballet with the contredance, the theme that has always been understood as a link to the *Prometheus* Variations and *Eroica* finale.

The Creatures of Prometheus proved to be seminal for Beethoven because of its carry-through to the cluster of related instrumental works forged at Heiligenstadt. In this regard it is important to note that the early genesis of the *Eroica* also stems from Beethoven's time in the countryside. The symphony first appears in correspondence in May 1803, but some sketches for the *Basso del tema* in the *Kessler* Sketchbook are not in keyboard format, and Beethoven likely envisioned the possibility of an orchestral work based on the *Prometheus* theme earlier than has been recognized. Sketches related to both the *Eroica* Symphony and *Prometheus* Variations appear not far into the *Wielhorsky* Sketchbook. Moreover, it seems that Beethoven had already begun to use the next sketchbook, the *Eroica* Sketchbook also known as *Landsberg 6*, before he had finished sketching in *Wielhorsky*. Beethoven composed the first two Marches for Piano Duet op. 45 at Heiligenstadt, as is described in detail in a colorful account from Ferdinand Ries and documented by a letter from the composer. Sketches for these marches are found in pages 44–48 of the *Eroica* Sketchbook, marked by folds similar to those for the second draft of the opening movement of the *Tempest* Sonata in *Kessler*. Beethoven apparently had assembled the *Eroica* Sketchbook by October 1802, allocating generous sections of the beginning of the book for the first movement of the new symphony. For that reason, when he needed space to notate the marches, he leafed ahead, which explains the otherwise puzzling placement of these entries amid his later sketches for the *Marcia funebre* of the symphony.

Beethoven repeatedly devised major piano works in association with large compositions in other genres. The *Appassionata* and *Waldstein* Sonatas parallel aspects of *Fidelio*; the Sonata in A♭ Major, op. 110, invites comparison to the Agnus Dei of the *Missa solemnis*. The affinity between the *Prometheus* Variations and the *Eroica* finale is the first important example of this practice, and as we have seen, both pieces grew directly out of Beethoven's preoccupation with *The Creatures of Prometheus* and followed up its performances at Vienna in 1802.

The most explicitly political of these pieces is the *Eroica*, but its symbolism often has been misunderstood. Fundamental to Beethoven's aesthetic attitude is the notion of resistance, of a confrontation with adversity leading ultimately to a renewal of creative possibilities. In this context, the relationship between Beethoven's incurable deafness and his artistic development merits scrutiny. Despite his initial fears, and now-discredited attempts to characterize his later style as a degeneration resulting from a lack of hearing, Beethoven's art became richer as his hearing declined. His half year spent at Heiligenstadt was crisis ridden yet remarkably productive in its innovative approaches, some of which may even reflect a response to his debility. A moving passage in the testament describes the despair Beethoven felt when "someone standing beside me heard a flute in the distance and I heard—nothing! or someone heard a shepherd singing and again I heard—nothing!" This description matches to a passage in the reminiscences of Ries, who was often Beethoven's hiking companion at the time. Can art address or repair the deficiencies of life? One thinks in this regard of the conclusion of Florestan's aria in the dungeon in the 1814 version of *Fidelio*, when the starving, delirious prisoner hallucinates. Florestan's imagined projection of Leonore as "angel of freedom" is initiated by the sound of a woodwind instrument—an oboe—rising into higher registers, those sound-spaces that were the first to be lost through the gradual erosion of Beethoven's hearing.

Elsewhere in the *Heiligenstadt Testament*, Beethoven writes that "I would have ended my life—it was only *my art* that held me back"; "It was thanks to virtue and to my art, I did not end my life by suicide." Seen in context, these suicidal thoughts need not be taken quite literally. The idea of a symbolic enactment of the artist's own death in order that he might start anew—in short, the notion of a "rebirth"—may be implied by Beethoven's references from about this time to a "new path" or "a completely new manner" in reference to his art. When Beethoven bade farewell to Heiligenstadt in closing his testament, his hopes for improvement in his hearing had withered like autumn leaves, but his art had advanced. The task of the artist held social implications, as is embedded in tensional innovations in the music, features indebted in turn to Promethean symbolism. The Prometheus contredance with its joyful reincarnation of the suffering-artist figure inspired Beethoven, and prepared him for two major monuments of his "heroic" style: the *Eroica* and *Fidelio*.

Path to the *Eroica*

Beethoven's creative rivalry with Haydn surfaces in an anecdote from 1801 related to his "heroic allegorical" ballet *The Creatures of Prometheus*. The Prometheus myth was attractive as a metaphor for innovative creativity, especially following the successful performances of Haydn's great oratorio *The Creation* beginning in 1799. Haydn supposedly told Beethoven that "I heard your ballet yesterday and it pleased me very much!" whereupon Beethoven replied: "O, dear Papa, you are very kind; but it is far from being a *Creation*!" Surprised and almost offended by the comparison of the younger composer's effort with his mature masterpiece, Haydn replied: "That is true; it is not yet a *Creation* and I can scarcely believe that it will ever become one."

In realizing his path to the *Eroica*, Beethoven built upon the ballet while surpassing it. How do we best understand the narrative and symbolism of the symphony? Revealing clues are offered by the fascinating allegorical portrait of Beethoven reproduced on the cover of the present book, a picture that dates from late 1804 or early 1805, the time when Beethoven completed the *Eroica* and Napoleon assumed absolute power. This portrait is by Willibrord Joseph Mähler, and is housed in the new Beethoven Museum in Vienna/Heiligenstadt that opened in 2017 (fig. 4.1). In Habsburg Vienna, where words were often subject to strict censorship, the nonverbal arts of painting and music could convey meanings not subject to such restriction.

Beethoven treasured the portrait. He kept it until his death and hung it in his last lodgings. This richly suggestive symbolic portrayal invites interpretation in a political context. Its treat-

4.1 Portrait of Beethoven by Willibrord Mähler, 1804–1805 (Wien-Museum, Vienna).

ment of landscape with darkness and light, the composer's gesture toward the Temple of Apollo in the background, the likely presence of "arbres de la liberté," and even Beethoven's haircut "à la Titus" are conspicuous in this regard.

Willibrord Mähler was eight years younger than Beethoven and, like the composer, came from the Rhineland. He was born at Ehrenbreitstein near Koblenz, the village south of Bonn where

Beethoven's mother was born and spent her young years. Like Beethoven, Mähler eventually moved away from the Rhineland in the wake of the upheavals and military conflicts of the 1790s. Unlike the composer, Mähler did not come directly to the Austrian capital, but first studied painting at Dresden with the noted portrait painter Anton Graff. Mähler met Beethoven in Vienna during the fall of 1804, when he was introduced to the composer by another fellow *Rheinländer*, Beethoven's close friend Stephan von Breuning.

Since the painter lived until 1860, Beethoven's American biographer, Alexander Wheelock Thayer, could interview Mähler shortly before the artist's death. The interview includes the following:

Another young Rhinelander, to whom Beethoven became much attached, and who returned the kindness with warm affection for him personally and a boundless admiration for his genius, became known to the composer also just at this time [in 1804]. Willibrord Joseph Mähler, a native of Coblentz—who died in 1860, at the age of 82 years, as pensioned Court Secretary—was a man of remarkably varied artistic talents, by which, however, since he cultivated them only as a dilettante and without confining himself to any one art, he achieved no great distinction. He wrote respectable poetry and set it to correct and not unpleasing music; sang well enough . . . as [an] "amateur singer," and painted sufficiently well to be named . . . "amateur portrait painter." He painted [a] portrait of the composer, about 1804–5 . . . and a second 1814–15 (Mr. Mähler could not recall the precise date) . . .

Soon after Beethoven returned from his summer lodgings to his apartment in the theatre building [in the *Theater an der Wien*], Mähler, who had then recently arrived in Vienna, was taken by Breuning thither to be introduced. They found him busily at work finishing the "Heroic Symphony." After some conversation, at the desire of Mähler to hear him play, Beethoven, instead of beginning an extempore performance, gave his visitors the finale of the new Symphony; but at its close, without a pause, he continued in free fantasia for *two hours*, "during all which time," said Mr. Mähler to

PLATE 1
Portrait of Beethoven by Willibrord Mähler, 1804–1805 (Wien-Museum, Vienna).

PLATE 2

Portrait of Julie von Vering by Willibrord Mähler (Wien-Museum, Vienna).

PLATE 3

The raising of the liberty tree on the Marketplace at Bonn, October 1794;
oil painting by François Rousseau. Bonn Stadtmuseum/Bonn City Museum,
SMB 1992/103; Stadtmuseum (www.bonn.de/stadtmuseum).

PLATE 4
Angel denigrating the king and glorifying Voltaire, Paris, 1791. Anonymous print
Journée du 21. Juin. Le Faux-pas. L'Homme immortel from the series *La fuite à Varennes*,
referring to the royal flight to Varennes. Musée Carnavalet, Histoire de Paris G.26280.
Used with permission © Musée Carnavalet/Roger-Viollet.

the present writer, "there was not a measure which was faulty, or which did not sound original." He added, that one circumstance attracted his particular notice; viz.: "that Beethoven played with his hands so very still; wonderful as his execution was, there was no tossing of them to and fro, up and down; they seemed to glide right and left over the keys, the fingers alone doing the work." To Mr. Mähler, as to most others who have recorded their impressions of Beethoven's improvisations, they were the *non plus ultra* of the art.

Several aspects of the interview merit attention. The chronology and basic substance of Mähler's report seem reliable. Beethoven was indeed putting finishing touches on his *Eroica* Symphony that autumn. The first private rehearsal of the symphony took place at the Lobkowitz Palace on 9 June 1804; the first public performance occurred at the *Theater an der Wien* on 7 April 1805. It makes sense that at this time Beethoven would have played from the *Eroica* finale at the keyboard for his visitors. As we have seen, his springboard for the symphony was the contredance he used in the ballet music *The Creatures of Prometheus* in 1801 and again as the basis for the Variations for Piano in E♭ Major, op. 35, in 1802. Beethoven's work on the symphony reaches back at least to the end of his crisis-ridden yet highly productive half year spent at Heiligenstadt, up to October 1802. The creation of the symphony began with its finale, whose musical material was drawn from the Piano Variations op. 35 and whose mythic symbolism derived from the *Prometheus* ballet.

The connection to Stephan von Breuning points to a biographical context in which Mähler played a part. The Beethoven Museum in Vienna holds another Mähler portrait, one of Stephan von Breuning's first wife, Julie von Vering, the daughter of Beethoven's doctor Gerhard von Vering (fig. 4.2). The marriage of Stephan von Breuning and Julie von Vering took place in April 1808, but she died already in 1809, at the age of nineteen. Beethoven dedicated his Violin Concerto op. 61 to Stephan von Breuning, who served as librettist for the revision of Beethoven's opera *Leonore* in 1806; the composer dedicated to Julie von Vering the version of his Violin

4.2 Portrait of Julie von Vering by Willibrord Mähler (Wien-Museum, Vienna).

Concerto arranged as a piano concerto, op. 61a. Mähler's portrait of Julie von Vering reflects the close interpersonal network connecting Beethoven and Mähler. The depiction of Julie with fragrant roses calls to mind Florestan's intoxicated vision of Leonore; other features bear comparison to the Beethoven portrait.

That portrait shows an evocative landscape as the setting for Beethoven's self-conscious artistic mission. Mähler himself drew attention to the presence in the portrait of an Apollo temple to the left of the composer, who is holding a lyre or type of lyre-guitar.

The composer was keenly interested in the mythology of antiquity. Starting around 1801, Beethoven began to identify with Apollo as the god of music, poetry, and song, as the source of inspiration for singers and poets. By that time, Beethoven was no longer just a successful composing keyboard virtuoso, but an ambitious symphonic composer and soon thereafter a creator of major choral and operatic works. Through his allusions to and aspiration toward the eternal divinity of Apollo, Beethoven could distance himself from quibbling journalistic criticism, as when he wrote in 1801 concerning a Leipzig critic that "one just lets them talk, certainly no one will receive anything enduring from their chatter, just as they cannot take eternity away from someone who receives it through Apollo." Beethoven sometimes regarded fellow artists metaphorically as "brothers through Apollo" and himself as a priest or son of Apollo. Beethoven valued a kinship between the arts and the ways in which painting and music should both strive toward an enduring significance. To his acquaintance the portrait painter Alexander Macco he wrote in 1803 that

> You paint—and I write notes and so we will be—eternal?—yes perhaps live on eternally.

> Mahlen sie—und ich mache Noten und so werden wir—ewig?—ja vielleicht ewig fortleben.

Beethoven himself was surely involved in the planning and conception of this unique portrait. This picture differs from Mähler's other paintings as well as the numerous portraits of his teacher Anton Graff. While traditional models can be identified for some aspects of the picture, we can distinguish layers of modeling, and specify what is most unique about this portrait of Beethoven.

The most fundamental level is that of the seated artist with lyre, evoking the classical image of Apollo or Orpheus. A point of comparison is offered by ancient frescos at the House of Augustus on the Palatine Hill in Rome. In ancient legends, Orpheus received a golden lyre from Apollo, who taught him how to play it. These two figures are closely linked. In some versions of the myth, Apollo is the father of Orpheus.

This reference to antiquity is complemented by other features. Mähler's picture depicts the status and activity of the artist. Conspicuous are the dynamic posture of the figure and the striking position of Beethoven's outstretched right hand. This hand of the keyboard virtuoso points toward the light and the Apollo temple in the background of the scene; the introspective gaze of the artist is directed toward the onlooker. The uplifted-hand gesture in the context of this symbolic landscape invites interpretation in relation to his personal crisis and suicidal thoughts in the *Heiligenstadt Testament*, that "it was only *my art* that held me back."

Mähler himself described the hand gesture: ". . . the right hand is extended, as if, in a moment of musical enthusiasm, he was beating time . . . ." This depiction of Beethoven thus relates to three different dimensions of musical activity: the allusion to instrumental performance conveyed through the Orpheus lyre held in the left hand; an implied perception of the flow of music through time as signaled by the dynamic gesture of the right hand and arm; and an impression of intense listening expressed through the thoughtful countenance and intense gaze of the figure.

In his study *Allegory: The Theory of a Symbolic Mode*, Angus Fletcher defines allegorical progress as a "symbolic action," and finds that "fictions of this type necessarily have double meanings, and necessarily have daemonic agency and cosmic imagery." Fletcher understands allegory in the sense of a "questing journey" and observes that "There is usually a paradoxical suggestion that by leaving home the hero can return to another better 'home' . . . Sometimes, having made the journey, the hero comes back to his original home so much changed that he cannot any longer hold his former position."

This idea applies to Beethoven's situation. Leaving Bonn for Vienna in 1792, the young composer embarked on a "questing journey"; for him, return to the Rhineland was impossible because of the French occupation, which swept away the system that had supported the young court musician. Bonn as a center for the progressive Enlightenment convictions was formative during Beethoven's youth; it was there that he became acquainted with literature, poetry, and philosophical ideas. Beethoven cherished his friendships stemming from the Rhineland as being loyal and true. He wrote in 1801 praising his new friend from Vienna, Karl Amenda, that "you are no Viennese friend, no, you are like one of those who grew up on my native soil."

Beethoven thought about moving to Paris by around 1804. More than a decade later, around 1816, he weighed the prospect of an extended trip to London, such as Haydn had undertaken during the 1790s. In the end, there was no such physical relocation, nor did Beethoven ever return to Bonn. His restless quest took an artistic, spiritual form, embracing a passionate commitment to the principles of the French Revolution, that striving toward liberty and equality that so often proved incompatible with actual political conditions. While divorced from any physical destination, the quest was no less urgently envisioned as a desired goal, or "effigy of the ideal," in Schiller's words.

Beethoven's simultaneous attraction to and rejection of Napoleon can be viewed in this broader context, as part of his commitment to principles that inspired his art but were often negated in the political sphere. His self-image during his first decades at Vienna was reflected in his characteristic mode of dress, haircut, and devotion to the symbolism of creativity and politics. Disinclined already during the 1790s to wear a wig and court dress, he appeared instead in "freer ultra-Rhenish garb, almost carelessly dressed," as one witness put it. Beethoven's hairstyle was "à la Titus," an imitation of old Roman style through French influence, and he favored long sideburns, which were sometimes regarded as potentially provocative as well in the reactionary environment of Viennese court circles. Carl Czerny commented on Beethoven's "jet-black hair, cut *à la Titus*, which made him look shaggy."

Mähler's painting of Julie von Vering also embodies an allegorical dimension, as expressed through a tensional polarity modulating from below to above (fig. 4.2). She gazes toward the onlooker, though without the searing intensity of the depiction of

Beethoven, while the upraised right hand again assumes importance. The symbolic action is expressed here above all through the long green scarf bearing stars that she holds. This scarf is lifted upward, becoming an ethereal blue banner that seems to rest on the clouds on the upper right, defying gravity. The picture's "cosmic imagery" is conveyed through the miraculous discontinuity of the banner, in its upward-striving, floating quality. One recalls the dictum Beethoven was fond of citing, drawn from the end of Schiller's play about Joan of Arc: "I dare not come without my banner!"

In the Beethoven portrait, the dark forest to the right of the figure is set into sharp opposition with the brighter cultivated sphere on the left, with the illuminated Apollo temple seen behind the composer's upraised hand. That the large tree on the right to which Beethoven turns his back is associated with the past and with decline is implied by its aged, gnarled appearance, with dead branches visible. The alert, energetic posture of the figure is coordinated with this dramatic opposition, as if Beethoven were on his way out of the dark forest toward the clearing with the Apollo temple. The big tree or German oak embraces a different temporal dimension from the young evergreen trees on the left symbolizing change or renewal. Because of its dynamic tension, this representation of Beethoven seems more Dionysian than Apollonian.

What is a possible model for this allegorical depiction? The closest model derives not from traditions of landscape painting, nor from mythic symbols from antiquity, but instead from those symbolic depictions of Napoleon Bonaparte that achieved wide currency during his years as First Consul of the French Republic beginning in 1799. Consider the Allegory of the Good Government of Napoleon Bonaparte, a print by Alexis Chataigner from 1801, *Le Soutien de la France* ("The Support of France") (fig. 4.3). In this positive image, France is embodied in the feminine Marianne figure on the left, as Bonaparte in the role of First Consul rescues her from the abyss and destructive pull of Ignorance, drawing her to Justice and Abundance, the two allegorical figures on the right-hand side. These figures are illuminated, as is the Apollo temple in Mähler's picture, and Bonaparte's outstretched

4.3 Allegory of the Good Government of Napoleon Bonaparte by
Alexis Chataigner, entitled *Le Soutien de la France*, ca. 1801 (partial image
authorized by the Bibliothèque nationale de France).

arm and hand make the connection to
their sphere of righteousness and plentitude. Beethoven admired Bonaparte
while he was First Consul, and his attitude is confirmed as well by a statuette
he kept to the end of his life of Lucius
Brutus, the emblematic figure of republican duty (fig. 4.4). Voltaire's play *Brutus* enjoyed successful revival during
the French Revolution, when the actor
François-Joseph Talma, who played
the role of Titus, sparked a craze for a
"coiffure à la Titus," the short choppy
hairstyle that Beethoven also adopted,
as Czerny attested. The historical position of Lucius Brutus during the Roman
Republic suggested a parallel to Napoleon Bonaparte as First Consul. Just as
Brutus assumed legendary status as one
of the Roman Republic's first Consuls,
so did Bonaparte serve as First Consul

4.4 Statuette of Lucius Brutus
once owned by Beethoven
(Beethoven-Haus, Bonn,
D-BNba, R 12).

93

of the French Republic. Republican men cropped their hair short in imitation of the style of busts of Roman consuls of antiquity, such as the statuette of Lucius Brutus that Beethoven kept in his possession.

Important too is the pair of vigorous young evergreen trees placed near the source of light behind Beethoven's right arm, to the right of the Apollo temple. A suspicion that these stand for liberty trees receives support from the extensive historical context pertaining to *arbres de la liberté*. This history predates the French Revolution. A liberty tree at Boston assumed significance starting in 1765 during the resistance to the Stamp Tax, while other freedom trees were designated during the ensuing rebellion of the Americans against the British. In 1787, Thomas Jefferson stated that "The tree of liberty must be refreshed from time to time with the blood of patriots and tyrants." The liberty tree became a prominent and widespread French political symbol starting around 1790, before emerging into German-speaking regions during the following decade. A ceremony with a liberty tree took place on the Bonn *Marktplatz* on 12 October 1794, four days after the French troops reached Beethoven's hometown (fig. 4.5). They felled a tree from the nearby Kreuzberg and adorned it with cockade and Jacob's hat, symbols of the Revolution. The German onlookers as depicted in this painting from 1794 by François Rousseau are observant but display no enthusiasm. The house in which Beethoven was born is just around the corner from this market square.

The apparent allusion to liberty trees in Mähler's painting is not overt; no flags or banners confirm the association. Why should there be not one, but a *pair* of liberty trees? We recall in this connection Beethoven's idea of "Brüder in Apollo," of an artistic brotherhood between a painter and musician, as in his letter to Macco. The two freedom trees evidently stand for an alliance of arts and the friendship of Beethoven with his fellow *Rhineländer* Mähler. The case for the pair of freedom trees is supported by the allegorical framework of the painting as a whole, whereby the vigorous young liberty trees on the left are set against a decaying

4.5 The raising of the liberty tree on the Marketplace at Bonn, October 1794; oil painting by François Rousseau. Bonn Stadtmuseum/Bonn City Museum, SMB 1992/103; Stadtmuseum (www.bonn.de/stadtmuseum).

old tree on the right symbolizing the discredited *ancien regime*. Because censorship and political surveillance were rampant in Vienna and encouraged by Emperor Franz, it was risky if not foolhardy for an artist in Beethoven's position to express directly political opinions urging change, let alone resistance or revolution. An artwork, on the other hand, whether in music or painting, may absorb hidden meanings and subtle allusions; Mähler's Beethoven portrait is full of such suggestive hints, too extensive to be coincidental. Yet another eye-catching detail is the exposed glimpse of red lining in Beethoven's coat seen at his back facing the dark, decrepit tree. In John Clubb's words, this "intense dash of red in Beethoven's cloak" may "ignite the moribund Tree of Absolutism." Close scrutiny of the original painting, moreover, reveals something that is not well conveyed even in a good digital image of the whole portrait (plate 1). The spot of color is too bright, the red glint too intensely lit, in view of its distance from any light source. This does not reflect lack of skill on Mähler's part, but a purposeful strategy highlighting a suggestive detail. Noting the blue and white in Beethoven's attire, one might perhaps even be tempted to recognize in this dash of red the missing third color of the French *tricolore*. Yet another question concerns the luminous imagery and the time of day represented in the painting. Is it dawn or dusk? It seems likely that the onlooker views the figure from the south, with the setting sun shining on the Apollo temple and the composer's outstretched hand. The artist would then be pointing west, toward France. In a letter from early 1804, Beethoven justified his rejection of Emanuel Schikaneder's opera libretto *Vestas Feuer* in favor of a French subject in terms of the duality of darkness and light. Deploring its crude language and use of magic, he found Schikaneder's realm "completely eclipsed by *the light* of the clever and sensible French operas."

When he first met Mähler, Beethoven still referred to the *Eroica* Symphony as being "actually entitled Bonaparte," but it is especially the mythic context of the Prometheus legend that lends "daemonic agency and cosmic imagery" to the music. A tensional thrust animates Mähler's portrait of the composer, which takes a cue from Napoleonic depictions while avoiding their overt propagandistic character. Within the cultural sphere, Beethoven pursued a kind of rivalry with Napoleon, who as First Consul of the French Republic had raised expectations but then dashed those hopes through an insatiable ambition and pursuit of power. By 1802, Bonaparte had become "First Consul for Life"; in 1803 at Paris, he had the remaining liberty trees planted during the Revolution cut down. Shortly before his death, as we have seen, Beethoven confessed about Bonaparte that he was "mistaken about the shithead." His own legacy proved more enduring. Willibrord Mähler's remarkable allegorical portrait renders as a progressive symbolic action some of those ideas and attitudes that fueled Beethoven's artistic creativity.

Beethoven likely encountered the ballet master Salvatore Viganò during the period 1793 until 1795—when Viganò resided in Vienna and the composer wrote a set of piano variations on a ballet theme, the "Menuett à la Viganò" by Mozart's brother-in-law Jakob Haibel from *Le nozze disturbate*, WoO 68. Viganò returned to Vienna for several years beginning in 1799. Their collaborative undertaking of the *Prometheus* ballet was a competitive response to Haydn's *Creation* that made subtle allusion to French Revolutionary events. The ballet was somewhat influenced by the political poem *Il Prometeo* by the Neoclassical Italian playwright Vincenzo Monti, who drew an analogy between the mythic titan and Napoleon's political and military deeds during his Italian campaign of 1797.

The *Prometheus* ballet casts light on the link between Beethoven's *Eroica* Symphony and Napoleon Bonaparte. As his student Ferdinand Ries reported, Beethoven's enthusiasm for the French leader arose when Bonaparte was First Consul of the French Republic: "at that time Beethoven held him in the highest esteem and compared him to the great consuls of ancient Rome." Since Bonaparte was an enemy of Austria, Beethoven could hardly express such convictions openly. It makes sense that Beethoven contemplated dedicating his *Eroica* to Bonaparte at the time he considered moving to Paris.

As we have seen, Prometheus is a rebellious figure who is spiritually free, a proud, implacable enemy of tyrants and benefactor of humanity. In the version that Beethoven set to music, the ballet is launched with an introductory "La Tempesta" movement reflecting the flight of Prometheus with the stolen fire. Overcoming the storm of wrath, he makes his way to clay sculptures of a man and woman; with the kidnapped fire he burns a heart in each of them. The ensuing action unfolds in two acts, focused on the efforts of Prometheus to instill higher awareness into his two statue-like "creatures"—the archetypal original man and woman. A review of the first performance, drawing on the original playbill, summarized the work as follows: "Prometheus lifts the people of his time up out of their ignorance, makes them more refined through scholarship and art, and gives them manners." One statement in the playbill held special meaning for Beethoven: "In the present ballet two statues appear coming to life, and they are made responsive to all the passions of human life through the power of harmony." The ballet centers not on the Promethean sacrifice but on the aesthetic awakening of his human beneficiaries. When Prometheus first appears on stage with his proto-human creatures, they seem blank and emotionless. The music for the creatures at the outset of both acts (nos. 1 and 4) is confined to soft disconnected chords in the strings. As the second act unfolds on Parnassus at the Court of Apollo, Prometheus still fails to arouse a response from his two "children." In this context, the "Tragica scena" (no. 9) proves decisive. The muse Melpomene acts out a tragic scene, enacting how death ends life. With her dagger, she slays Prometheus, a doleful act impacting on his creatures, who sought but failed to restrain her. As Prometheus is subsequently restored to life, his pupils display enhanced awareness. The ballet concludes with an apotheosis of Prometheus as celebrated by the two creatures. They at last show appreciation for his actions in festive dances, with the E♭ contredance assuming prominence.

Despite its key role in Beethoven's creative development, it is not the ballet music but the *Eroica* Symphony that embodies an achievement of Promethean stature, a work eminently worthy of being viewed as a "creation." Beethoven himself expressed disappointment that "I have composed a ballet; but the ballet master has not done his part very successfully." Yet the mythic narrative of the ballet stimulated his imagination, and the symphony owes more to the earlier work than has been recognized. This affinity is embedded in the narrative continuity of its multi-movement design. The version of the myth enacted in the ballet shifts the dramatic emphasis from the defiant martyr to the reception by humankind of the Promethean gift of culture. When the titan's efforts are not understood, Prometheus's dilemma comes to resemble the plight of a misunderstood artist. A joyful resolution is achieved in that last section of the ballet that is most easily recognized as a link to the *Eroica* Symphony. The shared theme is the lively contredance that Beethoven used in the ballet, as well as in the Variations in E♭ Major, op. 35, and the *Eroica* finale.

The connection to the Prometheus myth is not limited to the symphonic finale. The narrative of the symphony's four movements of the symphony outlines a larger progression: struggle—

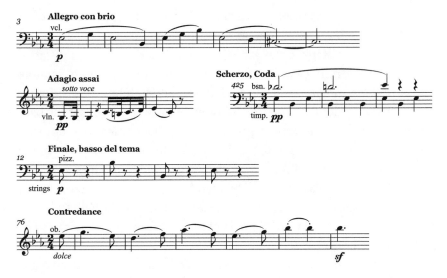

4.6 Thematic relations in the *Eroica* Symphony.

death—rebirth—apotheosis. The parallel with Beethoven's own despair, thoughts of suicide, and discovery of his new artistic path is hardly coincidental. But the heroic symbolism of the *Eroica* is too deeply embodied in the artwork to be interpreted only in terms of Beethoven's biography, or in relation to an individual historical figure such as Napoleon.

What Beethoven explores in the *Eroica* are universal aspects of heroism, centering on the idea of a confrontation with adversity leading ultimately to a renewal of creative possibilities. Prometheus placed humanity's welfare first, even at his own peril. How then can we understand the overarching narrative of the symphony? A quality of gigantic simplicity connects the movements to one another. Figure 4.6 shows some elements of this design. The *Eroica* finale became the generating movement of the entire symphony. No other Beethovenian work is based on a preexisting theme—the E♭ contredance from the *Prometheus* ballet—that had already been developed in a major composition—the op. 35 Variations.

The contredance was recognized at the time as a politically progressive dance: through its exchange of partners, it reflected the erosion of class divisions around the turn of the nineteenth century. In devising the op. 35 Variations, Beethoven expanded his treatment of his contredance by deconstructing the theme. Rather than beginning with the full theme, he started with the bass alone, the *Basso del tema* as he labeled it in his sketches. In fashioning this fragmentary opening followed by variations on just the bass, Beethoven illustrated a process of forethought leading in turn to the contredance and to the many transformations of that theme. The name Prometheus, we recall, designates one who shows forethought. The understated, skeletal *Basso del tema* is also suggestive of the initial music for the proto-humans in the ballet; the stiff accents and awkward silences of the bass line signal their need for refinement and development.

If the *Eroica* finale represents a metaphor for creativity, how do we understand the earlier movements? Clues are embedded in the musical motives. The triadic turning theme at the outset of the opening *Allegro con brio* rests solidly on the tonic note E♭, which is played at the outset of each of the first four measures. The stress on E♭ is framed by the B♭s below and above. The figure resembles the *Basso del tema* of the finale, sounding in the same register. Beethoven's earliest notated sketch for this theme in the *Wielhorsky* Sketchbook is still closer to the *Basso del tema* in using the scale steps 1–5–5–1. A later sketch begins with the rising third E♭–G, matching the head of the contredance melody. In shaping the symphony's opening theme, Beethoven elaborates and disguises the thematic substance of the contredance and its bass, but the affinity remains audible.

A heroic character suggestive of struggle is embodied in the opening *Allegro con brio*. Conflict is exposed already in measures 4–5, with the chromatic descent from E♭ to C♯. This dissonance—an open wound in the radiant tonality of E♭ major—triggers throbbing syncopations on high G in the violins, a seminal moment in a movement of great rhythmic tension. The dissonant gesture cannot be narrowly identified with the titan's theft of the fire, chaining to the rock, or torments from the eagle, though it may in the broadest poetic context evoke such impressions. Audacious action strains the framework of expectations against which it assumes meaning. A determined quality lends coherence to a narrative that resists a segmentation of form.

The immense scope of the first movement is reflected in a continuously evolving treatment of thematic material. Elements of dramatic tension are felt from the outset. The two powerful opening chords intensify the single *fortissimo* sonority that served as preface in the op. 35 Variations. The mysterious, low C♯ in measure 5 carries implications that are explored much later, at the beginning of the recapitulation, when Beethoven reinterprets this pitch as D♭, with a downward resolution leading to an extended solo for horn in F major. Beethoven vastly expands the development section and coda. With its 245 measures the development dwarfs the exposition, while the coda approaches the length of the recapitulation.

A treatment of tensional rhythm—syncopated jolts—generates decisive outcomes overturning musical conventions. This is most evident in the heart of the development section, the passage leading to measure 280 (fig. 4.7). Beethoven indulges here in rhythmic foreshortening, whereby phrases are curtailed into progressively shorter units. His Piano Sonata in F Minor, op. 2, no. 1, opens with a modest example of this technique. In the sonata, the initial four-measure unit is compressed to two bars, one bar, half measures, and then single beats before the opening salvo is brought to an arresting silence, a pregnant pause. The effect of the device is to thrust the music forward, while focusing attention on those motivic elements that survive the process of curtailment.

In the great syncopated passage in the *Eroica*, a protracted compression series flattens and nearly annihilates the thematic material, reducing it to a dissonant combination of F-major and A-minor triads, an "evil" chord, as it was deemed by one commentator. Repetitions of this chord serve as springboard to the strongly accented silence of measure 280, a moment paradoxically *soundless*. Accented silences are an important resource in Beethoven. In his sketches for the *Egmont* music, he notated that "the death could be expressed through a pause." This rest in the

4.7 Climax of the *Eroica* Symphony/I, mm. 274–297.

Eroica does not stand for death, but it marks a decisive pivot, after which everything seems changed.

This climax dissolves the thematic material into nothing at that point when the recapitulation would normally be expected. Instead of leading his musical narrative back to familiar territory, Beethoven confronts us with something unprecedented, a kind of black hole that forecloses a predictable continuation. The approach to this accented acoustic void delivers a shattering climax: after a chain of massive syncopated chords, the collision of A-minor and F-major triads marks the peak of intensification. The strongest rhythmic impulse falls on the empty beat, four measures before the appearance of a new theme in E minor. Beethoven discharges here the almost unbearable tension of the dissonant syncopations while preparing the fresh formal episode that fills much of the remainder of the development section. The E-minor theme is not entirely new, partaking as it does in the far-reaching motivic network of the *Eroica*. The theme calls to mind the three-note *dolce* motive with dotted rhythm heard already by measure 45. In the development, this same figure contributes to the energetic gestures that trigger the syncopated climax.

At a rehearsal of the symphony, Beethoven's student Ferdinand Ries mistook the premature horn entry just before the recapitulation as an error. The unlucky Ries blurted out, "Can't the damned horn player count?—it sounds infamously false!," a remark that enraged the composer. Beethoven layers the harmonies at this point, diffusing the moment of recapitulation into a larger process. The second horn anticipates the recapitulation before it occurs in the full orchestra, bringing about the harmonic superimposition. The resulting dissonance is acute, despite the soft dynamic level, and this helps motivate the powerful *fortissimo* outburst that ushers in the "true" recapitulation.

In many ways, the *Eroica* reflects Beethoven's self-professed goal "to keep the whole in view." In the coda of the first movement, following a recall of the "new" theme from the development, the woodwinds play a rising semitone motive *pianissimo*, outlining B♭–B–C and C–C♯–D (mm. 605–611). This motivic gesture prepares the rising semitone figure to come at the end of the scherzo, while inverting and counteracting the descending chromatic dissonance from the outset of the work. The resolving gesture paves the way in turn for the ensuing statements of the main theme starting in the horns and spreading by stages emphatically through the entire orchestra. The main thematic idea is thereby completed, and then framed in the closing chords by sonorities similar to those that had launched this *Allegro con brio*.

In its epic grandeur and dramatic power, the *Marcia funebre* in C minor of the *Eroica* commemorates the death of the hero. In 1821, upon hearing of the death of Bonaparte, Beethoven commented with dry irony that he "had already composed the music for that catastrophe." Napoleon had by the time of the *Eroica* already forfeited his heroic status, with his earlier Promethean deeds reflected in the work of art. On a mythic Promethean level, the funeral march corresponds both to the symbolic death of the titan in the ballet and to the universality of myth itself. Heroic deeds outlive individuals. A narrative interpretation of the symphony is not stymied but supported by the presence of two movements after the hero's funeral. The Promethean narrative we have discerned—struggle—death—rebirth—apotheosis—emerges through the contribution of each movement to the narrative design.

For Beethoven, heroism arises from a commitment to humanistic causes—freedom, enlightenment, creativity—goals that are pursued at risk or cost of death. In the Prometheus scenario, the death and revival of the mythic hero are explicit, while the outcome of the narrative brings dawning recognition of the creative principle by humanity's representatives. Glorifying the transformative possibilities of the imagination, the *Eroica* finale shows how unpromising scraps—the bare bones of a grotesque *Basso del tema*—can be turned into artistic coinage as an apotheosis of play. We should not forget the underdog status of Beethoven's symbolic heroes. Prometheus has his Zeus; Leonore and Florestan their Pizarro; Egmont his Alba. Confronted by brute power, each is vulnerable; death threatens or claims them all. Most important is the *principle* for which they undergo sacrifices. From this viewpoint, an individual who succumbs to the lure of power and authority for its own sake is *disqualified* from heroism, as was Napoleon after he crowned himself emperor. Napoleon's regression to the role of an absolute monarch surrounded by flatterers negated his heroic stature long before his military downfall and exile a decade later.

The title Beethoven gave to the work at its publication in 1806 was "Sinfonia Eroica . . . composta per festeggiare il sovvenire di un grand Uomo." This reference to a "great man remembered" resonates with Friedrich Hölderlin's unfinished "Ode to Napoleon" of 1797: "Poets are sacred vessels wherein the wine of life, the spirit of heroes, is preserved." What is aesthetically embodied in the *Eroica* assumes a meaningful expressive shape in sound and time. In the evolutionary trajectory of the first movement, the post-climactic "new" theme in E minor in the development represents an indispensable thematic *complement* that is achieved through fortitude and determination. This hard-won "second theme" of the *Allegro con brio* bears a conspicuous audible affinity to the opening subject of the *Marcia funebre*, linking the two opening movements to one another.

The heroism enacted in the funeral march does not belong solely to the past. Following the somber strains of the march, the music turns to C major with the oboe outlining the rising triad C–E–G, that elemental pattern given expression in "Der freier Mann" and the finale of the Fifth Symphony. As in the Fifth Symphony, this trio section reaches an ebullient *fortissimo* climax before trailing off into a void, as the funeral procession resumes in C minor. Now, more powerfully than in the *Sonate pathétique*, we sense a resistance to depressive forces. Beethoven telescopes the return of the march, which unfolds into a gripping fugato passage. This second half of the *Marcia funebre*, from the fugato to the conclusion, forms the emotional core of the symphony. Its power has to do with the way Beethoven handles a rising motive of the fourth, and spreads this gesture by degrees throughout the orchestra. In his sketchbook, he tagged the related figure of a stepwise falling fourth in a long-short-short-long rhythm from the march. Inverted to an ascending motive, the gesture signals an exertion of will, of urgent human motivation. Two measures long, and shaped in interactive counterpoint, the motivic statements enable all the instruments to join by stages, gradually filling the sound-space. Once the double basses pick up the figure, the effect is overwhelming; the rhythmic intensity resonates in the repeated-note figures of the violins.

What is asserted is haunted by doubt if not futility. The funeral march resumes, haltingly, in G minor. The violins posit a poignant high A♭, a question posed without hope, against an indifferent sky. The melodic climax of the processional march had also been placed on A♭, a pitch that assumes special importance throughout. Now, following the luminous C-major climax with trumpets and drums and the harrowing fugato, the pause on the mysterious unharmonized A♭ resembles a gaze into the abyss. The ensuing silence is broken by an emphatic answering A♭ in the low register, before a powerful continuation brings a varied reprise of the processional march.

In the closing passages of the slow movement, the march itself starts to disintegrate. Rests intrude on strong beats, creating a stumbling effect, with holes torn in the melodic fabric of the theme. Beethoven's very last sketch for the symphony in the *Eroica* Sketchbook is devoted to this passage. The device was not entirely new for Beethoven. He had already effected such a disintegration of a main theme at the close of the *Largo e mesto* of his Piano Sonata, op. 10, no. 3, and would use the technique again in his *Coriolan* Overture.

The subtle beginning of the scherzo—a soft indistinct stirring that starts *pianissimo* and *staccato* with strings in the lower registers—is surely connected to the symbolic reincarnation of Prometheus. But the progression of *Marcia funebre* to scherzo in the *Eroica* reaches far beyond the scope of the ballet. When in the *Creatures of Prometheus*, Melpomene as muse of tragedy turns her sword against Prometheus, it is a form of play-acting that contributes to the education of the proto-human subjects. In the symphony, Beethoven raises this tragic episode to another level. His thoughts about suicide and a "new path" in his art applied the lesson from the allegorical ballet to his own life situation. A struggle against destiny may fall short, yet still prove artistically worthwhile as a glorious failure, a cultural deed posited against intransigent conditions. The last two movements of the *Eroica* blend Schiller's notion of the "effigy of the ideal" with Promethean activity, pointing toward a path of creative renewal.

This perspective is compatible with a suggestion made in the nineteenth century that Beethoven alludes in the main scherzo melody to a saucy folk song or soldier's song. The text is "And what I won with the lyre one day, flees at night with the wind, wind, wind, wind, wind"; the melody was prominent during the Napoleonic period, as a carefree drinking song often sung in canon, an imitative texture present in the scherzo. Beethoven was keenly interested in folk song, and this example fits into the framework of contrasts that lends such vibrancy to the symphony. If this association is valid, the prominent repeated notes of the scherzo theme may allude to the transience of the wind, and thereby to renewal of the vitality of life. An early reviewer heard in this music a spontaneous quality of "raging rapture," finding that "pleasure is the goal of life; every joy wants to be tasted, every sensual pleasure put to the test. Away with wisdom, with its foresight!"

A heroic note is sounded in the trio, with its soloistic use of three horns—a special feature of orchestration that parallels Leonore's aria in act 1 of *Fidelio*. The musical character is joyous, reflecting a quality connected to the rehabilitation of Prometheus. On a page of his sketchbook next to the chords for the horns, Beethoven scrawled a word that may be discerned as "vereh[rung]," meaning reverence or homage.

The end of his scherzo absorbs a motivic reference to the outset of the opening *Allegro con brio*, clarifying the narrative of the whole symphony. Moments before the close, the rising chromatic figure $D\flat$–D–$E\flat$ is played twice in the high register in the woodwinds, while the timpani pivots between $E\flat$ and $B\flat$. In his sketchbook, he labeled the ascending motive as "fremd," as strange or unfamiliar. This is the long-range resolution of the mysterious downward shift $E\flat$–D–$C\sharp$ that was first heard in measures 6–7 of the opening *Allegro con brio*. That dissonant inflection brought the first hint of strife and tension; the syncopations of the first violins emerged in response to the falling chromatic figure, foreshadowing the rhythmic force of passages to come. As the scherzo closes, this breach is closed. The wound is healed. The struggle embodied in the first two movements is left behind. The resolving effect of this gesture reinforces a repeated phrase in the trio, in which the first horn outlines the rising fourth from B♭ to E♭. The chromatic variant echoes the earlier horn gestures, with their heroic associations.

In the finale, the association with Prometheus becomes explicit through the presence of the contredance from the ballet. This is surely the kind of music Beethoven would imagine while pointing toward the Apollo temple in Mähler's portrait. We may envision ourselves in the roles of those *Urmenschen* whose hearts burn with the impress of divine fire, those stolen sparks concealed by Prometheus in the fennel stalk he smuggled out of Olympus. The gentle *pizzicato* of the *Basso del tema* is an easy access point, which served as the generating kernel for the symphony as a whole. The bass theme enters on tiptoes, barely audible, effectively setting off the *fortissimo* octave strokes in the woodwinds, brass, and timpani at the start of its second half. Following two variations on the *Basso del tema* for strings, the Prometheus tune emerges in the woodwinds, with the oboe assuming prominence, as it does elsewhere in the *Eroica*.

The ensuing multiplicity of transformations of the contredance, played by a diversity of instrumental combinations in the orchestra, conveys a participatory social environment of shared creativity. In two later works, the Choral Fantasy and the choral finale of the Ninth Symphony, Beethoven extended this approach to embrace vocal forces as well. More than in op. 35, the variation chain is blended with a rondo design, enriched by adventurous fugal episodes and a robust, imposing marchlike central section in G minor, with dotted rhythms and rising scalar figures that mark the intervallic space spanned by the *Basso del tema*.

In composing the *Eroica* finale, Beethoven lavished special care on the concluding sections, which find no close parallel in op. 35. A meditative *Poco Andante* unfolds, leaving behind the *Basso del tema*, as the winds and especially the oboe assume prominence. This thoughtful hymnlike variation is reinforced by an emphatic *fortissimo* variation featuring the horns. What remains is the coda, which occupied Beethoven intensively during the compositional process. The music retreats into an unsettled, tonally ambiguous passage before plunging into a G-minor flourish at the *Presto*, marked *fortissimo* and scored for full orchestral forces.

This loud tempestuous outburst recalls the introductory preface to the finale, the *Allegro molto* that began with *fortissimo* unison octaves on D. As the sketches show, Beethoven carefully compared these two passages, weighing them in relation to the first movement's opening. After considering a preface to the initial *Allegro con brio* on a non-tonic harmony, he decided instead to begin with two emphatic tonic chords, firmly grounding the harmony before the side-slipping chromatic fall to C♯ ensues in measure 7. That crucial C♯ had resolved to an accented D in measure 9, reaching a G-minor harmony. In this context, the darker G-minor passages of Beethoven's finale provide the needed foil and counterweight to set into relief the affirmations of E♭ major, as the whole orchestra takes up the dotted figures initiated by the horns, leading to the triumphant conclusion. While keeping "the whole in view," Beethoven absorbed the Promethean symbolism from the ballet into a unique symphonic cycle rich in allusion, a work evoking "all the passions of human life through the power of harmony."

Leonore as
"Angel of Freedom"

Beethoven's only opera is a gritty tale of fortitude and rescue rooted in actual events. In tackling *Fidelio*, or *Leonore* (the title he would have preferred), he discarded the opera text he had been given by the theater director, Emanuel Schickaneder. That subject, *Vesta's Feuer* (*Vesta's Fire*), left him cold, and after sketching the music for several numbers, Beethoven gave up. By the beginning of 1804 he declared that "Schickaneder's realm has been totally eclipsed by the *light* of the clever and practical French operas" and added that "I have had an old French libretto adapted, and am beginning now to work on it."

Dizzying changes had occurred in France since the outbreak of the Revolution fifteen years earlier. The author of the "old French libretto," Jean-Nicolas Bouilly, was a judge belonging to the Military Commission during the Reign of Terror in 1793–1794. His role within the revolutionary regime served as a cloak, helping him shield innocent persecuted persons. Bouilly describes his *Léonore, ou L'amour conjugal*, which reached the stage at Paris in 1798 with music by Pierre Gaveaux, as depicting "a sublime act of heroism and devotion by one of the women of Touraine, whose generous efforts I had had the pleasure of assisting." Assuming male disguise, that heroine finds employment in the prison, and ultimately succeeds in liberating the imprisoned.

As originally performed at Paris, this *opéra-comique* was described as a *"Fait historique"* ("historic fact"), signaling a link to actual events. The composer Gaveaux impersonated the role of the tortured political prisoner Florestan, who is saved by his wife Léonore. A shift of the action to Spain was a thin disguise: the political setting remained transparent, owing to the wide circulation of a revolutionary song by Gaveaux from 1795, *The Alarm of the People Against the Terror*, a hymn often sung in opposition to Republican songs like the *Marseillaise*. The opera's local figures, Roc, Marceline, and Jaquino, speak in dialect; the role of the villain, the tyrannical Governor Pizare, is not sung at all but only spoken. The benevolent Minister Don Fernand, who sets things right at the end, stands in for the original librettist, Bouilly, who claimed "the pleasure of assisting" a real courageous heroine like Léonore.

The Revolution began on 14 July 1789. Since the opera's prison holds political detainees, its captives parallel those released with the storming of the Bastille, but the malign governor in *Léonore* stands for those excesses of arbitrary power that came later during the Reign of Terror. This motive is absorbed into Beethoven's *Fidelio*, along with the layout of seven main characters and basic plot from *Léonore, ou L'amour conjugal*. After the fall of Maximilien Robespierre ending the Reign of Terror in 1794, about 10,000 detainees were released within a few days. That event came too late to rescue Beethoven's former professor at Bonn, Eulogius Schneider, who passionately embraced the Revolution and was evidently the first to translate into German the words of the *Marseillaise*. Having himself played a role in the Terror, Schneider perished on the guillotine in 1794.

Beethoven's *Fidelio* exists in three versions stemming from 1805, 1806, and 1814, spanning most of the eventful period of Napoleon's unbridled power up to his downfall. Joseph von Sonnleithner was librettist for the first version based on translation of Bouilly's text; Beethoven's friend Stephan von Breuning aided him with changes in 1806. For the final, substantially revised version, Georg Friedrich Treitschke served as librettist. In the end, after immense labors, Beethoven felt he had earned a "martyr's crown" for his efforts.

Due to its prolonged genesis, the consideration of *Fidelio* forces an adjustment in the chronological flow of our narrative. The present chapter focuses on the opera and those works most closely connected to it. Chapter six offers a complementary perspective on this same period, beginning with Beethoven's conflict with Prince Karl Lichnowsky in 1806 and extending to the time of Napoleon's final downfall in 1815.

Through the extensive revision process, *Fidelio* became increasingly distanced from its origins in the "old French libretto," especially regarding the handling of Florestan and Leonore. In *Fidelio*, themes of unjust imprisonment at the hands of a tyrant and heroic valor in the name of freedom are expressed in a way not merely realistic but deeply symbolic and archetypal in import. The character of Leonore bears a certain affinity to the feminine liberty symbol of the French Revolution, and to the positive ethical potential that was betrayed during the upheavals of the 1790s.

The importance of *Fidelio* for Beethoven is often underestimated. The opera covers a vast range of dramatic character, from comic banter to the heroic sublime. Beethoven's engagement with the opera's dramatic themes in his instrumental music is reflected in the four overtures to *Fidelio*, especially the *Leonore* Overtures nos. 2 and 3, but his operatic preoccupation also exerted impact on his sonatas and quartets.

The political implications come into focus once we examine the role of Beethoven's artistic models and closely related works, including Schiller's play on Jeanne d'Arc, *Die Jungfrau von Orléans*, and Beethoven's own music to Goethe's drama *Egmont*. Beethoven's irritation with Mozart's great Italian operas, and particularly *Così fan tutte*, lurks behind his exalted musical depiction of the disguised heroine Leonore. In various ways, the story of Beethoven's struggle to find an optimal shape for his opera is a political tale.

When Emanuel Schikaneder sought to entice Beethoven to write an opera, his generosity backfired. Beethoven was well disposed toward the Bavarian playwright, who wrote the libretto of Mozart's *Magic Flute* and had assumed the role of Papageno. As part of the deal to compose the opera for the *Theater an der Wien*, the composer received free lodging in the theater, enabling him to attend many performances. French repertoire abounded. These were the "clever and practical French operas" whose "light . . . totally eclipsed . . . Schickaneder's realm." Beethoven was drawn most to the rhetorical manner of the operas and overtures of Luigi Cherubini. When he first began sketching music for *Fidelio* in 1804, he greased the wheels by copying out ensemble passages from Cherubini's *Les deux journées*, another French Revolutionary opera with text by Bouilly, alongside passages from Mozart's *Don Giovanni* and *The Magic Flute*.

Beethoven admired Mozart's music but was troubled by the subject matter of his operas with librettist Lorenzo da Ponte: *The Marriage of Figaro*, *Don Giovanni*, and *Così fan tutte*. According to the musician Ignaz von Seyfried, Beethoven considered *The Magic Flute* "Mozart's greatest work" but found that "'Don Juan' still is fashioned altogether in the Italian style and, besides, art, which is sacred, should never be degraded to serve as a pretext for so scandalous a subject." Another witness, Ludwig Rellstab, quoted Beethoven as follows: "I could not compose operas like 'Don Giovanni' and 'Figaro.' I hold them both in aversion. I could not have chosen such subjects, they are too frivolous for me."

If Beethoven found *Don Giovanni* and *Figaro* "too frivolous," *Così fan tutte* must have disturbed him more because of its skepticism toward ideals and its ironically tolerant view of fallible human relationships. In *Così*, the "philosopher" Don Alfonso, aided by his paid deputy Despina, designs a partner-swapping experiment aiming to prove the transient nature of emotional commitments and the fragility of vows of faithfulness in view of the volatile passions of real people. Don Alfonso sets forth a theory of human nature, according to which ideals always prove vulnerable when tested by human beings.

Così fan tutte radically destabilizes those bonds between the sexes that Beethoven glorifies through the elevation of spousal virtue in *Fidelio*. Beethoven's "aversion" toward such "scandalous" subjects and his convictions about "sacred" art were rooted in the humanistic background of his youth at Bonn, especially his lifelong interest in Schiller's works and ideas. Initially enthusiastic about the outbreak of the French Revolution but horrified by the Reign of Terror, Schiller tried to show how the cause of freedom could be promoted instead through aesthetic means. The strengths of Beethoven's *Fidelio*, however, lie not only in its ethical idealism but in its solid grounding in commonplace life.

Fidelio can almost be viewed as two operas: a drama centered on noble, elevated personages—Florestan and his heroic wife Leonore—inlaid into the humble, *opera-comique* plot inhabited by Rocco the jailor, his daughter Marzelline, and her jealous boyfriend Jacquino. The world of these latter figures is cramped and gray, marked by annoyance and peevish resentment. Rocco displays petty bourgeois satisfaction, self-importance, and a materialistic worldview. It is revealing that Beethoven, having withdrawn Rocco's "Gold" aria in the 1806 version, wisely restored it in 1814. We all know people like Rocco: while not inherently evil, he is a collaborator, morally compromised by his dependence on Pizarro.

This world of narrow horizons is conveyed in the duet of Marzelline and Jacquino, which became the opening number in 1814. Distracted by tender thoughts about Fidelio (the disguised Leonore), Marzelline is plagued by the attentions of Jacquino, who presses her to marry him. Their squabble is reflected in Beethoven's music, which alternates between the keys of A major and B minor, while the rhythm of persistent knocking that annoys Jacquino is deftly shifted to Marzelline's negative response to his appeals. This is a vivaciously tensional musical setting, such as Beethoven had developed in his instrumental works in a comic cast. The Piano Sonata in G Major, op. 31, no. 1, is launched by a similar shift between keys.

The quandary that lies behind the surface of things is first exposed in the canonic quartet, "Mir ist so wunderbar." As Marzelline and Rocco express their happiness, Leonore is beset by doubts whether her risky plan holds promise. Her rhyming counterpoint to Marzelline's "wunderbar" ("wonderful") is "Gefahr"

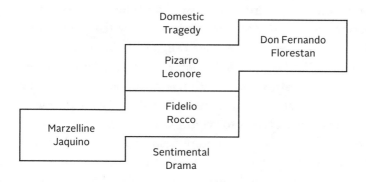

5.1 Configuration of seven main characters in *Fidelio*.

("danger"); her inner soliloquy laments: "wie schwach der Hoffnung Schein!" ("how dim the appearance of hope!"). This contemplative ensemble freezes a moment in time, as ethereal music joins incompatible perspectives. Here, and again in Leonore's big solo aria, Beethoven reshapes musical models from Mozart's *Così fan tutte*.

Leonore's critique of Marzelline's perspective—the clash of "Gefahr" against "wunderbar"—is double-edged irony. According to Jean Paul Richter, whose voluminous treatise on aesthetics appeared in the same year Beethoven began his labors on the opera, humor is the inverted sublime. In *Fidelio*, finitude and infinity—complacent realism and idealistic principles—collide. The handling of the embattled couple and chorus of inmates in *Fidelio* goes beyond the original French opera and the other early operas based on this material by Fernando Paer and Simone Mayr. Those works do not exploit the mixture of genres in Bouilly's plot that is heightened in the German version by Beethoven's first librettist, Sonnleithner. The disposition of the seven main characters is shown in figure 5.1. Two theatrical traditions, that of the *comédie larmoyante* (sentimental drama) and *tragédie bourgeoise* (domestic tragedy), are combined, yielding a dramatic form poised between classical tragedy and comedy. This configuration sets Leonore and Florestan into conflict with the tyrannical Pizarro as part of a symmetrical plot design. Since the central protagonist, Leonore, is disguised, she functions on two planes of action. Disguised as Fidelio, she interacts with Rocco, Marzelline, and Jacquino. Revealed as Leonore, she confronts Pizarro, shields Florestan, and is extolled by Don Fernando at the conclusion.

Leonore's ethical motivation is paramount. Pizarro's prisoners are incarcerated for political reasons. The warning Pizarro receives in act 1 refers to "victims of arbitrary power," so Florestan is not the only one. That impression is confirmed by Florestan's cruel punishment after his attempt to expose Pizarro's abuses. Rocco too is aware of injustice. When asked by Leonore whether the unnamed prisoner in the dungeon is a "great criminal," Rocco responds that he may "have great enemies; that amounts to much the same thing." During the Reign of Terror, such a *prison d'état* might have been housed in some great *château* crammed with innocent prisoners. In this context, it is important how Leonore's role as liberating agent goes beyond her own self-interest. In act 1, she urges allowing the prisoners into the light and air of the garden, foreshadowing their later collective liberation. In act 2, before knowing the identity of the solitary prisoner in the dungeon, Leonore exclaims that "Whoever you may be, I shall rescue you."

The depiction of the incarcerated Florestan in his dungeon cell posed problems. Chained in the dungeon on diminishing rations and close to death, he is a passive hero who must just endure, and somehow survive. As the victim of vengeful retribution, Florestan is powerless. Only intervention from Leonore can save him.

How can such a character be brought effectively to the operatic stage? How should a starving prisoner veiled in darkness be portrayed as a principal vocal role?

In *Léonore*, as in Beethoven's opera, Florestan's appearance in the dungeon is reserved until the last act. Decisive changes were made in the original French text when it was adapted. In Bouilly's version, the prisoner stares at a miniature portrait of the beloved and wishes for death. In Beethoven's opera, the suicidal wish is deleted from Florestan's soliloquy and the image of the beloved is transformed. Instead of a futile effort to sustain hope focused on a visual likeness of the beloved, Beethoven's Florestan experiences something quite different: an ecstatic vision of Leonore as an angel of freedom suspended in rosy illumination and embodied in sound, a vision promising deliverance from imprisonment while sustaining life.

This vision as portrayed by Beethoven becomes the inner climax of the opera. The musical embodiment of Leonore's uncanny presence in Florestan's dark cell counteracts the terror imposed on an isolated individual, aiding his self-preservation through virtuous endurance. Drawing on the resources of his symphonic style, Beethoven shaped the culmination of Florestan's aria in the dungeon as a nodal point of the dramatic narrative.

Beethoven's artistic strategy shows kinship with Schiller's ideas. In his 1801 essay "On the Sublime," Schiller illustrates the sublime in terms of the relationship between Odysseus and Penelope in Homer's *Odyssey*. For long years, Odysseus is held captive by the goddess Calypso. Book 1 of the *Odyssey* relates that "Odysseus alone, filled with longing for his return and for his wife, did the queenly nymph Calypso, that bright goddess, keep back in her hollow caves, yearning that he should be her husband." For Schiller, the captivity of Odysseus is eventually overcome by a sublime longing that enables his freedom and return to Ithaca. Beethoven's familiarity with Schiller's idea is implied from his plans for an opera with Theodor Körner, the son of Schiller's intimate friend Christian Gottfried Körner. When Beethoven met with Körner in 1812, they settled on the subject of *The Return of Ulysses* (Ulysses is the Latin variant of Odysseus). These plans fell through when the younger Körner died in 1813 fighting Napoleon's forces, but a connection to Homer and Schiller surely helped inspire Florestan's delirious vision as culmination of his aria.

Florestan's vision brings together two symbolic archetypes: the distant beloved and the liberating angel. The distant-beloved trope assumes importance for Beethoven as an "entfernte" or "ferne Geliebte" (as in his song cycle *An die ferne Geliebte*) or as an idealized "unsterbliche Geliebte" (Immortal Beloved, as in his famous love letter from 1812). Another such distant beloved is the Penelope of Homer's *Odyssey*. The sublime longing of Odysseus or

5.2 Liberty statue with the guillotine, Place de la Révolution, Paris, ca. 1793. Painting by Pierre-Antoine Demachy: *Une execution capitale, Place de la Révolution*, Musée Carnavalet, Histoire de Paris. Wikimedia Commons.

Florestan is akin to that expressed in Beethoven's Goethe setting "Wonne der Wehmut" ("Bliss in Sorrow") of 1810, in which the "tears of eternal love" should "Dry not!," conveying a poignant, even masochistic conflict within the protagonist.

The idea of a distant beloved can absorb other associations. In this respect let us consider the background of feminine liberty symbols in the post-Revolutionary period. Unlike in many other revolutions, the upheaval in France involved not just destruction of monuments of authority, of the king, but the frequent *replacement* of the monarch's image by a timeless idealistic symbol: a classically robed goddess of liberty. After the statue of King Louis XV was knocked down and replaced by the feminine embodiment of liberty, the plaza was renamed Place de la Révolution; during the Reign of Terror, many executions took place in front of the liberty statue. One such event is depicted in a painting by Pierre-Antoine Demachy (fig. 5.2). Belying this history, the plaza was subsequently renamed Place de la Concorde.

Feminine symbols of liberty could embody the collective spirit of a people or nation, echoing older traditions reaching back to Athena in ancient Greece. This type of symbol is transnational but was named "Marianne" in France and "Germania" in German-speaking regions. The character of these archetypal depictions reflected changing political conditions. The famous gift of the French to the Americans is a familiar example: the Statue of Liberty in New York harbor. The alliance of a feminine embodiment of *liberté* with freedom trees or *arbres de la liberté* found a precedent in antiquity in the figure of Athena, whose gift of an olive tree made her the emblematic goddess of ancient Athens, with the olive branch itself symbolic of peace or reconciliation.

In *Fidelio*, the figure of Leonore became a magnet for meaning drawn from several sources. Beethoven with his librettists augmented the French plot that had ignited their imagination, indulging in complexities conforming to what Friedrich Schlegel considered ironic: hovering, elusive visions to be grasped through the imagination, not the understanding. One key source for the figure of Leonore became the fifteenth-century teenage heroine Jeanne d'Arc (Joan of Arc), as mediated through Schiller's play *Die Jungfrau von Orléans*. Despite Habsburg censorship of some of Schiller's dramas, this play reached the stage at Vienna in January 1802; Beethoven owned a copy of the text. His musician friend Ignaz von Seyfried stated that "Beethoven never was seen in the street without a little note-book in which he jotted down his ideas of the moment. When by chance this was mentioned, he would parody the words of Joan of Arc: 'I may not come unless I bear my banner!'" This allusion refers to the end of Schiller's play, when the mortally wounded Johanna asserts her fidelity to the cause that sustains her. The remark asserts Beethoven's own attitude toward his art as a higher calling, but also bears irony. Beethoven's attachment to Schiller's *Die Jungfrau von Orléans* is reflected in two canons he wrote in 1813 and 1815 on "Kurz ist der Schmerz, ewig ist die Freude" ("The pain is short, the joy is endless"). These lines come from the end of the play, the last words uttered by Johanna before her death.

Parallels between Leonore and Schiller's heroine include the gender ambiguity of a woman in masculine garb and Johanna's description of herself as a "Retterin" ("rescuer"), the term of praise attributed to Leonore in the jubilant finale of act 2 of *Fidelio*. Another allusion appears in Leonore's recitative "Repellent one! Where do you rush?" when she responds to the malign Pizarro in act 1. What sustains her fortitude is the vision of a consoling rainbow that she perceives before her, illuminated above dark clouds: "so leuchtet mir ein Farbenbogen, der hell auf dunkeln Wolken ruht." The inspiration for this luminous image—which was added to the opera in 1814—derives from the end of Schiller's play, when the dying Johanna asks those around her, "Do you see the rainbow in the air?" The musical setting employs a shift to a sustained C-major chord in the woodwind instruments in a slow *Adagio* tempo, opening an expressive space of celestial self-possession that stands in stark contrast to Pizarro's destructive rage. The inclusion of this luminous vision for Leonore enriches the drama while critiquing the realistic level of the action.

Such interpolated visions call for metaphorical interpretation. Although separated, Leonore and Florestan embark on a joint quest that surmounts fear and danger. Neither of them would succeed without a powerful conviction about a reality that lies beyond. This utopian conviction or "effigy of the ideal," in Schiller's formulation, gives to each of them the strength to persevere. In his creative process, Beethoven sought musical means to embody these positive symbols, lending sensuous embodiment to an ideal representation. In narrative terms paralleling Homer's *Odyssey*, Leonore threads her way through treacherous situations, guided by a sublime longing. When we first observe Leonore, she carries chains for use in the prison; in the closing scene, she unchains Florestan and has enabled through her actions the liberation of all the prisoners.

Stages of Leonore's odyssey are revealed in the canonic quartet "Mir ist so wunderbar" and her aria "Komm, Hoffnung" ("Come, Hope") in act 1. In these pieces, Beethoven drew upon Mozartian models but inverted their dramatic meaning. Mozart's vocal canon for Fiordiligi, Dorabella, and Ferrando in the finale of act 2 of *Così fan tutte* (no. 31, *Larghetto*) helped inspire "Mir ist so wunderbar." Mozart's ensemble, like Beethoven's, unites conflicting perspectives, and a fourth participant, Guglielmo, declines to join in the canon at all. Leonore's aria "Come, Hope" responds to Fiordiligi's "Per pieta, ben mio perdona" ("Dearest love, I beg your pardon") earlier in act 2 of *Così fan tutte*. Both arias are set in E major, beginning *Adagio*, with the prominent single horn in Fiordiligi's piece becoming three horns in Leonore's aria.

Unlike Leonore, Fiordiligi does not remain faithful to her partner. Her immersion in the present supplants her loyalty to the past. In this respect, *Fidelio* offers an alternative to Mozart's work, with the undimmed memory and spiritual conviction of Leonore and Florestan becoming crucial enabling factors. In the face of uncertainty and seemingly insuperable barriers, yet strengthened by the "duty of true conjugal love," Leonore appeals in her aria to the "last star" to "illuminate her goal, however distant, in order that love reach it." The registral ascent to her peak note of high B is achieved at the word "erreichen" ("reach"). In another E-major *Adagio* written soon after the opera, the slow movement of the second *Razumovsky* Quartet, Beethoven again invokes a contemplative vision of the "starry heavens."

Beethoven's operatic preoccupation impacted on his pair of big piano sonatas conceived by 1804, during the composition of *Fidelio*. The *Waldstein* Sonata, op. 53, in C major, parallels the festive, ebullient atmosphere of *Fidelio*'s last-act finale; the *Appassionata* Sonata, op. 57, in F minor, reflects the tragic environment of Pizarro's dungeon. If Florestan's "God!—what darkness here!" might serve as commentary on the outer movements of the *Appassionata*, the choral text "Hail to the day! Hail to the hour!" at the end of *Fidelio* might serve as motto for the jubilant coda to the finale of the *Waldstein*.

Beethoven's sketchbooks show how these sonatas evolved during his labors on the opera. Their key symbolism mirrors the central dramatic polarity in *Fidelio*. C major is the tonality of the great overtures to the opera—the second and third *Leonore* overtures—in which the overarching drama is set forth in symphonic terms. In the opera, Beethoven also employed C minor/C major as the key of Marzelline's aria, originally the opening number. Above all in the choral finale of the last act, C major shines forth as the brilliant soundscape for the stirring choral conclusion.

This background explains a puzzling aspect of the compositional genesis of the *Waldstein*. Before it was published, Beethoven often performed the piece at the palaces of his aristocratic sponsors, and the slow movement attracted special praise. Beethoven begrudgingly dubbed this movement "Andante favori" or "favorite Andante" in response to its popularity. Yet he then decided to remove it from the sonata for which it had been composed. In its place he composed a much shorter replacement movement, a mere introduction to the *Waldstein* finale.

A main reason for the substitution was undoubtedly to supply expressive and registral contrast, setting the lofty opening theme of the rondo finale into sharp relief. Beethoven begins his substituted *Introduzione* on a low-octave F, a sound grounded on the deepest available tonic pitch in F major. The motives in the right hand gradually strive upward out of the bass region, while the left hand moves in contrary motion into the depths of the bass. The lowest F becomes a low reference point in sound, until the rondo melody is heard, emerging softly without a break above a deep pedal point in the bass, nuanced with sensitive pedal effects.

The mysterious dark realm of sound embodied in the *Introduzione* enhances the expressive world of the entire sonata. Its aesthetic meaning points beyond the sphere of "absolute" music, a term ill suited to Beethoven if it implies an abstract autonomy. For the *Introduzione* embodies a process of discovery, a shift out of the depths to reach the threshold of the rondo in its gleaming C major. This process parallels the opera in its symbolic ascent from darkness to freedom and illumination. Something of this experience should be conveyed in every adequate performance of the sonata.

A more direct link to *Fidelio* is felt in the *Appassionata*, one of the very few Beethovenian works maintaining a tragic solemnity throughout. A motivic key to its character lies in the first three notes descending through the tonic chord of F minor and marked by a dotted rhythm. The main theme of the finale elaborates this same idea (fig. 5.3). Beethoven's student Ferdinand Ries related how he witnessed his teacher in the throes of conceiving the music during a long rambling walk:

> We went so far astray that we did not get back to Döbling, where Beethoven lived, until nearly 8 o'clock, [and] he had been all the time humming and sometimes howling, always up and down, without singing any definite notes. In answer to my question what it was he said: "A theme for the last movement of the sonata has occurred to me" [in F minor, op. 57]. When we entered the room he ran to the pianoforte without taking off his hat. I took a seat in the corner and he soon forgot all about me. Now he stormed for at least an hour with the beautiful finale of the sonata. Finally he got up, was surprised still to see me and said: "I cannot give you a lesson today, I must do some more work."

The *Appassionata*'s opening movement harbors a subtle connection to the famous *Marseillaise*, the French national anthem. Originally entitled "Chant de guerre pour l'Armée du Rhin" ("War Song for the Rhine Army"), the *Marseillaise* was written by Claude Joseph Rouget de Lisle in 1792 in Strasbourg, the city that had

Beethoven, Sonata in F minor, op. 57, first and last movements

Claude Joseph Rouget de L'Isle, *La Marseillaise*

5.3 *Appassionata* Sonata, op. 57: comparison of first and last movements.

Beethoven, Sonata in F minor, op. 57/I, mm. 35-37

dolce

Claude Joseph Rouget de L'Isle, *La Marseillaise,* mm. 3-5

[Pa] - tri - e! Le jour de gloire est ar - ri vé.

5.4 Second theme of the *Appassionata* Sonata/I and the *Marseillaise.*

become the residence of Beethoven's former professor Eulogius Schneider one year earlier. As a revolutionary song, the *Marseillaise* exhorted citizens to patriotic defense against foreign invasion. In 1795, the National Convention adopted the *Marseillaise* as the French national anthem.

Prominent in the *Marseillaise* is a threefold pattern of three-note descending figures, beginning at "patrie" ("country"). The beginning of the *Appassionata* already reproduces the three-note figure in F minor (fig. 5.3), but the lyrical second subject evokes a broader audible parallel to the *Marseillaise* because of its almost obsessive repetitions of the motivic dotted figure together with a swinging triadic melodic contour in the major mode (fig. 5.4). These rhythmic inflections lend a distinctive anthem-like character to the theme. The French text for these inflections in the *Marseillaise* refers to the day of glory ("le jour de gloire arrivé"), with the rhythmic figure set to "jour de gloi[re]" corresponding to the head motive at the outset of the *Appassionata.* A more emphatic statement of the threefold dotted figures in the *Marseillaise* refers to the raising of the bloody flag. Understandably, Beethoven alludes to the character and repetitive rhythmic swing of the *Marseillaise* but does not cite it openly and directly. The affinity is a veiled allusion, not a quotation. In his travel memoires from 1802, Johann Gottfried Seume related how he disrupted the "reverent silence" of a Viennese coffeehouse simply by whistling the *Marseillaise,* causing startled consternation.

In composing the sonata, Beethoven fashioned this lyrical second subject as an interpolation, framed by ideas of agitated, tragic character. During most of the movement, when the lyrical subject appears, it trails off into mysterious silence or is brutally negated. In the *Presto* coda, however, this theme appears in F minor in the high register racked by dissonance and rhythmic agitation; it is not guillotined, but itself leads the way to the scaffold. The entire sonata evinces a quality of gigantic simplicity that contributes to its terrible expressive power. Its motives and themes exploit tensional half steps, as in the four-note motto D♭–D♭–D♭–C in the bass of the opening theme. The slow movement eventually collapses onto shattering dissonant chords; the trajectory of the perpetual-motion finale is burdened by a sense of tragic doom. The *Appassionata*, like the *Waldstein* and *Fidelio*, projects a gripping sense of register, of musical height and depth. The lowest possible F marks weighty arrival points. It seems almost evocative of a dungeon floor.

The powerful opening movement of the *Appassionata*, with its lyrical episodes allusive to the *Marseillaise*, some of which are cut off and virtually decapitated, seems haunted by the ghost of Eulogius Schneider and the nightmarish events of the Terror of 1793. Before Schneider left Bonn in 1791, he had been a key figure for Beethoven. The idea of commemorating the death of Emperor Joseph II with a musical work—the origin of Beethoven's *Joseph Cantata*—came from Schneider. Although the text of the cantata is by Severin Anton Averdonk, formulations such as "Ungeheuer Fanatismus" ("The monster of fanaticism") in the recitative (no. 2) derived from Schneider's poetic *Elegie an den sterbenden Kaiser* (*Elegy to the Dying Emperor*). Once in Strasbourg, Schneider assumed a potent political influence, and translated the *Marseillaise* for the largely German-speaking Alsatian populace, as we have seen. Allied with the Jacobin faction, Schneider joined the Revolutionary Tribunal at Strasbourg in 1793, and authorized the execution by guillotine of numerous persons accused of opposing the Revolution. The earlier critic of fanaticism succumbed to the monster.

The reception history of the *Appassionata* includes responses from famous political figures. The German chancellor Otto von Bismarck reportedly commented that if he "listened often to music" like the first movement of the *Appassionata*, "he would always be very brave." Vladimir Lenin was drawn to several Beethovenian works whose accents have seemed to evoke thoughts about revolution or conflicts related to political upheaval. For Lenin, these included the *Sonate pathétique*, the *Egmont* and *Coriolan* Overtures, the Ninth Symphony, and the *Appassionata*. Such affinities encourage us to enlarge our view of Beethoven's *Fidelio* by taking into account his contemporaneous pieces in other genres. It is not only *Fidelio* that sheds light on Beethoven's instrumental works, but conversely, those pieces enable us to read more into the opera. Some of these compositions, like the *Waldstein* Sonata, with its symbolic ascent out of the darkness to freedom and self-assurance, likely contributed to Beethoven's revision process of his opera, which reached its final version only in 1814.

A deliciously ironic aspect of Beethoven's opera is the name of the disguised Leonore. To whom does Fidelio owe fidelity? Biding time, waiting for her chance to change sides, she is forced to prepare her husband's grave in the dungeon. Her official task is to help Rocco, as they open an old cistern that is supposed to serve as tomb for the prisoner after he is murdered. Rather than remaining subservient, Leonore then intervenes to save Florestan, unmanning the despot Pizarro as she reveals herself to be a woman.

This brings us back to Florestan's vision, which is no mere hallucination. It does not belong to the genre of operatic "mad scenes," despite the direction in the score that Florestan's psychic state verges on insanity ("Wahnsinn"). The stage direction specifies Florestan's inner state as "close to madness, but a quiet enthusiasm" conveying self-possession. The music for Florestan's vision is linked to other passages in the opera, and could have been conceived only at a late stage in the genesis of the opera. What Beethoven conveys here is something uncanny. Leonore appears here as a supernatural presence, an angel.

As Florestan senses this ethereal presence in his dungeon cell, a gentle breeze and rosy light animate his "grave," as he puts it. Moments before, a melody has arisen in the solo oboe, sounding above a quiet syncopated accompaniment in the strings (fig. 5.5a). This high *dolce* oboe melody evokes Leonore as a luminous spiritual presence consoling the prisoner. The oboe soars in dialogue with the voice, so that the falling pitches G–E–C–B of the high instrument are echoed by Florestan to his words "an angel, Leonore." He continues: "Leonore, so like my wife, who leads me to freedom, to the heavenly sphere."

Nowhere else in the opera are the boundaries between imagination and reality so challenged. The "heavenly realm" of freedom—is it to be realized in life, or in death? The final section of this aria is one of Beethoven's contributions to the idea that the current of subjectivity, of spiritual activity, of the individual's apprehension of *value*, is more real than external reality.

Closely connected to Florestan's vision is the ensuing melodrama, with spoken dialogue for Leonore and Rocco interspersed with orchestral music. Leonore enters the dungeon without recognizing the prisoner. As the two gravediggers stare at the unmoving captive, Rocco quips dryly: "Maybe he is dead." Leonore: "Do you mean that?" Rocco: "No, no, he is sleeping." When Florestan then makes a movement, a snippet of the oboe melody in F major is heard, a near-quotation from the end of Florestan's aria, heard just before (fig. 5.5b). This quotation mimics the hovering oboe phrases at Florestan's words "an angel, Leonore."

What is the meaning of this correspondence? From the perspective of the gravediggers as they peer toward the motionless prisoner, it seems that he might be dead. What has preserved Florestan's vital forces is an idealized, spiritual experience—a sustaining vision of Leonore as angel of freedom. The aria of the prisoner, especially its culminating F-major section, is inward and psychological, not an outward display or physical performance. The oboe excerpt in the melodrama signals how his life is sustained through his vivid imagination and virtuous inner conviction; it identifies this inward state with the climax of the preceding aria. We best understand these two events as not successive

5.5a *Fidelio*, act 2: Florestan's vision of the angel of freedom.

5.5b *Fidelio*, act 2, melodrama with Florestan asleep.

but *simultaneous*: "No, no, he's sleeping" coincides with an inner vision that soon becomes more real than external conditions. The prisoner's aria reveals his inward state; it is a metaphor with predictive force. For the object of aspiration and agent for change has just entered the forbidden chamber, and Florestan's imminent death is about to be averted.

Treitschke described his struggle together with Beethoven to conceive this passage. Finding it problematic for a prisoner on the verge of death to sing a bravura aria, Treitschke sought words conveying a "last flaring up of life" before Florestan's impending demise. Oddly, Treitschke does not mention the poetic image of the angel of liberty, which closely parallels an earlier work of Beethoven's and thereby aided the composer in finding an artistic solution. Beethoven was initially uncertain about the orchestration at that crucial moment when Florestan perceives Leonore as angelic apparition in his prison cell. Beethoven's sketches imply that this psychological projection—or supernatural presence— was at first to have been represented musically by the flute. In changing the instrumentation from flute to oboe, he surely became cognizant of striking affinities pointing beyond his opera.

Beethoven drew here on an intensely political work he had composed in 1810: his music to Goethe's *Egmont*. The relaxation of censorship in Austria during the French occupation of 1809 and its aftermath had enabled performances with music of political dramas by Schiller and Goethe: *Wilhelm Tell* and *Egmont*, respectively. Beethoven's preference was for *Wilhelm Tell*, but he was assigned *Egmont*. In the first performances, "Clärchen" was played by Antonia Adamberger, fiancée of Theodor Körner. After that young Saxon poet-patriot was killed fighting Napoleon's troops, he became for generations the most famous martyr for the cause of the liberation from French domination. Inspired by Körner's poems, the student Karl Sand assassinated the conservative dramatist August von Kotzebue in 1819, an action that triggered the Karlsbad Decrees of 1820, marking a notoriously repressive period of the Metternich regime during the reign of Emperor Franz.

In the *Egmont* music as in *Fidelio*, Beethoven shapes his music to convey narratives involving apotheosis of an envisioned but not achieved goal, an "effigy of the ideal." The political context Beethoven experienced offered unpalatable choices, with Napoleon, despite all disillusionment and resistance, still sometimes seen as preferable to rulers such as Emperor Franz. Beethoven did not waver in his support between Napoleon and anti-Napoleonic Austrian nationalism. By 1804, his attitude toward both sides was ambivalent to negative; it was a matter of weighing the lesser of two evils.

In 1820 Beethoven discussed the political situation with educator Joseph Blöchlinger von Bannholz, who found that whereas the period from 1809 until 1813 had brought some progressive developments in the German lands,

Now it is again miserable.

––––––

It was earlier much better, NB. Before 1813.

––––––

The *aristocrats* found support once more in Austria, and the *republican spirit* only just glows in the ashes.

These entries from a conversation notebook used by the deaf composer imply that he concurred with Blöchlinger's pessimistic view. Beethoven and his friends felt bitter disappointment about the repressive political developments after the Congress of Vienna, and were supportive of the oppressed, not of the representatives of authority.

Goethe's *Egmont* shares the same historical setting as Schiller's *Don Carlos*. Like *Fidelio*, it is grounded in actual historical events. In his play, Goethe explicitly envisioned a role for music. The historical Count Egmont in the sixteenth century opposed the Inquisition and became a victim of the infamous "Council of Blood" erected by the Duke of Alba, a ruler dubbed "the Iron Duke" by Protestants in the Low Countries because of his cruelty. The dialogue between Egmont and Alba in Goethe's play (act 4, scene 2, 85–86) touches on these themes:

EGMONT. Religion, it is said, is merely a splendid device, behind which every dangerous design may be contrived with greater ease; the prostrate crowds adore the sacred symbols pictured there while behind lurks the fowler ready to ensnare them.
ALBA. This must I hear from you?
EGMONT. I speak not my own sentiments! I but repeat what is loudly rumored, and uttered now here and now there by great and by humble, by wise men and fools. The Netherlanders fear a double yoke, and who will be surety to them for their liberty?

When Egmont faces execution by the Spaniards, he accepts his fate proudly, like Jeanne d'Arc, and he predicts the liberation of his country. At the end of Goethe's play, the imprisoned Egmont describes his dream vision of his beloved Clärchen:

With blood-stained feet the vision approached, the waving folds of her robe also were tinged with blood. It was my blood, and the blood of many brave hearts. No! It shall not be shed in vain! Forward! Brave people! The goddess of liberty leads you on!

Egmont's dream projection of his role as martyr of Flemish freedom foresees an uprising—the revolt of the Netherlands in the Eighty Years' War (1568–1648). Goethe's direction that his play culminates in a *Siegessymphonie* (*Victory Symphony*) inspired Beethoven to write the prescribed music, which is associated with resistance to arbitrary authority and tyrannical brutality.

In the *Egmont* Overture capped by the *Victory Symphony*, Beethoven expresses the relation between the personal fate of Count Egmont and the liberation for which Egmont sacrifices himself. The pause near the end of this stern, concentrated overture is important—in his sketches Beethoven wrote that "the death could be expressed through a rest." After this portentous silence, the tragedy is overturned through the *Victory Symphony*, with its thrilling apotheosis of the fallen hero. The use of musical silence symbolizing death occurs elsewhere in the *Egmont* music, in no. 7 "(Representing Clärchen's death")" and in the melodrama, no. 8 ("indicating Egmont's death"), a passage that leads to trumpets asserting the spirit of freedom, the crowning of Egmont as martyr, and once again to the *Victory Symphony*, as the F-major coda of the overture is recaptured.

When Beethoven revised *Fidelio* in 1814, he drew on the symbolism and dramatic strategies developed in the *Egmont* music. That the F-major coda of Florestan's aria and melodrama in the dungeon displays affinities with *Egmont* is shown as well by the orchestration, including the prominent role of the oboe. Florestan's aria culminates in a dream vision, an embodiment of consequential creativity. Count Egmont and his beloved Clärchen do not survive the action; she dies before the melodrama, in which her spirit as liberating angel crowns him with laurels. In *Fidelio*, by contrast, Florestan's ecstatic vision of the angel of freedom presages the positive outcome of the drama: Leonore's triumph over Pizarro and the closing collective scene of liberation.

The angelic symbolism merits attention. In the wake of the French Revolution, following the abdication and execution of King Louis XVI, feminine allegorical images of *liberté* often replaced those of patriarchal authority. The substitution of the hereditary patriarchal ruler by a symbolic feminine image reflected a shift from absolute monarchy to a civil society, whose collective unity was no longer represented by a monarch or a single human individual. In the context of *Léonore* and *Fidelio*, the notion of conjugal devotion unites separate individuals, implying family and community. The "sublime heroism" of Fidelio/Leonore is pitted here against the villainous figure of the corrupt prison governor. Pizarro's "Tigersinn," his "tigerish heart" steeped in fierce hate, covets a fanatical exercise of power, pointing toward political regression in authoritarian or fascist terms.

During the Revolutionary period, angelic symbolism could assume a double aspect. A caricature of the pantheonization of Voltaire from 1791 scorns royalty while extolling a formidable cultural figure famous for biting critiques of authority, who even spent prison time in the Bastille during the *ancien regime*. In this depiction, an angel as allegorical symbol of fame blows two different trumpets, one lampooning the king as a "faux pas," a false step or blunder, one glorifying Voltaire as an "immortal man" (fig. 5.6). A crown of stars and the winged horse Pegasus mark the greatness of Voltaire; the landscape around the king is barren apart from scattered weeds. The irreverent, bare-bottomed figure desecrates the king, referring to the treasonous flight and the capture of the monarch on 21 June 1791. One recalls the ignoble sounds of an anus trumpet in canto 21 of the *Inferno* by Dante Alighieri, in which Barbariccia, the head demon, makes "a trumpet of his ass." The tensional motion of the angelic figure points away from

5.6 Angel denigrating the king and glorifying Voltaire, Paris, 1791. Anonymous print
Journée du 21. Juin. Le Faux-pas. L'Homme immortel from the series *La fuite à Varennes*,
referring to the royal flight to Varennes. Musée Carnavalet, Histoire de Paris G.26280.
Used with permission © Musée Carnavalet/Roger-Viollet.

the bleak empty landscape on the left toward the splendor of the
pantheon. Voltaire was well known for his advocacy of freedom
of speech and religion. The inscription below the depiction of the
internment of Voltaire's ashes in the pantheon reads that "All
true citizens have finally restored public liberty. We no longer fear
tyrannical power." The pantheon provided a consecrated space for
revolutionary heroes; Voltaire was the first of the *philosophes* to
be so honored.

The target of disdain in Beethoven's *Fidelio* is not authority as
such, but the misuse of authority. Pizarro is obsessed by his jealous grip on power and desire for vengeance. The collision of his
thirst for revenge with Leonore's defensive response in the dungeon provides the dramatic climax of the drama. The quartet "Er
sterbe!" ("He dies!") enacts a transfer of power, knocking Pizarro

off his pedestal. The governor dominates the first section, disclosing his identity to Florestan as he prepares to kill him. Florestan mocks Pizarro's pretense as an avenger: "A murderer, a murderer stands before me." As Pizarro closes in, he tries to seize the moment: "only just a moment, and this dagger." Leonore's first intervention comes after his word "Dolch" ("dagger") on a high G♯: "Zurück!" ("Back!"). She then seizes control over the musical trajectory, exploiting her feminine control of higher pitch registers. A crux comes at her words "kill first his wife!," whose vocal setting springs up a fifth from E♭ to the peak pitch of high B♭. These vocal high points establish her musical dominance over her adversary, with none more bound up with her femininity than "Weib!" ("woman"), set to a piercing unaccompanied B♭ at the top of her range.

Leonore's most decisive intervention, as she wields a pistol to silence Pizarro, seizes key pitches from his associated key of D, forcing him into submission. As Pizarro utters "to death with him!," Leonore blocks him. At her word "todt!" ("dead!"), the trumpet sounds in the distance from the ramparts, announcing the arrival of the minister Don Fernando. At this moment, Leonore's triumph over Pizarro reaches beyond the prison and the stage. The irony of the trumpet fanfares should not be overlooked. These signals stem not from Don Fernando, but from Pizarro, who had earlier commanded the soldier on pain of death to sound the trumpet to give him warning of the minister's approach. Florestan is rescued not by Don Fernando, but by Leonore. The offstage trumpet freezes the action at the moment of her shielding intervention, validating her achievement. Pizarro's cautionary signal becomes a *tuba mirum spargens sonum*—a trumpet casting a wondrous sound—at this moment of dramatic transformation.

The political dimension of *Fidelio* unfolds on a collective level. The finale of act 1 centers on the prisoners' chorus. At Fidelio's insistence, the prisoners are granted access to the warmth and light of the open air. Among their first words is the phrase "in freier Luft" ("in the free air"), whose liberating tones are emphasized through the music. Their hopeful appeal, "O freedom, will you come?," is juxtaposed with whispered warnings that the guards are listening; the atmosphere is that of a concentration camp. In its first version of the opera, this act had closed instead with a number for Pizarro and the chorus of guards. In 1814, the role of the prisoners' chorus was enhanced through the addition of a stirring setting of the text "Farewell, you warm sunshine," sung as the men return reluctantly to their cells. Through the revision process of *Fidelio*, the chorus came to stand increasingly for all of suffering humanity.

The prisoners' chorus struck home in the staging by Christine Mielitz at the Semper Oper in Dresden that premiered on 7 October 1989, just as widespread unrest began to topple the East German regime. Political demonstrations involving 10,000 persons ensued on the plaza outside the opera house. One month later, the government collapsed. *Fidelio* had often been performed in East Germany, but only then did the identification of the populace with the opera's prisoners become a real as distinct from a theatrical event in the sense of *parabasis*, breaking boundaries to reach the threshold of revolution. The pivotal moment occurred in nearby Leipzig two days after the *Fidelio* premiere, as the crowd chanted "Wir sind das Volk" ("We are the people"), seizing the rhetoric and turning the tables on their discredited political leaders.

The stage set of the Mielitz production evoked the prisons of East Germany and the Nazi concentration camps from earlier times (fig. 5.7). Such merging of an artwork with political conditions provokes thought. No other opera so potently critiques regimes that deny human freedom. As we have seen, the lack of such resistance during the Nazi era troubled the writer Thomas Mann, who asked pointedly in 1945: "How could it happen that Beethoven's *Fidelio* . . . was not forbidden in the Germany of the last twelve years?"

A shift from contemplation to action characterizes the opera's last *tableau*. Don Fernando, in an afterthought, asks Leonore to remove Florestan's chains. Beethoven here absorbs the hymnlike theme from his youthful *Joseph* Cantata from 1790, set there to the words "Da stiegen die Menschen ans Licht" ("There the peo-

5.7 *Fidelio*, act 1, prisoners' chorus. Production directed by Christine Mielitz,
Semper Oper, Dresden 1989 (Historisches Archiv der Sächsischen Staatstheater,
photograph by Erwin Döring).

ple ascended into the light"). The use of oboe in this emblematic
theme in F major set to Florestan's text "Oh inexpressible sweet
bliss!" recalls the coda of his dungeon aria, with its vision of
Leonore as angel of freedom. Florestan, in that clairvoyant state,
envisions his liberation by Leonore; in so doing, his music anticipates the oboe in F major that will mark his actual liberation. In
some uncanny way, as Beethoven's musical design implies, this
sustained ethical vision has kept Florestan alive until his rescue
by Leonore. Fittingly, Beethoven recycles the hymn theme he
conceived to honor the enlightened Emperor Joseph II in order
to crown this shared contemplative moment of thankful joy. In
productions by Mielitz and others, the donning of ordinary street
clothes by the chorus has encouraged an identification of the audience with this enactment of community.

The final revision of Beethoven's opera altered the final scenes,
removing the uncertainty that originally hung over the heads of

Florestan and Leonore even after the trumpet calls, while shifting the final choral sections from the prison into the light and air of the parade grounds. This change boosts the festive atmosphere of the conclusion, even with some lowering of dramatic tension. The shift from darkness to light, from a dystopian to a utopian environment, enables an inclusive celebration of conjugal love, since with the liberation of prisoners many couples have been reunited.

Strange parallels exist between Jean-Nicolas Bouilly and Eulogius Schneider. Both men held influential positions during the Reign of Terror, both were prolific authors, both exerted impact on Beethoven. Schneider's interest in poets like Klopstock and Gellert, and his talent as a charismatic orator, surely impressed the young Beethoven, entirely apart from his passionate embrace of the French Revolution. While at Bonn, the publications of this feisty "secular priest" elicited massive protest from the conservative clerics at Cologne. Schneider's public protest against suppression of his works led to his dismissal; during his time at Strasbourg, Schneider became increasingly radicalized as he rose in the ranks to become part of the Revolutionary Tribunal. If Schneider tried to make heads roll while at Bonn, he succeeded at Strasbourg, where he oversaw the execution by guillotine of more than thirty persons before being himself beheaded at Paris in 1794.

Bouilly followed an opposite path from Schneider, defanging the "monster of fanaticism." His most enduring legacy is the stirring human drama of *Léonore*, whose libretto served as touchstone for Beethoven. Unlike many operas and ceremonies from the time of revolutionary fever and waves of terror in France, *Fidelio* displays a Schillerian integrity and restraint. Its embedded political content avoids overt symbolism and propagandistic pageantry. The handling of Leonore as Florestan's imagined angel of freedom is an ingenious metaphor, an unconsummated symbol.

By contrast, François-Joseph Gossec's opera *Le Triomphe de la République, ou le Camp de Grand-Pré* from 1793 indulges in blatant spectacle, as a costumed Goddess of Liberty descends from the ceiling to fraternize with the troops while singing of freedom. When Notre Dame Cathedral was recast as an atheistic Temple of

Reason later that year, the ceremony paid homage to a personage clad in the blue, white, and red tricolor, an opera singer similarly personifying the Liberty Goddess. Another ceremonial climax was the deistic Festival of the Supreme Being promoted in June 1794 by Maximilien Robespierre, who soon thereafter was himself devoured by the monster, bringing to an end the Reign of Terror.

Beethoven caps his opera with a different kind of finale, an energetic closing chorus, whose text begins with yet another Schiller quotation, this time with two lines from *An die Freude* that would also find their way into the Ninth Symphony, joined to the last two lines praising Leonore as "Retterin":

Wer ein holdes Weib errungen
Stimm' in unsern Jubel ein.
Nie wird es zu hoch besungen,
Retterin des Gatten sein.

Whoever has won a noble woman
join in our jubilation.
Never will it be too highly praised
to be rescuer of your partner.

The premiere of Beethoven's *Fidelio* in its final incarnation took place in May 1814, the time of Napoleon's first exile to Elba but before the Battle of Waterloo and his banishment to St. Helena. With Napoleon's departure, a new era of absolutist power politics loomed. The opera's stage directions specify that a statue of the king be seen in the parade grounds at the conclusion, but the heroine assumes a stature rich in implications. Unmistakable is the symbolism of chains and unchaining: Leonore's unlocking of Florestan recalls the opening of Jean-Jacques Rousseau's *Social Contract*: "Man is born free, and everywhere he is in chains." The double allusion to Schiller, joining praise of the "rescuer" with the quotation from the *Ode to Joy*, presages a work from a decade later: the Ninth Symphony.

In *Fidelio*, Beethoven and his collaborators raised a monument to the ideals, not the actuality of the French Revolution. The drama involves a penetration into the depths followed by a reemergence into a light that stands for Enlightenment, as fidelity and justice triumph over tyranny. Celestial symbols and whispered warnings enhance the action. The promise of this story of rescue from post-Revolutionary circumstances applies to all those oppressive events that continue to litter human history. In our own age, the symbol of the angel of freedom as "effigy of the ideal" endures. We need such a guardian angel more than ever today.

From Grätz to Wagram and Leipzig

During Napoleon's second occupation of Vienna in 1809, the French transported animals from the menagerie at the royal summer place at Schönbrünn to Paris. They were most interested in European bison, wild oxen facing extinction in the wild. Their expropriation of such creatures during Napoleon's reign as emperor was motivated by the earlier depletion of the French royal menagerie during the Reign of Terror from 1793 to 1794. One hardened survivor of the anti-royalty fervor of the Terror was an old lion, formerly held at Versailles, a creature that while held at the Jardin de Plantes was mistreated and spat upon for being not only a "creature of royalty" but even "the King of Beasts."

Another Austrian export item of the period was those archduchesses who became queens or empresses of France. Marie-Antoinette was not so lucky as the old lion, the bars of whose cage ensured his survival. Before she met her demise, Marie-Antoinette was demonized as an Austrian "she-wolf" or "arch-tigress." Nearly a generation after Marie-Antoinette lost her head, Napoleon married the eighteen-year-old Austrian archduchess Marie-Louise in 1810, as part of his strategy of consolidating his empire in central Europe. Napoleon became thereby the great-nephew of King Louis XVI and Marie-Antoinette, the royal couple who had been guillotined at Paris during 1793. Marie-Louise's tenure as empress was curtailed, lasting only as long as Napoleon's power, and she was unsuccessful in dissuading her father, Emperor Franz of Austria, from entering the Wars of Liberation against France in 1813.

The paradoxical conflict of politics and culture strongly impacted Beethoven's life during these years. Ironies abound. Such tensions had already surfaced earlier in the composer's relationship with his most generous patron up to 1806, Prince Karl Alois Lichnowsky. Lichnowsky supported Beethoven handsomely, offering the young composer lodging and a regular income. The prince had impeccable musical credentials. He was himself a composer, had been a Masonic lodge brother of Mozart, and was acquainted with Johann Nikolaus Forkel, first biographer of Johann Sebastian Bach. Beethoven's concert tour to Prague, Dresden, Leipzig, and Berlin during 1796 was arranged by Lichnowsky, who had sponsored Mozart on a similar trip in 1789. Beethoven's engagement with chamber music during the later 1790s benefited from the string quartet supported by Lichnowsky, which provided the workshop environment for the *magnum opus* of Beethoven's first decade in Vienna, the six string quartets, op. 18. The prince even gave Beethoven a valuable set of quartet instruments, which Beethoven mentions in his *Heiligenstadt Testament*.

The event that nearly brought Beethoven to blows with the prince and broke their long-standing friendship unfolded in October 1806. Beethoven paid an extended visit to Lichnowsky at his country estate at Grätz Castle in Austrian Silesia, now in the Czech Republic near the Polish border. In the wake of Napoleon's military victories and the expansion of French influence, Lichnowsky, presumably worried about protecting his interests and property holdings, sought to cultivate cordial contact with French officers. The prince asked Beethoven to perform for his French military visitors, and he persisted when the composer was reluctant. Surely Lichnowsky did not anticipate a refusal from an artist to whom he had extended such support. Nor was it in Beethoven's interest to lose Lichnowsky's generous patronage.

This episode occurred after Napoleon's crushing double victory over the Prussian and Saxon forces at Auerstädt and Jena on 14 October. The dramatic defeat of Prussia and its aftermath in Napoleon's blatant politics of expansion represents a historical turning point marked by the rise of Francophobia and anti-

French patriotism in the German regions. After hearing that news of Napoleon's triumph, Beethoven declared: "Too bad that I don't understand the art of war the way I understand the art of music—I would conquer him!"

In response to Lichnowsky's pressure, Beethoven left Grätz Castle abruptly, walked several miles through a storm of wind and rain to the town of Troppau, stayed overnight with a physician friend, and then made his way back to Vienna, where he smashed the bust of Lichnowsky he had in his lodgings. He wrote to Lichnowsky that "Prince, what you are, you are through chance and birth; what I am, I am through my own labor. There are many princes and there will continue to be thousands more, but there is only one Beethoven." Beethoven's principled refusal to perform as requested for the French officers recalls Schiller's recommendation that individuals as moral agents shield their creativity against arbitrary force, such that a *"relationship*, which is disadvantageous . . . *be completely and utterly nullified*, and the power . . . *be destroyed in concept."*

The eighteen-year-old poet Joseph von Eichendorff was in Troppau at precisely this time, having traveled there with a group from his family's estate in Lubowitz, fifty miles away. He recalled "threatening weather from the West" with lightning and thunder coinciding with the "bolt out of the blue" of Napoleon's decisive victory. In his diary entry for 30 October 1806, Eichendorff reports returning to Lubowitz in the rain, while being "truly shattered" to learn of Napoleon's closing of the University at Halle, news he heard with "black anguish."

The soggy weather during Beethoven's departure and return journey to Vienna left its imprint on his music manuscripts. Water stains can be seen on his manuscripts of the second *Razumovsky* Quartet, op. 59, no 2, and the *Appassionata* Sonata. This sets the *Appassionata* into the context of the tensional scene with Lichnowsky and the visiting French officers. The sonata's connection to the dungeon scenes of *Fidelio* and its evocative allusion to the *Marseillaise* come to mind. The conflict at Grätz surely had to do with the intended audience and not merely Beethoven's interaction with the prince. Beethoven's anger over Napoleon crowning himself emperor two years earlier flared up in response to the military events of 1806. However, his relationship with Lichnowsky must have been repaired by 1811, when his C-major Mass was performed at Troppau and Beethoven once more stayed in Grätz.

Beethoven nevertheless later turned the French incursion into German lands to his personal advantage. In August 1808 he received an invitation to become *Kapellmeister* for Napoleon's brother Jérôme Bonaparte, who had been installed as king of Westphalia at Kassel in the wake of the French occupation. He declared his intention to leave Vienna to work at the court of Austria's enemy. As a counteroffer, Beethoven received in the spring of 1809 a lifetime annuity from three Viennese aristocrats, on the condition he remain in Austria. His three supporters were Archduke Rudolph, Prince Lobkowitz, and Prince Ferdinand Kinsky. A black sheep in the royal family whose interests centered on music and theology, Archduke Rudolph was Beethoven's long-term student and important patron in the royal family. Rudolph was the youngest son of Emperor Leopold II. That Leopold's brief regime had been less repressive than that of his son Franz was partly a matter of timing: Leopold died in 1792, before the Reign of Terror in France and ensuing armed conflicts during the 1790s, which strengthened the reaction away from constitutional reform and toward centralized absolutism in Austria. By 1800 the state required from its bureaucrats a yearly oath of loyalty.

The *Kapellmeister* at Jérôme's court in Kassel during 1807–1808 was the composer and author Johann Friedrich Reichardt, who knew Kant, Herder, and Goethe. Like Beethoven, Reichardt had embraced the principles of the French Revolution but was dismayed by Napoleon's assumption of absolute power. Reichardt resided in Vienna during late 1808 and early 1809. His *Vertraute Briefe* or "trusted letters" are a revealing source of information about Viennese musical life.

Beethoven's restless desire to impress his aristocratic allies and improve his financial conditions resulted in the most extraordinary single concert of his career and perhaps in the entire history of music: the *Akademie* held in bone-chilling cold at the *Theater an der Wien* on 22 December 1808. His options of dates were limited, and the chosen evening was unfavorable because another concert held the same night limited the availability of players and reduced the audience. Beethoven complained bitterly about conspiratorial actions undermining his concert, pointing blame at Antonio Salieri. The program included the premiere performances of the Fifth Symphony in C Minor, op. 67, and the Sixth Symphony in F Major, op. 68, the *Pastorale*. This pair of symphonies was joined by several other pieces, including the aria "Ah perfido!," two movements from the Mass in C Major, op. 86, the Fourth Concerto in G Major, op. 58, with the composer at the piano, and a solo improvisation, which was almost certainly the basis for Beethoven's Fantasy, op. 77.

The concert had its shortcomings, due to lack of rehearsal and the fact that the hall remained unheated in the frigid weather. Reichardt reported that "I accepted with hearty thanks the kind offer of Prince Lobkowitz to let me sit in his box. There we continued, in the bitterest cold, too, from 6:30 until 10:30, and experienced the truth that one can easily have too much of a good thing." Despite the large amount of music to be performed—enough for two concerts—Beethoven directed his energies to completing yet another work to serve as the crowning final piece of his *Akademie*: the Choral Fantasy in C Major for piano, orchestra, and chorus, op. 80. Its performance did not run smoothly: at one point in the middle, Beethoven was obliged to stop the orchestra and begin again.

Reichardt found Beethoven's Concerto in G Major to be a piece of "monstrous difficulty, which Beethoven executed astoundingly in the most rapid tempi." He perceived its slow movement in performance as a "masterful piece of beautifully developed song, which [Beethoven] sang on the instrument to convey a profoundly melancholy character, which also moved me." This *Andante con moto* evokes the mythic atmosphere of Orpheus taming the Furies, with the pianist confronting an initially hostile, implacable body of strings. One is reminded of the Orpheus pose in Mähler's portrait of the composer; Beethoven's early sketches for the concerto date from the same period as the portrait. Beethoven bases the movement's narrative on the principle of gradual transformation, so that the bare, harsh orchestral unisons at the outset are eventually replaced by a soft, sustained E-minor harmony at the conclusion. Although the pianist eventually compels the orchestra to yield, the soloist's confident tone later experiences a crisis in a climactic, despairing cadenza featuring a prolonged trill. This is surely part of that "profound melancholy" that touched Reichardt. Has the apparent rhetorical triumph of the soloist masked a hidden weakness? Does the cadenza harbor implications of a Pyrrhic victory?

A sense of human vulnerability also deepens the Fifth Symphony, a work whose rhetoric and overall narrative bears inescapable political implications. Few works of art have so impressed posterity. The efforts of the National Socialists to expropriate Beethoven's legacy recoiled upon them with the Fifth, whose famous opening figure became so widely associated with resistance to their tyranny. The short-short-short-long rhythmic figure has a telegraphic equivalent in the letter *V*, expressed in Morse code as dot-dot-dot-dash. The "V for Victory" campaign of the Allies was identified starting in 1941 with Beethoven's Symphony V, as is illustrated by the postcard showing "V for Victory," together with Beethoven's opening motive and the flags of the Allied forces (fig. 6.1). In the symphony, staunch opposition to Hitler's regime could be symbolized not only by the riveting opening upbeat motive and its ramifications but through the entire narrative design of the four closely interconnected movements, with a luminous C major conquering C minor. This narrative of overcoming found a prime political target in the brutality of the National Socialists.

A postcard from 1939 by the French artist Paul Barbier depicts Beethoven and Goethe as horrified representatives of the legacy of German humanism. They point accusingly at Hitler's raging, bloodthirsty destruction, as the brutal dictator tramples on treaties and scowls over his innocent victims. Beethoven and Goethe exclaim, "Malheur! Qu'as tu fait de L'Allemagne!!!" ("Tragic! What have you done to Germany!!!") (fig. 6.2).

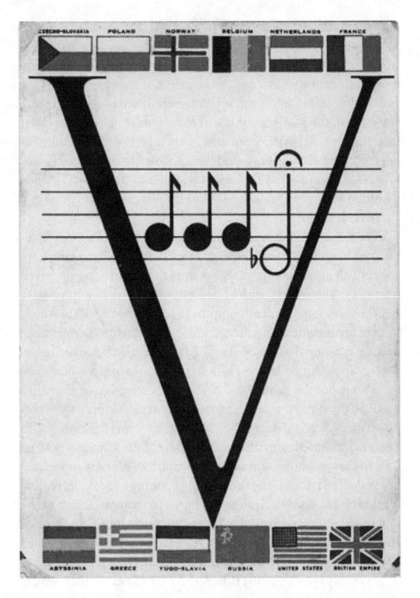

6.1 Poster with V for Victory and the beginning of Beethoven's Fifth Symphony, 1941. Wikimedia commons.

6.2 Postcard by Paul Barbier showing Beethoven and Goethe accusing Hitler, 1939. Biblioteca Beethoveniana, Carrino Collection, Muggia (Trieste).

In the December 1808 program, the *Pastoral* Symphony preceded the Fifth. The two works represent a contrasting work-pair. Although their opening movements are opposites—terse, dark drive in the Fifth, relaxed repose in the Sixth, initially inscribed "Pleasant, cheerful feelings aroused on arrival in the countryside"—the pieces share distinctive features, above all the culminating role of the finales following harrowing penultimate movements: the scherzo in the Fifth, the storm in the Sixth. The F-major Symphony is not simply a mirror of rustic country life, as is reflected in the middle movement, the "Merry gathering of villagers" with its medley of dances. Deeper meaning resides in its portrayal of nature. In writing that the work was "more an expression of feeling than tone painting" ("mehr Ausdruck der Empfindung als Malerei"), Beethoven draws attention to an important aspect of subjective engagement.

His song "Der Wachtelschlag" ("The Call of the Quail"), WoO 129, deserves attention in this context. In this 1803 setting of a widely circulated poem by Samuel Friedrich Sauter, the text begins with an admonition to careful listening: "Ach, wie schallt's dort so lieblich hervor" ("Oh, how do those lovely sounds come forth"). Beethoven uses a concise three-note figure of repeated tones with a dotted rhythm to signal the warning cry of the quail, in music beginning *Larghetto*. This rhythm is true to the bird's actual call. The bird calls "Fürch-te Gott! Fürch-te Gott!" ("Fear God! Fear God!"); its motive is then set to the words "Love God!," "Praise God!," "Thank God!" In the later sections of this remarkable *Lied*, variants of the quail's three-note figure are set to "Plead with God!" and "Trust God!" in relation to the nourishing, but fragile and threatening, aspects of nature. "He frightens you in the storm, the Lord of Nature: Plead with God! Plead with God!"

Such a warning call was embedded already in two piano sonatas Beethoven wrote in 1801: the first movement of the so-called *Moonlight* Sonata, op. 27, no. 2, and the coda of the second movement *Andante* of the *Pastoral* Sonata, op. 28. An intriguing manuscript that surfaced in the 1990s suggests that Beethoven's poetic idea for the *Adagio sostenuto* of op. 27, no. 2, was bound up with a publication from 1801, *The Aeolian Harp: an Allegorical Dream*, by F. H. von Dalberg, as well as a romance from the operetta *Annette et Lubin* by a composer who adopted the name Martini il Tedesco but was born as Johann Paul Ägidius Schwarzendorf. Martini was a Freemason who moved to Paris and became an administrator of the *Conservatoire de Musique*. Martini's romance was printed and Dalberg's book advertised in different issues from 1801 of the music journal the *Allgemeine musikalische Zeitung*, which Beethoven read avidly. Martini's piece is a lyrical arioso accompanied by a texture of rising broken chords suggestive of the harp. Beethoven copied out eighteen measures of Martini's music on his sketchleaf, and employed a similar texture of rising arpeggios in the *Moonlight* Sonata, in which a sense of the windblown mystery of the Aeolian harp is conveyed through his direction that "the whole piece be played very delicately and with the sustaining pedal held down." In view of its poetic association with nature, it is conspicuous how Beethoven uses the quail figure of repeated notes and dotted rhythms in the haunting opening movement of this Sonata in C ♯ Minor, with the title *Sonata quasi una Fantasia*.

In the *Pastoral* Sonata, one can find pedal points in the outer movements and occasional bagpipe fifths. Various passages especially in the scherzo are rustic in character. The *Andante* in D minor has a processional, ballade-like atmosphere; the melody of its main theme is suggestive of speech. In the coda Beethoven juxtaposes the opening phrases of this main theme with a disturbing, dissonant transformation of the innocent, bucolic contrasting subject—a glimpse of the abyss, followed by a close in bleak resignation. The transformed motive is the quail figure, which on its third repetition becomes a heart-rending cry: "Plead with God!"

Toward the end of the second movement of the *Pastoral* Symphony, the "Scene by the Brook," the quail gains companions in a trio of birdcalls: nightingale, quail, and cuckoo. Beethoven names each bird next to their corresponding instruments: flute, oboe, and clarinet, respectively. The presence of the quail's warning in this *Andante, molto moto* is poignant in view of the later storm movement. Raymond Knapp observes about the prophetic birdcalls that benevolent nature becomes "an imperiled paradise to be reclaimed in the finale through the devout faith expressed in the shepherd's hymn." The ensuing movements are directly connected to one another. Beethoven interrupts the dancing merrymaking of the peasants with a deceptive cadence, as the natural elements force their attention on the country folk. The storm, with its wind, rain, thunder, and lightning, is a frightful emanation of the "Lord of Nature," in Sauter's words. Hector Berlioz described the climax of this *Allegro* as "no longer just a wind and rain storm: it is a terrible cataclysm, a universal deluge, the end of the world." This is a window out of the work into the world, a psychic storm that encourages the listener to reevaluate his or her aesthetic response to the music.

In an age of global warming, humanly altered weather patterns, and political indifference to environmental degradation, the *Pastoral* Symphony is more pertinent than ever before. In 2017, the "Beethoven Pastoral Project" became part of a global initiative against climate change. In this vein, the finale of the *Pastoral*, with its reclamation of the imperiled paradise, is richly allusive, containing Alpine *Kuhreigen* evocative of Switzerland, the land whose freedom struggles are associated with *Wilhelm Tell*. Beethoven's meditations on the natural world are documented in his annotated copy of Christoph Christian Sturm's voluminous work *Betrachtungen über die Werke Gottes in der Natur* (*Observations about the Work of God in Nature*) in an edition from 1811, which shows his deistic or pantheistic inclinations. In one passage, Beethoven writes next to the poetic text the inscription "appropriate material for music," and marks the entire text in pencil, with its evocation of a transformative force in nature, manifested in the sun and flowers, bees and trees, weather and landscape. Divinity reveals itself in a violet, in a storm. Musical allusions also appear, to "my weak song," and to "the sound of the harp."

The passage in question carries the inscription "God's Omnipresence," and depicts a divine force as embodied in light and darkness and in all phenomena. "Hear my weak song, and hear, omnipresent one, the sound of the cherub's harp at the foot of your throne." The message with which Beethoven identified expresses a humble prayer of thanks and expression of reverence for a spiritual presence manifested in the external physical world of nature. The *Pastoral* Symphony conveys similar sentiments, as a ferocious storm yields to a pantheistic sense of harmony in the shepherd's hymn. This attitude provides a basis for environmental ethics, with its imperative of defending the threatened paradise of our increasingly endangered planet.

At the time of Beethoven's concert in 1808, Alexander von Humboldt had recently completed his *Essay on the Geography of Plants*, the first of his many publications promoting the idea of nature as an interconnected organic whole, a web of life. In the introduction of the German edition, Humboldt referred to Friedrich Schelling's *Naturphilosophie* or philosophy of nature, which rejected the notion of any "irreconcilable chasm between the internal and the external—between the subjective world of the Self and the objective world of nature." Humboldt also expressed his indebtedness to Goethe's organicist views of nature, and dedicated this work to the Weimar poet. The frontispiece of the book with its dedication to Goethe depicts Apollo, the immortal god of music and poetry, lifting the veil of the goddess of nature, images that were crucial for Beethoven. We have seen how an Apollo reference was incorporated into Mähler's allegorical portrait of the composer. The veil of Isis, or Mother Nature, was no less important to Beethoven, who in later years kept an epigraph under glass at his desk to remind him of the sublimity of this idea.

The political character of the Fifth Symphony, on the other hand, is reflected through its affinities to French Revolutionary idioms. Its concentrated first movement invites comparison to Luigi Cherubini's *Hymne du Panthéon*. Such allusions are absorbed into an overreaching narrative rich in contrasts. It has been suggested that "the fame of the Fifth Symphony has its biographical match in Beethoven's deafness," and that the inspiration for the soft, spectral transition from the scherzo to the finale was connected to Beethoven's impediment. At the reprise of the scherzo, its substance is transformed into shadowy accents, with *pizzicato* strings and muted sounds in the winds. Its dark humor fades into deeper obscurity as a cadence is reached in the low register, with the strings marked triple *pianissimo*. We reach here a turning point at the threshold of audibility.

The transition begins with a deceptive harmonic shift, as the cellos and basses settle onto a long-held A♭. As the strings try to pick up the thread of the scherzo, they dwell as if hypnotized on a repeated motivic fragment. The motivic scrap from the scherzo is quietly repeated above the pulsating rhythm in the timpani, drifting ever higher until it converges into the chord for full orchestra that resolves to the emphatic beginning of the finale in C major, marked by the first appearance of trombones in the symphony.

The finale of the Fifth absorbs the character of an *éclat triomphal*, heroic passion whose power derives from the gigantic overreaching polarity of minor and major that embraces the whole symphony. Yet Beethoven reminds us of the conditional, perhaps provisional, status of his triumphant final movement by recalling the C-minor scherzo in the development section of the finale. The moment of recapitulation brings not just a return of the exposi-

Chan-tons la Li - ber - té,   cou - ron - nons___ sa sta - tu - e

6.3 Claude Joseph Rouget de L'Isle, *Hymne dithyrambique:*
"Chantons la liberté, courron nous sa statue."

6.4 Beethoven, Fifth Symphony, finale, passage evoking "la liberté," mm. 119–123.

tion, but reinterpretation of the entire expressive transition linking these contrasting movements. As the scherzo is recalled, the
presence of the oboe recalls the expressive oboe cadenza at the
recapitulation of the opening movement, a moment of respite in
the furious temporal drive of that *Allegro con brio*.

In the finale, the most visceral resonance to French Revolutionary music is to the *Hymne dithyrambique*, a hymn celebrating
the fall of Robespierre written by Claude Joseph Rouget de L'Isle,
composer of the *Marseillaise*. Rouget de L'Isle declaims the key
word of the revolution, "li-ber-té," as a rising major third in long
notes. A phrase containing this figure bears the text "Chantons
la liberté, courron nous sa statue" ("We sing of liberty, we crown
its statue") (fig. 6.3). Beethoven alludes extensively to this idea in
his slow movement, marked *Andante con moto*. The rising third
first appears *piano* and *dolce* in A♭ major. Following a dissonant
transitional chord, the same melodic idea emerges more forcefully
in C major, *forte*, with reinforcement from the horns, trumpets,
and timpani. Such a progression unfolds three times without ever
fulfilling its potential. A vision comes to the threshold of realiza-

tion, before the music withdraws, mysteriously veiled. To the end, the *Andante* remains unsettled, suggesting the premonition of a desired goal that cannot yet be achieved.

In the finale, Beethoven develops the "li-ber-té" figure of a rising third in two surpassing passages placed in the middle and toward the conclusion of this powerful *Allegro*. Since the motive is played here as a four-note figure with upbeat, it evokes the words "la li-ber-té," while the famous four-note "ta-ta-ta-taaaa" motive of three eighths and a quarter in the orchestra offers affirmative echoes in compressed rhythm (fig. 6.4). Motivic development compresses the figure further, building up the music into a great ascending arch of sound. These two passages are interconnected as images of failure and success: the first fails, collapsing into the reprise of the ghostly scherzo in the minor; the second succeeds, then delivering the C major that cannot be followed. The first stammers on the edge of silence; the second celebrates in the coda with rhythmic frenzy and extravagant orchestration, with a fresh elaboration of the rising triadic motive crowned by the piccolo trill on high G. A dichotomous mythic pattern is imposed on the overall artistic sequence, guiding the interconnected chain of musical forms. The musical design is not abstract, but absorbs a concrete relation to historical reality: embrace of the inspiring principles of the French Revolution cleansed from the abuses of Jacobin terror.

During the weeks following his December concert, Beethoven successfully exploited his aforementioned job offer from Jérôme Bonaparte, the new king of Westphalia at Kassel. The composer claimed that he was "compelled at last through intrigues, cabals, and low tricks of all kinds to leave the only German Vaterland," but he accepted the counteroffer of a lifelong annuity provided he remain in Austria, with support extended by the three aristocrats, most notably his own student Archduke Rudolph. Toward Napoleon he remained fascinated but deeply ambivalent. Even during the ensuing period of the French occupation of Vienna, the Baron de Trémont reported about Beethoven that "his mind was much occupied with the greatness of Napoleon . . . through all his resentment I could see that he admired [Napoleon's] rise from such obscure beginnings; his democratic ideas were flattered by it." Trémont gained the impression that Beethoven would have felt flattered by any mark of distinction from Napoleon. Beethoven himself conducted his *Eroica* Symphony on 8 September 1809 at Vienna, likely hoping Napoleon would attend, but the emperor had left the city one day earlier. He even considered dedicating his C-major Mass to Napoleon.

In early May of that year, as his army occupied Vienna, Emperor Napoleon placed a guard of honor at the doorstep of the frail seventy-seven-year-old Haydn, who was moved by the singing of a French officer of an aria from *The Creation*. At this time of Vienna's military occupation and Austria's imminent collapse, Haydn played his celebrated Austrian hymn "Gott erhalte Franz den Kaiser" ("God protect Emperor Franz") multiple times a day at the piano, before he died on 31 May. On that same day in the faraway northern German city of Stralsund, the Prussian officer Ferdinand von Schill was killed in action against French troops, an incident that helped ignite the resistance movement leading to the *Befreiungskriege* or Wars of Liberation against Napoleonic domination.

A few weeks later, Austria's main army unsuccessfully engaged Napoleon's forces on the outskirts of Vienna on 5–6 July 1809 in the battle of Wagram, the largest battle yet seen in the gunpowder age, which claimed about 80,000 casualties. In a letter from late July, Beethoven lamented the "disturbing, wild life all around, nothing but drums, cannons . . . human misery of all sorts" and found that his own work was "rather *for death* than *immortality*."

A piece that arose through the circumstances of Napoleon's occupation of Vienna in 1809 is the Piano Sonata in E♭ Major, op. 81a, entitled "Lebewohl" or "Farewell." This big three-movement sonata is one of a series of important works dedicated to Beethoven's benefactor Archduke Rudolph, and the first of several pieces in which he supplied movement titles in German. He objected to the use of the French title "Les Adieux" by which the sonata is commonly known, pointing out the more intimate associations of "Le-be-wohl" ("Fare thee well"), those three syllables that he placed over the three initial chords of the composition. Unlike the common leave-taking expression "Wiedersehen," with its clear expectation of further contact, "Lebewohl" implies a parting with a greater sense of finality, without anticipation of reunion.

At the time of the Napoleonic Wars, symbolic depictions appeared in connection with military mobilization. In 1813, four years after the founding of the Austrian *Landwehr* (militia) and at the time the Wars of Liberation culminated in the Battle of Leipzig, Johann Peter Krafft painted "Der Abschied des Landwehrmannes" ("The Departure of the Militia Soldier"). This painting shows a determined-looking young man in the uniform of the *Landwehr* taking leave of his family in its domestic setting in order to join the armed conflict. Emperor Franz obtained the painting in 1815 and had it publicly displayed to encourage patriotic feeling. A later, contrasting depiction of the *Abschied* theme modeled on Beethoven's music is a triptych, a painting by August Kühles entitled "Beethoven op. 81" that was subsequently reproduced as a postcard; its narrative stages "Departure—Solitude—Homecoming" respond to the "Farewell" Sonata (fig. 6.5). Beethoven does not stress the motive of military mobilization and the dedication of his piece is not to a soldier; the first two movements of the sonata do not emphasize patriotic fervor but the reflective sadness of the departure (*Abschied*) and solitude (*Abwesenheit*).

Beethoven entered into his score the date of Rudolph's departure from Vienna on 4 May 1809 in response to the French occupation, as well as the archduke's date of return to the city many months later, on 30 January 1810. Beethoven's sketches indicate that he delayed composition of the exuberant finale until the actual return of the archduke. The symbolism of this work is connected to the return of the ruling family to Vienna after withdrawal of the French Army, even though Austria remained under French influence at this time.

In its narrative design, the sonata's moment of strong assertion of the main key is postponed until the finale. The principal

Abschied.   Alleinsein.   Heimkehr.

6.5 Postcard showing departure—absence—return of soldier, 1920, based on August Kühles, "Beethoven op. 81." Biblioteca Beethoveniana, Carrino Collection, Muggia (Trieste).

motive of the first movement is the symbolic two-voiced horn figure, bearing associations with the village post horn and melancholy of leave-taking. The harmonic implications of the motive convey an evocative sense of distance, a quality bound up with leave-taking that resonates throughout the opening movement. In the development section of this movement, the original rhythmic form of the "Farewell" figure is juxtaposed with more rapid three-note figures in the left hand, forming a motivic combination that appears in a variety of keys in a labyrinth-like descending passage. We seem to hear multiple individual departures, which reminds us that during the war-torn conditions of 1809, many who bade farewell never returned. The musical continuation elongates the "Lebewohl" motive across an entire octave, before the music evokes somber drum rolls in the bass, and sinks into the static tonal space of C minor, the tonic key of the ensuing slow movement, marked "Abwesenheit" ("Absence").

The slow movement marked "Abwesenheit" ("Absence") takes on the character of a slow procession and continues directly into the finale. When the searching music of "Abwesenheit" at last glimpses an end to its melancholy waiting, the long-awaited break-through occurs on the harmonic threshold of E♭ major, carry-ing us into the finale, marked "Das Wiedersehen" ("Reunion"). Beethoven sustains the excitement of this irrepressible music, marked "Vivacissimamente." The unfolding duets of voices in the opening theme are reminiscent of the ecstatic music of reunion in *Fidelio*. Only after these passages do we reach a joyous explo-sion in which E♭ major is asserted *fortissimo* in textures rich and ingenious.

In the narrative design of the "Farewell" Sonata, the composer realized his aesthetic ideals while also celebrating his reunion with Archduke Rudolph, whose exceptional devotion to music found enduring value through his indispensable patronage of Beethoven. The aesthetic meaning of the *Lebewohl* Sonata, like that of the *Eroica* Symphony, goes well beyond any personal dedi-cation or homage, triggered as it was in this instance by the arch-duke's patronage and the circumstances of his departure from Vienna in 1809 and return in 1810. Unconstrained by the unpal-atable political alternatives, Beethoven set forth his innovative musical triptych in the spirit of a Schillerian symbol of the ideal.

Ironically, the French occupation of 1809 and its aftermath brought some relaxation of the restrictive censorship of the Austrian regime, enabling for instance the performances of Beethoven's *Egmont* music written for Goethe's play. As we have seen, Goethe's direction that the play culminate in a *Victory Sym-phony* glorifies Egmont's role, and inspired Beethoven to write the prescribed music. Explicitly associated with resistance to tyr-anny, the *Victory Symphony* projects a future goal that for Count Egmont remained remote. The stark contrast between the dark F-minor *Allegro* and delirious energy of the F-major *Victory Sym-phony* portrays the gap between a tragic fate overtaking a heroic individual, on the one hand, and the eventual triumph of his just cause, on the other.

Beethoven wrote another major work in F minor around this time, in 1810, but withheld the piece from publication until 1816, even stating that it was composed for a "small circle of connois-

seurs" and "never to be performed in public." This is his String
Quartet op. 95, titled *Quartetto serioso*, as befits its dark, vehement, laconic character. As in the *Appassionata* Sonata in this key,
the dissonant semitone D♭–C assumes special weight in the outer
movements, yet the astonishing coda to the finale, in F major,
leaves the brooding character of the rest of the work far behind.
A parallel emerges to the *Egmont* Overture—the *Victory Symphony*—in that the dramatic tensions are not resolved but tran-
scended in an exhilarating coda. How do we best understand this
conclusion? One commentator has described it in terms of ironic
idealism, as "neither *amusing* nor *victorious*, but rather both an
ironic and a utopian contradiction of what has gone before." Pertinent is the observation of the critic Carl Blum in 1814 that "in
the works of the greatest poets there is often an irony that hovers
gently above the whole but that breaks through incisively at times":
he names Shakespeare, Cervantes, and Goethe in this regard, and
continues that "Beethoven's compositions have not been considered nearly enough from this perspective; yet only in this way
will that which is *seemingly* unpleasant and alien be recognized
as exquisite and necessary."

One type of irony that "breaks through incisively" is political satire, as in the remarkable collaboration between Goethe
and Beethoven: Mephistopheles' "Song of the Flea" from *Faust*.
Although this text had attracted the composer's attention already
at Bonn, the song reached publication only much later, as the centerpiece of his op. 75 songs. In the caricature by Paul Barbier showing Beethoven and Goethe accusing Hitler, the poet grasps a copy
of his *Faust*, part 1 of which was published in 1808. The definitive
version of Beethoven's setting was completed in 1809 and issued
as op. 73, no. 3, "From Goethe's *Faust*," in 1810. This part of *Faust*
fascinated the composer and became firmly absorbed in his later
years into the lore of his jovial circle of friends and colleagues. If
Beethoven had ever undertaken an opera on *Faust*, he likely would
have assimilated the "Flea Song" into the larger unfolding narrative, just as Goethe had done in expanding the contents of his early
Urfaust into the monumental work we know.

In *Faust*, Mephisto's *Flohlied* is one of several bawdy drinking songs in Auerbach's Cellar in Leipzig. Immediately before Faust and Mephistopheles enter, the student Brander sings a satirical song, "There was a Rat in the Cellar Nest," in which his drinking companions Frosch, Siebel, and Altmayer enter boisterously as a "chorus" for the concluding rhyming line: "As if wasted by love." The rat feasts gluttonously on butter but then on poison. Following this ironic tale of the demise of the swollen rodent, Faust and Mephistopheles make their entrance, with Mephisto's strophic song, starting "There was once a king" and focusing on a much smaller creature: a flea. Mephisto's *Flohlied* or "Flea Song" serves as a counterpart to Brander's song, once again involving an emphatic shouting chorus to reinforce the last lines:

But we snap and smother
At once, if someone bites.

Wir knicken und ersticken
Doch gleich, wenn einer sticht.

The closing couplet—sung in this instance by the group only at the end of the entire song—encapsulates the political meaning. As the king's special favorite, the worthless flea receives undeserved honors and bears a star of state, benefiting his flea relations, who are immune from all critique. The unimpeachable political solidarity of flea culture is the target. The last stanza of the song can be provided with a different, less literal translation of the closing pair of lines conforming to the rhyme:

SOLO: At court they were distressed
as the queen and her maidens
were bitten by the pests.
And yet they dared not scratch them,
Or chase the fleas away.
If we are bit, we catch them
And crush without delay.

CHORUS: If we are bit, we catch them
And crush without delay.

Fleas are tiny parasitic creatures with prodigious jumping abilities. Beethoven devises motives reflecting these distinct qualities. The swift and nimble, diminutive being that can leap: in the opening ritornello in the piano, those features are adroitly mirrored in the semitone turn-figure (the motivic tag for the flea) that springs across entire octaves from the treble into the bass. The detached articulation of the falling octaves conveys the imagery of the leaping flea.

Mephistopheles delivers humor in Goethe's *Faust*. Yet even as he brings others in Auerbach's Cellar to lusty laughter, he himself hardly laughs. And he certainly is no great singer. Consequently, Beethoven keeps the vocal part simple, almost in the manner of recitative, with frequent repeated pitches. The text unfolds as a ballad-like narrative, in which, as we have seen, the last sentence is repeated emphatically at the conclusion by the chorus of drinkers: "Wir knicken und ersticken doch gleich, wenn einer sticht." Beethoven decisively weights the end of each strophe through an accented harmonic shift from G minor to G major, with the voice landing with emphasis on B♮. This closing four-measure phrase of each strophe shifts to *forte*, and a grotesquely parodistic echo follows in the piano, with strident grace notes and a trill on B♭, leading into restatement of the ritornello.

At the end of the entire song, the humorous effect is heightened through variation of the text. After the chorus has sung Mephisto's closing lines once, Beethoven adds the word "ja" ("indeed"), as we hear a syllabic setting in sixteenth notes up to the final word "sticht" ("bite") (fig. 6.6). The dramatic reinforcement of the conclusion is lent power through figurative gestures in the piano: the characteristic grace-note figure C–B♭ at "stik-[ken]" recurs melodically in the voice and piano before it is *replaced* by the highly emphatic repeated semitone C–B♮ played *fortissimo* in thirty-second notes in measure 79. The music has now settled decisively into G major, which underlines the message of the end-

6.6 Beethoven, "Flea Song" based on the Auerbach's Cellar scene
in Goethe's *Faust*, part 1; op. 75, no. 3, conclusion.

ing, shifting the level of discourse from that of a legendary bal-
lade to the present here and now, while the ironic tone from the
end of the first two stanzas is heightened to sarcastic glee. Yet the
motivic stress on the C–B step corresponds precisely to the opening ritornello in the second measure. The gestural subject remains
the tiny flea, whose nimble jumping animates each statement of
the ritornello.

As fingering for the last two measures, Beethoven writes "1 1"
over all of the two-note figures. Herein lies the core of the joke. He
thereby instructs the pianist to "knicken und ersticken" ("snap and
smother") at exactly those spots on the keyboard where a flea has
leapt. The flea circus is thereby brought to an abrupt end through
physical annihilation of the parasite! A very specific technique
is required to crush the flea(s): two adjacent notes are depressed
simultaneously, as the weight of the thumb settles on the lower
note. In a few fleeting moments of targeted manual action, the
piece is finished and the irritating flea(s) dispatched.

According to a report from Anna Pessiak-Schmerling,
Beethoven himself drew attention to the comic character of the
song, especially its ending:

Once Beethoven came with the manuscript of his song from *Faust*: "There was once a king who had a great flea." Aunt and mother needed to try it out. When they came to the end, Beethoven while laughing showed them how it had to be played, and took always two tones with the thumbs just as one would crush a flea.

The irony and sarcasm of Beethoven's setting was noted in a review by the former editor of the *Allgemeine musikalische Zeitung*, Johann Friedrich Rochlitz. Associated as he was with an effort to encourage Beethoven to write a larger work or opera based on Goethe's *Faust*, the critic became known in the composer's intimate circle as "Mephistopheles" Rochlitz. His commentary on the "Flea Song" appeared in the *Allgemeine musikalische Zeitung* in 1811:

> This single piece, as Mr. v[an] B[eethoven] has shaped it here from the first to the last notes, is worth more than entire volumes of mediocre songs. One must bear in mind thereby the whole wild scene and its meaning, the brilliant diabolical mood and the rhapsodic character: everything is contained in the adventurous, burlesque-like combination of music embracing the characteristic old-fashioned aura and an entirely modern pictorial imagination (especially in the chorus at the *crushing*).

In the political context of Austria after 1813 and extending through the repressive Metternich era of the 1820s and far beyond up to the present, the "Flea Song" holds acute relevance. In Goethe's *Faust*, a political tone is struck ironically at the outset of the Auerbach's Cellar scene in Frosch's two-line song "the endearing Holy Roman Empire, how holds it still together?" to which Brander replies dismissively: "An ugly song! Yuck! A political song!" During Beethoven's aforementioned conversation with the publisher Moritz Schlesinger from 1825, in which Emperor Franz is described as a "dumb beast," Schlesinger adds the following:

In *all* countries stupidity gains the upper hand principle of the *ministers*

In *allen* Landen nimmt die Dummheit Überhand Prinzip der *Minister*

The mention of a "principle of the *ministers*"—presumably meaning the unmerited advancement of stupid or corrupt government officials—comes quite close to the second stanza of Goethe's text of the *Flohlied*, whereby the worthless flea "immediately became minister and wore a large star."

Beethoven's "Song of the Flea" displays his delight in critiquing such problems with caustic wit from a protected distance, without any need to pretend or court favor from those in power. In this case, the conviction is expressed not merely through words or tones but through physical action—the symbolic crushing of the unworthy on the keyboard itself. In the shared aesthetic space afforded by the "Flea Song" and its closing chorus, Beethoven raises a spirited protest against the shortcomings of political life.

When Beethoven and Goethe finally met at the Bohemian spa resort Teplitz during the summer of 1812, their differences stood out, despite their enormous respect for one another. In part this was due to a difference between generations. Goethe's urbane diplomacy contrasted sharply with Beethoven's defiant individualism, as is most succinctly captured in the famous anecdote about the two artists passing the Austrian royal party at Teplitz. Whether or not the story is literally true, it matches to other documented attitudes and actions and has a strong ring of plausibility. As the two artists encountered royalty, Goethe stood aside and cordially removed his hat with deference, whereas Beethoven stubbornly continued on his way, while everyone yielded to him. Paradoxically, it was Beethoven and not Goethe who had a significant contact to a member of this royal party, namely Archduke Rudolph, his student and patron. Beethoven thought Goethe displayed too much regard for authority, delighting in the "court atmosphere far more than is becoming to a poet," whereas Goethe found Beethoven to be an "utterly untamed personality, not completely wrong in thinking the world detestable, but hardly making it more pleasant for himself or others by his attitude."

Rumors and speculation abounded that summer about the prospects of Napoleon's invasion of Russia, which had begun in late June 1812, and would lead to the destruction of his army that winter, and to his pivotal defeat at the "Battle of the Nations" at Leipzig in October 1813. Through Metternich's sly duplicitous diplomacy, Austria was poised to switch sides. As the tide turned, Jérôme Bonaparte, Beethoven's potential employer in 1809, hastily fled Kassel for France, accompanied by servile courtiers and the tattered trappings of royalty. His artificial short-lived realm had been set forth in 1807 as a model constitutional state curbing the aristocracy and abolishing servitude, but new hierarchies were promoted. While the "jolly king" indulged in lavish spectacle and vain pomposity, commissioning numerous portraits and busts of himself, many thousands of conscripted soldiers were forced to join Napoleon's army of invasion, never to return. A year later, after the battle of Leipzig, an army of Austrians and Bavarians sought to block Napoleon's retreat toward France at the battle of Hanau. The concert Beethoven conducted on 8 December with its premiere of the Seventh Symphony was to benefit wounded Austrian soldiers. The composer declared that "We are moved by nothing but pure patriotism and the joyful sacrifice of our powers for those who have sacrificed so much for us." The contemplative *Allegretto* of this ebullient symphony was encored when first heard, with its subsequent popularity promoted by numerous arrangements. Beethoven's idealism was directed against the French in 1813, but his work transcends that historical context. The Bacchic fury of its finale continues to inspire revitalizing renewal.

For those in Beethoven's circle, Napoleon's rise and fall was not just the saga of a foreign oppressor eventually overcome by patriotic allied struggle. Beethoven's acquaintance the customs inspector Franz Janschikh confessed in 1820 in one of the composer's conversation-notebooks that while he "as a German" felt initially opposed to Napoleon, he had come to regard things differently. The drift of his written entries implies that the composer shared similar feelings. Janschikh recognized that Napoleon appreciated art and science, defended the right of law, and overturned feudalism. For him, Napoleon's marriage to the Austrian "princess *Louise*" was his "highest point of *culmination* . . . the chance to promote world peace and good government without . . . any more conquests." Yet this chance for peaceful progress was squandered, yielding "through overambition [to] the greatest calamity."

During this same period, Beethoven's long-standing hopes for achieving happiness through marriage collapsed in the wake of his "Immortal Beloved" affair movingly documented in his letter from July 1812. Beethoven was repeatedly drawn to women whose aristocratic status was a barrier to him as a commoner and an artist. He was not especially successful with women, to judge from Magdalena Willmann's alleged comment that he was "ugly and half crazy," or the failure of his awkward attempt to broach the subject of marriage to Therese Malfatti in 1810. Beethoven especially sought marriage around the time of Napoleon's marriage to Marie-Louise of Austria. The identity of the "Immortal Beloved" of the famous letter remains unconfirmed, but the most plausible candidates—Antonia Brentano and Josephine Brunsvik Deym— had familial commitments that would have worked against the contemplation of marriage. In 1810, at the time of his rebuff from the Malfatti family, Beethoven confided his feelings to his friend Ignaz von Gleichenstein, who was closely connected to the Malfattis, and who married Therese's sister Anna in 1811. Beethoven confessed that "Your report plunged me again from the regions of highest rapture into the depths . . . Am I then nothing more than your musician or musician to the others? . . . I can therefore seek support only in my own heart; there is none for me outside of it. . . . So be it then, for you, poor B, there is no happiness in the outer world, you must create it in yourself."

In years to come, through the remarkable development of his art, Beethoven indeed sought to create happiness in himself, expanding the boundaries of his "empire of the mind" on an ambitious Napoleonic scale. Had he known it, Beethoven might have identified with Schiller's conviction from 1797 concerning the tensional relation of the political and spiritual realms ("das politische Reich . . . [und] geistige [Reich]"):

> The German dwells in an old house threatened with collapse but he himself is a noble tenant, and as the political sphere falters, the empire of the mind assumes an ever firmer and more complete realization.

> Der Deutsche wohnt in einem alten sturzdrohenden Hauß aber er selbst ist ein edler Bewohner, und indem das politische Reich wankt, hat das geistige sich immer fester und vollkommender gebildet.

Starting in early 1815, at the end of the Napoleonic era (but still before the battle of Waterloo and Napoleon's exile to St. Helena), Beethoven initiated and sustained a humorous correspondence with his publisher Sigmund Anton Steiner and his associates, assigning military grades to members of the firm. Beethoven himself assumed the highest rank of commander-in-chief, "Obergeneral" or "Generalissimo." As Napoleon departed from the main stage of European history, Beethoven metaphorically took his place, assuming the role of a commanding "Generalissimo" in the realm of musical art.

A Double Chill: Beethoven in Metternich's Vienna

"Abbé Gelinek complained a lot about you at the *Camel* [the restaurant *Zum schwarzen Kameel*]. He said you're a second [Karl Ludwig] Sand, you gripe about the Emperor, about the Archduke, about the ministers, [and] that you will end up on the gallows."

These comments, entered in 1820 into one of Beethoven's conversation notebooks, offer a vivid glimpse of the tense political environment that prevailed in Vienna during the composer's last decade. Joseph Gelinek was a long-standing pianistic rival of Beethoven's known for his critical jibes about the composer. Karl Ludwig Sand was a militant member of the *Burschenschaften*, the group of fraternal student associations that organized the Wartburg Festival at Eisenach in October 1817, commemorating the victory over Napoleon in October 1813 as well as the Reformation three centuries earlier. The *Burschenschaften* arose in 1815 in response to Napoleon's downfall and the restoration of monarchic power at the Congress of Vienna. The students called for "Honor— Freedom—Fatherland," condemning absolutism while promoting German unity. Social liberalism and nationalism became natural allies in opposing the conservatism of the Habsburg regime. In March 1819, inspired by the martyrdom of Theodor Körner, Sand murdered August von Kotzebue, the conservative dramatist and consul to Russia, whose *History of the German Empires* had been tossed on the bonfire at the Wartburg. Sand was beheaded in May 1820, soon after the entries in Beethoven's conversation book had been made. Kotzebue's assassination served as the pretext for Prince Metternich's infamous Karlsbad Decrees, which dissolved the *Burschenschaften*, restricted academic freedom, and intensified censorship and the surveillance of the citizenry. This era of a new Inquisition impacted artists such as Beethoven's acquaintance the playwright Franz Grillparzer, who wrote with some envy in another of Beethoven's conversation notebooks that "musicians are immune to the censors—if they only knew what you think about in your music!"

Beethoven's friend Joseph Karl Bernard, editor of the *Wiener Zeitung*, commented sarcastically to the composer about the deliberations leading to the Karlsbad Decrees that "at the congress they are drafting a law regulating how high the birds may fly and how fast the hare may run." Other entries in the same conversation notebook of the deaf composer reflect Beethoven's cultural commitment in the face of political disappointment. Bernard copies inexactly from Schiller's and Goethe's "To the Muses" the following lines:

What I would be without you,
you muses, I know not,
but I dread it, when I see
that so many are without you!

and from Goethe's *Faust* a quotation from Mephistopheles:

Should we art and science deny,
these strengths of humanity most high,
then soon we'll experience decline,
making brotherhood with swine.

In branding Beethoven "a second Sand" destined for the gallows, Gelinek depicted the composer as a subversive enemy of order. For Gelinek, Beethoven's artistic method was also suspect. He charged that all of Beethoven's compositions were lacking in internal coherence and . . . not infrequently they were overloaded. These things he [Gelinek] looked upon as grave faults of composition and sought to explain them from the manner in which Beethoven went about his work, saying that he had always been in the habit of noting every musical idea that occurred to him upon a bit of paper which he threw into a corner of his room, and that after a while there was a considerable pile of the memoranda which the maid was not permitted to touch when cleaning the room. Now, when Beethoven got into a mood for work he would hunt a few musical *motivi* out of his treasure-heap which he thought might serve as principal and secondary themes for the composition in contemplation, and often his selection was not a lucky one.

This anecdote stems from the Czech musician Jan Tomaschek, who reported that Gelinek was a "virulent opponent" of Beethoven. The two composers had been at first on good terms during the 1790s, but had a falling-out. After being defeated by Beethoven in a piano contest, Gelinek reportedly described his opponent as "a short, ugly, black and stubborn-looking young man" who was "not a human being, but the devil." Gelinek disapproved of Beethoven's artistic development after 1800. Abbé Gelinek was a successful but conventional composer who set his name on more than a hundred sets of variations. His special emphasis on variation form, and his own character and lack of originality, are all brought into play in a witty satirical verse penned by Carl Maria von Weber:

To the famous variation-forger Gelinek:

No theme on earth escaped your genius airy,
The simplest one of all—yourself—you never vary.

An den berühmten Variationen-Schmidt Gelinek.

Kein Thema in der Welt verschonte dein Genie,
Das simpelste allein—Dich selbst—variirst Du nie.

This opposition—between the facile and worldly, on the one hand, and the artistically challenging, on the other—is encapsulated in a quotation scrawled by Beethoven into the same conversation notebook cited above. The quotation echoes Goethe's "Flea Song":

The world is a king, and like a king,
desires flattery in return for favor;
but true art is stubborn—it will not submit
to the mold of flattery.

Die Welt ist ein König,
u. sie will geschmeichelt seyn,
Soll sie sich günstig zeigen—
Doch wahre Kunst ist eigensinnig,
Läßt sich nicht in Schmeichelnde Formen zwängen.

Beethoven did not resort often to flattery, but the best examples stem from several years earlier during 1813–1814, the politically volatile period preceding the Congress of Vienna starting in late 1814. The composer's creativity and personal well-being were then in crisis, likely triggered by depression following the "Immortal Beloved" affair in 1812. Comments about Beethoven's social isolation at this time stem from Nannette and Andreas Streicher, who described his despondent state of mind and noted the "deplorable condition" of his clothes and domestic affairs. According to the painter Blasius Höfel, Beethoven neglected his appearance and cleanliness such that his dining place at a favorite inn, although large, "was avoided by the other guests due to the very uninviting habits into which he had fallen."

At this juncture, more than at any other time in his career, economic and political factors exerted a decisive influence. Beethoven's patriotic compositions from 1813 and 1814 have often been neglected, but fascinating aesthetic issues are raised by such pieces as *Wellington's Victory*, *Germania*, and the festive cantata *Der glorreiche Augenblick* (*The Glorious Moment*).

In these works Beethoven appears as a pioneer of kitsch at the threshold of the era of mass production and modern commercial propaganda. This is a surprising role for a cultural hero of Beethoven's stature, yet one supported by the historical evidence. Beethoven's patriotic potboilers present the spectacle of a great composer lowering his art to gain economic reward and seek political favor. This episode in his career raises basic aesthetic and ethical questions. In order to evaluate these matters, let us review the critical literature devoted to art and kitsch.

In essays from 1933 and 1950, the author Hermann Broch defined kitsch as "evil in the value system of art." In his view, kitsch involves a false association between fundamental principles. Whereas the true work of art displays qualities of openness, originality, and irrationality, kitsch involves a closed and rational system of imitation. Broch regards kitsch as an anti-Christ, who looks like Christ and "acts and speaks like Christ and is nevertheless Lucifer." Broch asks:

> Wherein is the difference ultimately noticed? An open system . . . is an ethical one, that is, it offers the individual a guiding framework, within which he or she can act. A closed system, on the other hand, cannot go beyond fixed rules—even if these are given an ethical coloring—and it thus transforms those parts of human life that it touches into a game that is no longer ethical, but only aesthetic in nature.

Broch admits "that one is not infrequently very well disposed to kitsch," but insists at the same time that "the goddess of beauty in art" is "the goddess of kitsch." He insists, in other words, that beauty is insufficient as a basis for art. Rather, beauty needs to be integrated with other dimensions of the work in order that it does not become just an end in itself, or a simple play of effects. In that case we would be dealing not with art, but with kitsch.

Other thinkers on aesthetics have shared the conviction that art is concerned with more than mere beauty. Susanne Langer's concept of a successful artwork as an "unconsummated symbol," or Theodor W. Adorno's paradoxical description of a true performance as "a copy of a nonexistent original," point toward some irreducible essence. What is essential is that the symbolic artistic content be recognized without it being flattened or reduced, as in some programmatic interpretations in which the integrity of the work threatens to vanish behind an unequivocal verbal interpretation. The danger that arises thereby is of art being degraded into kitsch—a common enough tendency in the reception history of art.

Broch's insights can be refined on the basis of studies by Wolfgang Welsch, who uses the pair of concepts "aesthetic" and "anaesthetic." He writes that

> Whereas aesthetic experience increases out sensibility, the anaesthetic stands for a loss of sensibility . . . the anaesthetic is the converse of the aesthetic . . . Through anaesthesia we block out feeling—and the loss of a higher perceptive capacity is the direct result. The anaesthetic realm thus deals with the most elementary level of the aesthetic, and furnishes its condition and boundary.

This pair of concepts applies to the phenomenon of kitsch, and offers us a means of testing Broch's thesis. We can discern two opposing processes at work. In the Viennese Classical style, and in Beethoven's music in general, we observe tendencies to widen the boundaries of art. Artistic material can be absorbed from the commonplace, taken from the anaesthetic into the aesthetic realm. With kitsch we evidently encounter the opposite—what is offered as art demands no higher perceptive capacity and brings a regression; material from the aesthetic sphere returns to the realm of the anaesthetic. It would be mistaken, however, to regard art only as the expansion and kitsch as the surrender of aesthetic substance. According to Broch, kitsch wallows in beauty—its shortcoming is not aesthetic, but ethical. The boundary between aesthetic and anaesthetic experience is not to be understood merely negatively. As Welsch remarks, "one anaesthetizes, in order to avoid aesthetic pain"; and not a few artists, stoics, or mystics, for instance, "strive toward a transcendence of the senses in the attainment of 'another condition'"—which can be recognized as a type of anaesthetic state. These possibilities are contained in Broch's somewhat questionable attack on beauty as the "goddess of kitsch." Broch is undoubtedly right, however, that kitsch, if regarded as a system of imitation, can imply an ethical failure, if it embodies a false pretense.

Let us consider in this light Beethoven's "Battle Symphony" *Wellington's Victory*, which was composed in late 1813, well before the beginning of the Congress of Vienna. After Wellington's military victory in Spain on 21 June 1813, Johann Mälzel spotted a business opportunity in the form of a commemorative piece to be performed on his elaborate mechanical instrument, the Panharmonicon. Mälzel approached Beethoven, who agreed to take up the task. From the beginning the work was tailored for popular success, particularly in England. The plan of the piece, with its flourishes, marches, use of the hymns *Rule, Britannia* and *God Save the King*, and even the fugue based on the latter, had much to do with Mälzel, though Beethoven had long been interested in these themes and had written piano variations on them in 1802. In the end, the "Battle Symphony" was first given not by Mälzel's Panharmonicon but in a version for augmented orchestra at gala charity performances in Vienna in December 1813. Its enthusiastic reception led to more performances for Beethoven's own benefit. Tomaschek commented about *Wellington's Victory* that he was

> very painfully affected to see a Beethoven, whom Providence had probably assigned to the highest throne in the realm of music, among the rudest materialists. I was told, it is true, that he himself had declared the work to be folly, and that he liked it only because with it he had thoroughly thrashed the Viennese.

Wellington's Victory has been regarded as a "gigantic professional frolic" or even as a "masterpiece of its own genre," but we should resist the temptation simply to collapse the work into its historical context. In its style, the "Battle Symphony" departs radically from Beethoven's aesthetic norms. The crude realism of *Wellington's Victory* is illustrated in its first main section, which is devoted to the battle. After preliminary fanfares and national marches heard from the opposing ensembles representing the French and British forces, the engagement begins with an *Allegro*, sporting syncopations and lively motivic figures of descending scales. Initially, Beethoven favors these syncopated beats for his placement of the cannon shots, which are meticulously specified in the score with dark circles for the British and open circles for the French artillery. A well-known aspect of the historical battle was the British capture of the French guns; this is reflected in Beethoven's painstaking distribution of the 188 cannon shots. As the tide turns against the French, their cannons are heard less and less often and are then silenced altogether.

Characteristic of *Wellington's Victory* are insistent repetitions of a few basic figures on a broad, flat musical canvas. As the British launch their assault in the "Storm March," the music consists largely of twenty-four almost undifferentiated repetitions on the single note A♭, followed by sixteen strokes on A and sixteen more on B♭, leading to still more repetitions on B. Beethoven pushes up the music notch by notch, a familiar device in popular music. This is symptomatic of the almost complete absence, in the "Battle Symphony," of an integrating tonal and formal perspective such as we normally find in Beethoven. Wellington's soldiers have no need of subtlety; they force their way heavily and brutally into the French defenses.

There are still some finer points to Beethoven's musical depiction of the collapse of the French resistance. He employs a motive with a triplet figure and falling semitone to serve as a tag for the French forces—this turn of phrase stems from the "Marlborough" French marching song heard at the outset. As the British gain the upper hand, the motive is deprived of its downbeat, suggesting an effect of breathless panic. While the British cannons pound relentlessly, Beethoven dismembers what is left of the French motive. In the measures following the "double hits" of the cannoneers—as shown by two dark circles on successive beats—the "Marlborough" figure is reduced to a single note. The rout of the French Army is conveyed not only by the long descending lines and *decrescendo* but by a limping and forlorn F♯-minor version of the "Marlborough" tune. This dismal departure of the French Army makes room for the triumphant "Victory Symphony" that makes up the remainder of the work.

The occasional subtle touches do little to relieve the impression of pastiche and bombast. Some of the same rhetorical figures appear here as in Beethoven's important compositions, but an integrating aesthetic context is absent or undeveloped. The "Battle Symphony" is a fascinating historical artifact, but a dubious work of art. Elements of Beethoven's heroic style take on here a quality of parody or farce, as identifiable aspects of his aesthetic enterprise dissipate into the realm of the anaesthetic. The narrative design of the music is mainly extrinsic rather than intrinsic.

In response to these aspects, the critic Alfred Einstein described *Wellington's Victory* as "the lowest point in Beethoven's work." But a better candidate for that distinction might be *The Glorious Moment*, the cantata for chorus, orchestra, and soloists that Beethoven wrote during the autumn of 1814 in fawning tribute to the assembled dignitaries at the Congress of Vienna. *The Glorious Moment* was performed on 29 November and 2 December 1814 in a program containing *Wellington's Victory* and (as the reviewer in the *Wiener Zeitung* misleadingly put it) "a symphony composed to accompany" these works—the Seventh Symphony, an outstanding composition that Beethoven had completed earlier, in 1812. The ceremonial function of *The Glorious Moment* should be borne in mind in assessing this composition. It has been claimed that "democracy, by definition, is the failure of ceremony." The structure of this cantata is shaped by deference to royalty and monarchy, and the piece was written in tribute to the Congress of Vienna. On the other hand, as we have seen, Beethoven declared in 1814 that "I much prefer the empire of the mind, and regard it as the highest of all spiritual and worldly monarchies." This statement about the priority of "the empire of the mind (or spirit)" implies a Schillerian conviction about the latent political value of the work of art, regarded as an "effigy of the ideal." Beethoven will have been aware that this perspective was not widely shared. A report of Austria's secret police about the composer from this time states that "There are two factions, pro- and contra-Beethoven ... [with] a much larger majority of connoisseurs who do not want to hear anything composed by Herr von Beethoven." Another comment by Beethoven from 1814 attests that "my kingdom is in the air, like the wind, so do resonate the tones," a notion compatible with Leonore's vision of the rainbow above dark clouds or Florestan's awareness of her stirring presence suspended before him as a liberating angel.

The text of the cantata, by the deaf surgeon Alois Weissenbach, is an exercise in bathos. One recurrent motive is a hymn of praise to "the queen of cities," Vienna, or "Vindobona," the archaic name for the town, used in the fugal setting of the closing chorus. "I am Europe, give way, proud Rome," is the message in the aria in which the soprano becomes the voice of Vienna herself. *The Glorious Moment* is mostly sweetness and light, with a correspondingly "triumphant" musical setting. Moments of pathos are exaggerated. "Oh kneel down, people, and worship those who have rescued you!" are the words of the recitative praising the "gleaming crown heads" of Europe. To be "worshipped" are the same monarchs who were consolidating their restoration of political power. A few years later, as we have seen, Austria was to suffer the oppressive police state overseen by Klemens von Metternich. As time passed, the ideological content of this cantata became more disquieting than it had been during the Congress of Vienna.

Weissenbach's unrestrained, flamboyant writing style is reflected in his book with its Goethean title *Meine Reise zum Congress: Wahrheit und Dichtung* (*My Trip to the Congress: Truth and Poetry*). In one of several passages extolling Beethoven, he likens the composer to a special kind of bird, continuing that "this bird is a musical microcosm: he brings forth all the tones but each one belongs to him; when he sings, all others are silent and the stars come forth to hear him." Weissenbach closes his book with a reference to Emperor Joseph II as a "colossus," reflecting a nostalgia for the pre-Revolutionary period that became widespread in Vienna in later years.

The musical setting in the cantata alluding to the Austrian monarch, Emperor Franz, merits attention. Although many other dignitaries were present at the concert on 29 November 1814, Emperor Franz was not. Franz took little notice of Beethoven, and that response was mutual. Beethoven dedicated not a single work to his emperor, not even a trifle. Many entries in the sources voice profound disappointment with the political environment of the post-Napoleonic period.

Beethoven's lingering optimism about Napoleon and frustration with Franz correspond to the assessment of the historian Heinrich August Winkler, that "the positive echo Napoleon found in Germany was, in truth, based on the hope that he would help the original ideas of 1789—that is, a progressive agenda purified of Jacobin terror—to achieve success," whereas on the other hand "the peace settlement reached by the Congress of Vienna was like a declaration of war against German nationalism." Winkler finds that "After Napoleon's defeat, it was again possible to lord . . . over peoples and territories in the traditional style of absolutist power politics, and since it was possible, it was done."

Beethoven's critical attitude toward the ruling leaders at the Congress of Vienna is revealed in various sources from this time. To Georg Friedrich Treitschke, the librettist for the final revision of *Fidelio,* Beethoven confessed in 1814 that "it's better to deal with artists than with the so-called great ones (little tiny ones)." In the same letter he responded to the suggestion of a revival of his *Egmont* music at the *Theater an der Wien* by imagining a theatrical role for these "little tiny ones" as identified with the fierce and brutal Spanish: "the arrival of the Spanish, which is just implied in the work, could be shown by opening a large entry in the theater for the riffraff, with other stuff too offering a visual *spectacle.*" Around the same time, Beethoven reminded himself in his diary of the need for caution and discretion: "Never let people notice outwardly the disdain that they deserve, for one cannot know when one may need them."

In *The Glorious Moment,* the glorification of Emperor Franz is conspicuously placed at the end of the fourth movement, with the music set in the key in which the cantata began, A major. Weissenbach's rhymed stanza for the passage is as follows:

And God has drawn
this splendor, this glorious arch
through the whole
world in our Franz.

Und diesen Glanz,
und diesen Gloriebogen
hat Gott in unsern Franz
um eine ganze Welt gezogen.

Beethoven did not avoid emphatic setting of these lines, and he could not be accused of failing to mark through his music regal accents befitting an exalted emperor. Beethoven's music mimics the rhetorical exaggerations of Weissenbach's text. The commotion in the orchestra matches the effect of overstated pathos in the poem, with its dubious rhymed pairing of "Glanz" ("splendor") and "Franz." The repetitive rhythms and rising string arpeggios contribute to the emphatic yet rather facile *fortissimo* climax in the full orchestra. The overstated pathos of the words is reflected in the conventionally celebratory musical setting. This ceremonial cantata is an ample but glib musical canvas, whereby words and music are subordinated to the political adoration of authority. Beethoven's concern here was less with the "empire of the mind" than with the practical task of creating something appropriately flattering for the ceremonial occasion.

The hollow splendor of *The Glorious Moment* represents an overextended pretense in artistic guise. The glaring contrast with Beethoven's other music implies a conscious decision on his part to adjust priorities. To be sure, his occasional patriotic works indulge less in hedonism than in aggressive nationalist sentiments. In *The Glorious Moment*, a seductive wallowing in beauty remains a secondary and not a primary characteristic. It is not dreamy sentimentality but the underlying criterion of a false pretense that betrays the affinity of Beethoven's Congress of Vienna works with the sphere of kitsch.

It is a historical accident that the reactionary turn in post-Napoleonic politics coincided with another kind of chill: 1816 was the "year without summer," marking the onset of a global environmental shift with extreme weather and crop failures over multiple years that caused much widespread suffering. We have seen how in 1795, Beethoven described Russia as a "cold land" on account of its political repression as well as its robust climate. The impact of major volcanic eruptions has played a consequential but mostly unrecorded role in human history. An eruption of the Iceland volcano Laki in June 1783 caused abrupt cooling and crop failures, contributing thereby to the worsening problems in France during the years preceding the outbreak of the revolution. The first person to note the connection between volcanic eruption and an extreme cooling of weather was Benjamin Franklin, in a conjectural paper written in 1784.

Tambora, the great volcano on Sumbawa Island in Indonesia, erupted on 10 April 1815, just as the Congress of Vienna concluded on the other side of the world. While the protracted negotiations of the Congress representatives were nearing their end, Napoleon escaped from Elba and gathered forces for the final showdown at Waterloo on 15 June. Months earlier, one of those statesmen at Vienna, Prince Talleyrand, quipped that "The Congress dances but does not advance," referring to the dazzling array of receptions and balls held while steps toward promised constitutions or progressive causes lagged. More successful were those dispossessed aristocrats of the Old Regime who lobbied for their restored fiefdoms. The diplomat Emmerich von Dalberg commented gloomily that "We are completing the sad business of the Congress . . . the most mean-spirited piece of work ever seen."

Beethoven's own creative production during 1815–1817 lagged too, as some projects remained incomplete. He began a Piano Concerto in D Major in 1815, and a Piano Trio in F Minor in 1816, major pieces that if completed would have been his final contributions to these musical genres. My recording of a reconstructed torso of the first movement of the Piano Trio in F Minor is available online at press.uchicago.edu/sites/kinderman/. Beethoven's decline in productivity had multiple causes, including ill health and the demands of the guardianship of his young nephew Karl after his brother Caspar Carl's death in 1815. Beethoven was challenged by the guardianship role. Although he undoubtedly felt a Promethean calling of "divine and fatherly love" in relation to his nephew, he was not well equipped to sustain the practical aspects of parental responsibility.

Could the inhospitable weather of these years have also been a factor in his lowered artistic productivity? The temporary drastic climate change of those times distantly foreshadowed today's concerns about the natural environment. References to abnormal climactic conditions are contained in Beethoven's letters to Nannette Streicher. In July 1817 Beethoven begins a letter complaining "of bad weather . . ."; a few weeks later, another letter starts with "In spite of wind and rain." In yet another, he refers to "a second deluge," observing that "we are *bound* to get dripping wet, after rain continually pouring down from the sky." For an artist passionately devoted to nature and to the enjoyment of the out-of-doors, the sustained chilly, wet weather and lack of clear summer days were surely conspicuous. These abnormal climactic conditions lingered for about three years after Tambora's explosion, until 1818.

Beethoven's path to renewed and heightened creativity during the 1820s found its threshold in two gigantic piano compositions: the *Hammerklavier* Sonata, op. 106, completed in 1818, and the *33 Variations on a Waltz by Diabelli*, op. 120, a project begun in 1819 and completed in 1823. Beethoven predicted with some justification about the *Hammerklavier* that "It would give pianists something to do, and would be played fifty years hence." Similarly, decades passed before the Diabelli Variations began to receive serious attention. The reception history of this great set of variations continues to gain momentum. It has stimulated literary responses, even a Broadway play.

Beethoven liked to call Anton Diabelli "diabolus," and he reportedly at first declined the invitation to write a single variation for the publisher's collective project, which was designed to promote Diabelli's fledgling music-publishing firm. The timing of Diabelli's call soliciting variations on his vivacious German waltz or "Deutscher" was conspicuously close to Sand's assassination of Kotzebue, the trigger of the Karlsbad Decrees. The resulting collection—issued under the banner of a "Patriotic Association of Artists" (*Vaterländischer Künstlerverein*)—brought together fifty variations by a diversity of composers, including Carl Czerny, Franz Schubert, Jan Tomaschek, Archduke Rudolph, and the young Franz Liszt. The contributors showed a range of abilities. Beethoven was less than impressed by Anton Halm, whom he dubbed a "straw" or "blade of straw," negating the literal meaning of *Halm* as "blade." Another contributor was that prolific variation-forger who became Beethoven's "virulent opponent": Abbé Gelinek.

Gelinek responds to Diabelli with decorative embellishment of his waltz. Much remains unchanged: the key, meter, and basic harmonic structure with the "cobbler's patch" sequences remain intact (figs. 7.1 and 7.2). He adds some chromatic spice in a continuous rhythmic texture of running notes; an upward registral expansion marks the *forte* arrival point at measure 4. When the first half of the theme is repeated, Gelinek retains Diabelli's repeated chords, slipping a rising chromatic scale into the bass. At the close, the notes in the left hand are rendered as octaves. Gelinek's variation technique is confined to figurative elaboration. If we envision the theme as analogous to a person, it is as if the attire is adjusted while the individual remains the same. Diabelli remains the master, but dons a purple vest.

According to Jean Paul, as we have seen, "humor, understood as the inverted sublime . . . lowers the sublime, while . . . raising up the trivial, and . . . sets the trivial beside the sublime and so annihilates both, since in relation to the infinite everything is the same and nothing." Jean Paul's tensional duality of the Great and the Small fits well to Beethoven's engagement with Diabelli's theme,

7.1 Diabelli's waltz, beginning.

a response opposed to Gelinek's glib complacency. If Gelinek pictured Beethoven while composing as scavenging "a few musical *motivi* out of his treasure-heap," the Diabelli Variations show how from a handful of motives a vast "treasure-heap" of distinctive musical worlds could be shaped. Gelinek takes Diabelli's beer-hall waltz at face value—he fills in a few gaps with alternative figuration, without exploring the intrinsic nature of the artistic material. Beethoven's variations, by contrast, decide what *they* wish to extract from the theme. His transformations are rebellious, even revolutionary, overturning the hierarchies of conventional practice.

In his Variations, Beethoven counterbalanced the entire collective effort of Diabelli's "patriotic association of artists." There is no better example of an ambitious musical work grounded in the commonplace than Beethoven's transformations of this "well-known German waltz," as he described it. Hans von Bülow dubbed the composition "a microcosm of Beethoven's art," and Alfred Brendel calls it "the most comprehensive masterwork of the older piano literature." Yet this enormous musical edifice was built from a trivial waltz that Beethoven described as a "cobbler's patch."

7.2 Joseph Gelinek's variation on Diabelli's waltz, beginning.

Writing to Diabelli with tongue-in-cheek irony in 1823, Beethoven lauded the contributors: "Hats off to this, your Austrian Association, which knows how to handle the cobbler's patch most excellently." His designation *Schusterfleck* or "cobbler's patch" refers to the mechanical sequences in Diabelli's theme, with all of the voices moving in the same direction—a facile technique familiar in popular music. In appreciating Beethoven's Variations, we should savor their paradoxical origins. Not only did he ennoble Diabelli's theme by transforming it into a variety of shapes and characters, but he also subjected it to critique, poking fun at its more primitive aspects. His use of the term "Veränderungen" rather than "Variationen" in his title signals a transformational approach. The Diabelli Variations create a uniquely coherent design of vast dimensions, filling nearly an hour in performance time.

The genesis of Beethoven's Variations reaches back to 1819, soon after Diabelli circulated his invitation. Despite Beethoven having expressed an initial distaste for it, the theme triggered a creative brainstorm: he had soon conceived twenty-three variations, ten fewer than the final number. Beethoven's manuscripts have allowed new insight into the structure and import of the piece. After setting it aside for several years, he finally expanded his draft from within in 1823, adding variations 1, 2, 15, 23–26, 28, 29, and 31 to the preestablished order, while greatly elaborating the conclusion. During the interim period, in 1822, Beethoven completed another set of variations for piano whose genesis became intertwined with his set of thirty-three: the last movement of his last Sonata in C Minor, op. 111. My complete recording of the Sonata in C Minor, op. 111, is accessible online at press.uchicago.edu/sites/kinderman/.

While composing, Beethoven often de-emphasized or obliterated similarities between the variations in his sketches, while imparting to each finished variation a sharply defined individuality of character. Diabelli's waltz becomes a reservoir of unrealized possibilities out of which the variations generate an almost encyclopedic range of contexts. The psychological complexity of the Diabelli Variations arises above all from this tension between the commonplace theme as point of departure and the seemingly unlimited horizon of the variations. The range of pulse, movement, texture, and sonority explored here is so prodigious as to justify von Bülow's description of op. 120 as "a microcosm of Beethoven's art."

No other piece by Beethoven is so rich in allusion, humor, and parody. Trivial or repetitive features of the waltz, such as the C-major chords repeated tenfold with a *crescendo* in the right hand in the opening measures, can be mercilessly exaggerated as in variation 21, or dissolved into silence as in variation 13. Inconspicuous aspects of the theme, such as the ornamental turn heard at the outset, can assume astonishing importance, as in variations 9, 11, and 12, which are based throughout on this turn. Several variations allude to Mozart, Bach, and other composers. The most obvious of these is the reference, in the unison octaves of variation 22, to "Notte giorno faticar" from the beginning of Mozart's *Don Giovanni*. This allusion is brilliant not only through the musical affinity of the themes—which share, for example, the same descending fourth and fifth—but through the reference to

Mozart's Leporello. Beethoven's relationship to his theme, like Leporello's to his master, is critical but faithful, inasmuch as he thoroughly exploits its motivic components. Like Leporello, the variations after this point gain the capacity for disguise. Variation 23 is an *étude*-like parody of pianistic virtuosity alluding to the *Pianoforte-Method* by Johann Baptist Cramer, whereas variation 24, the Fughetta, shows an affinity in its intensely sublimated atmosphere to some organ pieces from the third part of the *Clavierübung* by J. S. Bach.

The work as a whole consists of one large form with three distinct regions. The opening variations generally remain close to the basic attributes of the theme but show gradually increasing freedom, which at last turns into dissociation with Beethoven's juxtaposition of two contrasting canonic variations (nos. 19 and 20), whereupon in no. 21 the structural parts of each variation half are themselves placed into opposition. In the opening measures of variation 21, a grotesque exaggeration of the turns and repeated chords annihilates the inward stillness of variation 20; this most shocking contrast is placed at the temporal midpoint of the entire cycle. The Janus face of no. 21 marks the extreme limit of the progression toward dissociation that began about ten variations before.

A sense of larger overreaching coherence is created in part through direct reference to the melodic shape of the original waltz in its original register in three of the variations inserted in 1823—nos. 1, 15, and 25. Variation 1 is an impressive but somewhat stilted march in which the bass initially spells out the descending fourth from the waltz; variation 15 is a miniature (the shortest of all thirty-three variations) with a static and peculiar harmonic plan, whose capricious two-octave skip in the bass has provoked "correction" from puzzled editors. By parodying the melody of the waltz directly in these variations, Beethoven made the theme into an indispensable foundation for the overall musical progression. If the elusive caricature embodied in variation 15 calls forth the theme again as a kind of hallucination at the very moment when drastic, bewildering contrasts have gained the upper hand, this allusion to the outset of the work is broadened in the following pair of march variations, nos. 16 and 17, which are counterpoised to variation 1 (the march more stilted in character). In variation 25, the waltz is reincarnated as a humorous German dance, but this image is gradually obliterated in the interconnected series of fast variations culminating in no. 28, in which harsh dissonances dominate every strong beat throughout. This series of variations also marks the beginning of a consolation in the form of the whole.

After variation 28, we enter a transfigured realm in which Diabelli's waltz and the world it represents seem to be left behind. A group of three slow variations in the minor culminates in variation 31, an elaborate aria reminiscent of the decorated minor variation of Bach's "Goldberg" set, but also foreshadowing the style of Chopin. The energetic fugue in E♭ major that follows is initially Handelian in character; its second part builds to a tremendous climax with three subjects combined simultaneously before the fugue dissipates into a powerful dissonant chord. An impressive transition leads to C major and to the final and most subtle variation of all: a Mozartian minuet whose elaboration through rhythmic means leads, in the coda, to an ethereal texture unmistakably reminiscent of the fourth variation of the *Arietta* movement from Beethoven's own last sonata, op. 111, from 1822.

The Diabelli Variations and last sonata reflect Beethoven's search for unity in diversity. The many parallels between op. 111 and the final Diabelli variation are structural in nature and extend to thematic proportions and the use of an analogous series of rhythmic diminutions leading, in each case, to the suspended, ethereal texture; but the most obvious similarity surfaces in the concluding passages outlining the descending fourth C–G, so crucial in both works. Herein lies a surprise: the *Arietta* movement, itself influenced by the Diabelli project, became in turn Beethoven's model for the last of the Diabelli Variations. The end of the series of allusions became a self-reference, a final point of orientation within a work of art whose vast scope ranges from ironic caricature to sublime transformation of the commonplace waltz.

In *Ludwig van: Hommage von Beethoven*, a contribution to the anti-authoritarian movement that paradoxically commemorated the 1970 Beethoven bicentennial, Mauricio Kagel took inspiration from the open concept embodied in the Diabelli Variations. His notion of an homage "from" and not "to" Beethoven is ironic; the indeterminate shape of *Ludwig van* is reflected in multiple realizations as film, score, and sound recording. Kagel's film version incorporates a mocking critique of Elly Ney, a pianist who piously embraced the National Socialist cause. The blend of parody and homage rooted in the Diabelli Variations takes flight in Kagel's theatricality. Shorthand permutations of Beethoven's name have marked many diverse responses to his music, from Kagel van Beethoven and Ludwig [a]van[t] garde in the 1970s to Yeethoven mash-ups today. It is understandable that Kagel found in the vast scope and allusiveness of the Diabelli Variations a springboard for *Ludwig van*.

One might be tempted to dwell on the goal-directedness of the conclusion of the Diabelli Variations, stressing Beethoven's sublime transformations of Diabelli's "cobbler's patch." In the last sections of this colossal work, Beethoven incorporates a series of allusions to other contexts and composers, ending with a self-reference to the last movement of his own last sonata. At the same time, he retains a keen memory of the original context. He ennobles the humble, the original waltz; the artistic journey encompasses many stages. There is something wonderfully paradoxical in Beethoven's open ending. Even the final chord is a surprise—the long-range backward glance and conclusion on a weak beat convey a sense of unfinished business, of a witty smiling gaze, suggesting perhaps that the creative process is not exhausted after all, and that even more variations *could* have followed.

Something of that overspill of creativity can be recognized in Beethoven's final sonata and last return to the "C-minor mood," the key of the Fifth Symphony and the *Eroica* funeral march, the *Coriolan* Overture, and *Sonate pathétique*. This piece is the focus of the lecture recital by Wendell Kretzschmar in the eighth chapter of Thomas Mann's novel *Doktor Faustus*. Kretzschmar asks why this sonata has but two movements instead of the more customary three, and he characterizes the end of the finale, the *Arietta* with variations, as an "end without any return." The dualistic contrast in op. 111 involves a transition from the turbulent dystopian landscape of the opening *Allegro* to the serenity and ecstatic utopia of the *Arietta* movement. An early sketch for the fugato used in the first movement shows that Beethoven intended to use it in a projected third movement, but soon changed his mind. The encompassing polar design of op. 111 begins with a tragic slow introduction comparable to the Crucifixion of his *Missa solemnis*, but concludes with a coda to the *Arietta* movement that is transfigured and celestial.

How is the transition achieved? Beethoven interpolates two passages of reflective intervention into the midst of the opening movement, episodes that confront its turbulent trajectory. Kretzschmar describes these as "passages of melodic loveliness by which the ravaged and tempestuous skies of the composition are at intervals brightened as though by faint glimpses of light." These episodes bring a shift to the major mode and broaden the tempo to *Adagio*, foreshadowing the character of the *Arietta* movement to come. The first of the episodes is abruptly cut off, brutally negated (mm. 55–56). The second interpolation became an intense focus of Beethoven's revisions during the creative process, as his manuscripts show. When the music "of melodic loveliness" reappears in C major in the recapitulation, it displays more resilience. Here, instead of a disjunctive break, Beethoven writes a new rising passage that links directly to resumption of the "tempestuous skies," that rapid agitated music in the minor with jagged rhythms and dissonant harmonies. The extreme nature of his efforts is reflected in the lofty register at that moment of connection (m. 132). His copyist asked, "Should I write so high?" since the top pitch, E♭, did not exist on most keyboard instruments of the day. Beethoven included the high E♭. But a crucial aspect of the larger passage centers on a single chord, a major-ninth sonority containing the pitches F, G, and A (mm. 120–121; fig. 7.3). Like an uncanny vision, this gentle utterance prefigures the *Arietta* movement. This enhanced presence of the brighter major mode is sustained

7.3 Beethoven, Sonata in C Minor, op. 111/I, mm. 120–121.

at the end of the first movement. Three plagal cadences assert C major, balancing the turbulence from the outset of the slow introduction. The last of these cadential gestures corresponds to the earlier moment when the first passage of "melodic loveliness" had been negated, but now the outcome is reversed. The consoling shift into C major opens a gateway to the ensuing *Arietta*.

Kretzschmar describes the *Arietta* as "destined to vicissitudes for which in its idyllic innocence it would seem not to be born," but it was markedly influenced by Diabelli's "cobbler's patch" tune: Beethoven altered his initial idea to reflect the falling fourth and fifth from the waltz in the same key, while refining the phrase structure and thematic proportions. The ensuing transformations of the *Arietta* embody an adventurous journey. In Mann's literary description, we read about "what now happens to this mild utterance, rhythmically, harmonically, contrapuntally, to this pensive, subdued formulation; with what its master blesses and to what condemns it; into what black nights and dazzling flashes, crystal spheres wherein coldness and heat, repose and ecstasy are one and the same, he flings it down and lifts it up; all that one may well call vast, strange, extravagantly magnificent, without thereby giving it a name, because it is quite truly nameless."

The two overreaching principles are Being and Becoming, endurance and change. The returning presence of the theme embodies stasis, but the overall progression is evolutionary and exploratory. The movement could not conclude with a literal repetition or *da capo* of the original theme. While maintaining the basic tempo in his variations, Beethoven gradually intensifies the rhythmic activity. The slow tempo and broad spaces of the theme are filled up from within with moving voices. Variation 2 attains the dance-like character resembling his initial sketches for the main theme. The process of rhythmic compression of motivic figures creates an agitated, jazzlike character notated in 12/32 meter in variation 3. One critic in Beethoven's time found this section inscrutable, like a discourse in a foreign language written in an unknown alphabet. Beethoven launches the motivic material here with mathematical rigor, with inversion of the right-hand figuration in the left hand.

Variation 4 exploits a contrast of low and high registers, spinning out the 9/16 meter in transfigured, hypnotic patterns, rhythmic tremolos, and suspended arabesques, in which "repose and ecstasy are one and the same," in Kretzschmar's words. At the end of this variation, the music lingers on high G, corresponding to the accented melodic peak at the end of the *Arietta* theme. The extension of the structural model of the theme leads to a culminating stage of rhythmic compression. This is a rapid musical texture in unmeasured motion, which can stand for an inner stillness or pulsation: the trill, a vibrating resonance between adjacent pitches.

Beethoven's handling of the ensuing climactic passage transfigures the *Arietta*, revealing unsuspected potential in the original theme. By this point, Beethoven has fully prepared the cadence and resolution to the tonic key that marks the outset of the recapitulatory fifth variation (mm. 130–131). The inner climax (mm. 106–130) is a formal interpolation that seems to suspend the passage of time, with a shift to E♭ major as multiple trills resonate simultaneously. In Mann's colorful description, Kretzschmar echoes the opening three-note motive of the *Arietta* with his shouts while playing the trills: "Dim-dada!" The three-note figure, with its long-short-long rhythm, initiates a triple trill, as the music penetrates new expressive regions. The modification of the head motive in multiple voices *creates* the suspended texture with multiple trills. After the onset of the long trill on D, the additional voices set ablaze through trills are derived motivically through the head motive of the *Arietta* theme. This conveys a sense of intense introspection brought to sound, as the pitches of the new key of

E♭ vibrate together, having been assembled through an enlarge-ment—a still, suspended, meditative vision—of the motives of the *Arietta*.

If the cadenza-like interpolation develops the trill as a logical outcome of the large-scale process of rhythmic diminution, the recapitulatory variation 5 signals the consolidation of the over-all form. By bringing together components that had earlier been heard separately, this variation embodies a synthesis. The *Arietta* theme returns here in its original register, but the rhythm of other parts of the texture recalls variations 1 and 4, enabling us to experience as a simultaneity what had earlier been heard suc-cessively. Being and Becoming are forged into a single entity. At the end of this variation, Beethoven writes a *crescendo* over five measures, a passage that reaches its outcome at the major-ninth chord marked *forte* in measure 158. This climax brings to sound a rich dissonance, as the high A is heard against G, F, and B in the other voices (fig. 7.4). This is the sonority that was foreshadowed at the pivotal *Adagio* in the first movement (fig. 7.3).

The expanded temporality of Beethoven's artistic strategy merits recognition. In *Fidelio*, as we have seen, the soaring oboe of Florestan's vision foretells and merges with Leonore's actual approach; in op. 111, the uncanny *Adagio* gesture in the first move-ment prefigures this memorable climax in the *Arietta* movement. In his study *Art & Physics*, Leonard Shlain stresses the role of overlapping fields and need to go beyond mere understanding in grasping the complementarity of space and time. Contem-plating Édouard Manet's painting *A Bar at the Folies-Bergève*, Shlain dwells on its double exposure, with the same scene experi-enced from different perspectives and moments in time. Decades before Manet, Beethoven explored parallel possibilities in music. Moments of disjunction can signal connection; opposing aspects of reality enable us to move forward toward a heightened percep-tive capacity as in this very passage, with the ecstatic climactic chord generating another ringing, vibrating trill.

The coda brings another synthesis of rhythmic and textural lev-els: a reprise of the original theme in the highest possible register

7.4 Sonata in C Minor, op. 111/II, mm. 157–158.

combined with the ethereal passagework in triplet sixteenths from variation 4, as well as with a sustained trill on G, prolonging the rich dissonance from the end of variation 5. This exquisite texture is followed by just six measures, in which the passagework is first carried upward, touching the registral ceiling of the entire piece before echoes of the original opening motto from the *Arietta* bring the sonata to a quiet, understated close, opening into the ensuing silence. In its synthesizing quality, earlier stages in the movement are recalled and combined. The overall trajectory is directional, with a sense of goal-directedness conveyed through a texture of plentitude in the fifth variation and coda. The limits of execution are tested, as the coda brings a climactic distillation of content drawn from the movement as a whole. At the same time, the utopian character of the end of the *Arietta* movement is counterpoised to the dystopian character of the opening movement. The encompassing polar design of op. 111 begins with a tragic slow introduction comparable to the Crucifixion of his *Missa solemnis*, but concludes with a coda to the finale that is transfigured and celestial.

In contemplating this music, we are reminded of the inscription from ancient Egypt that Beethoven kept framed on his desk during the last decade of his life:

I am all that is, that was, and that will be, no mortal human being has lifted my veil.

Ich bin alles, Was ist, Was war, und Was seyn wird, Kein sterblicher Mensch hat meinen Schleyer aufgehoben.

This veil of Isis is an allegorical motive, with infinite nature personified and covered by a mantle representing the inaccessibility of nature's secrets. Beethoven's creativity was fired by such imagery. In his *Critique of Judgement*, Immanuel Kant commented about this dictum that "Perhaps nothing more sublime was ever said and no sublimer thought ever expressed than on the Temple of Isis (Mother Nature)."

In a letter from 1819, Beethoven referred to his artistic goal by coining the idiosyncratic term "Kunstvereinigung" or "artistic unification," a notion connected to the aging composer's intense assimilation of the music of Handel and Bach. His convictions parallel those of Friedrich Schelling, a pivotal figure in the circle at Jena in the 1790s that included Schiller, Hölderin, and Hegel. These thinkers followed a philosophical quest for an intuition prior to the distinction between subject and object, a project with social, political, and religious implications, since what was sought was a unity with all being (*Vereinigung*). Schelling's concept of the natural world, like Beethoven's, was organicist; for him, mind itself was seen as emanating from the unending activity of nature. In his *System of Transcendental Idealism* of 1800, Schelling granted an exalted role to the artwork in displaying an original harmony of object and subject, unconscious and conscious, nature and freedom. Schelling found that since philosophy is reflection, it must wait for art to produce a consciousness of the unity of nature and freedom. This perspective offered philosophical justification for the claim, attributed apocryphally to Beethoven, that the revelation of art was "higher than all wisdom and philosophy." It is in light of this effort of the Jena circle to transcend the limits of Kantian and Schillerian aesthetics that we may view the artistic enterprise that Beethoven himself provocatively dubbed *Kunstvereinigung*.

A quest for an ethereal essence, for an elusive unity amid diversity, is embedded in Beethoven's Diabelli Variations and last sonata. This quality resonates with our current worldview. Recent developments in physics have revived the older notion that the phenomenon of light must be vibrations of an unknown medium called aether, which necessarily had to fill the whole universe. With the advent of quantum physics and recognition that the vacuum is not void with its vacuum fluctuations, the notion of the aether has reemerged in a new modern light. A mysterious tension pointing beyond itself invests this music. In the coda of the *Arietta* movement, for instance, the tremolo texture in undulating triplets alternates between E and C, with the accented first notes of each triplet group of the 9/16 meter shifting between these two pitches. Out of the gently pulsating movement of this figuration, a larger triplet pattern emerges, unfolding once with each group of nine smaller notes. A hypnotic, bell-like resonance results, as intervals vibrate as parts of themselves on different temporal levels. The high trill resonating above this texture suggests a spiritualized transformation of the piccolo trill on these notes in the coda of the finale of the Fifth Symphony.

Beethoven's final sonata attests to his conviction that solutions to the problems facing humanity may lie within our grasp if they can be confronted by models of transformation. Projections of human goals and desires are richly realized in such masterpieces of art, which supply a source of renewable energy capable of promoting changes in the relations between human beings. In this context, art is not just an escape or haven from social and political life, but it offers a potential link between these realms of experience. Among Beethoven's instrumental works, op. 111 assumes a special position as an "effigy of the ideal," in Schiller's formulation, and every adequate performance must reenact something of this process, reaching beyond the purely aesthetic dimension to touch the sphere of the moral and ethical.

Then and Now:
The Ninth Symphony

In 2012, in Sabadell, Catalonia, a city in Spain near Barcelona, a flash-mob rendition of Beethoven's Ninth was captured on video. By the time of this writing, the event had received more than 90 million viewings on YouTube. The flash mob is a twenty-first-century phenomenon, whose seeming spontaneity in a public space is carefully staged. On a lovely day in May, a young girl tossed a coin in a hat, triggering a dapper double bassist in the street to begin playing. The child received more than expected. One by one, other orchestral players arrived, then members of the chorus. Their stirring performance was admirably preserved on video. The role of Beethoven's "Joy" theme as anthem of the European Union fits to the larger contextual meaning, with no hint of the tensional political relation between Catalonia and the rest of Spain.

Friedrich Schiller's poem "To Joy" from 1785 makes reference to the "millions" as an all-embracing gesture of inclusion. "Be embraced millions, this kiss to the whole world," forms part of the "chorus" in the original text. Though Schiller's words were never officially certified as part of the anthem for the European Union, they shape the appeal of this music to communities across the globe. The attraction and widespread familiarity of the "Joy" theme in parts of Asia matches that in Europe or America. Beethoven's Ninth Symphony has become a seemingly unsurpassed model of affirmative culture.

Nevertheless, controversy remains. Collective joy is an irresistible but slippery notion, which might seem politically naïve and ideologically risky. Never was this so much the case as during the reign of the National Socialists in Germany, the dozen years from 1933 until 1945. Writing in exile in California during this grim chapter of German history, Thomas Mann in his novel *Doktor Faustus* pitted the culminating work of his fictional composer protagonist, Adrian Leverkühn, against the luminous message of Beethoven's Ninth. Leverkühn's last piece is a great Faust Cantata entitled *Des Fausti Weheklag* or "Lament of Faust," a multi-movement work with an orchestral finale that negates Beethoven's optimistic message. Mann describes Leverkühn's piece as "the opposite trajectory of the Song to Joy, the negative image of that transition in the symphony into joyous vocality, a taking back," or revocation, in Mann's formulation. His fictional narrator, the humanist Serenus Zeitblom, comments about this "Song of Sorrow" in *Des Fausti Weheklag* that "without doubt, it was written in response to Beethoven's Ninth, to form its counterpart in the most lamenting sense. Not only does this signal a formal shift into the negative, a taking back into negativity, but it also embodies a negation of the religious dimension."

The hard-edged dualism of Thomas Mann's framework in his novel sets into relief issues of musical symbolism and dramatic narrative important to Beethoven's aesthetic enterprise. This question can be approached from two interlocking perspectives, historical and contemporary. Inspection of the genesis of Beethoven's work sheds light on the challenges the composer faced in closing his final symphony with the choral setting of Schiller's poem. The remarkable reception history of this music up to the present is instructive in another way. Like that little girl in Sabadell, we witness an astonishing, open-ended process attesting to the growing resonance of Beethoven's legacy in an increasingly globalized world.

A historical perspective uncovers doubts on Beethoven's part about the choral finale. More than a century ago, the pioneer scholar of Beethoven's voluminous sketchbooks, Gustav Nottebohm, noticed that interspersed with Beethoven's sketches for the choral finale of the Ninth Symphony are entries for an alternative, a "Finale instrumentale" or orchestral finale. Much more recently, reexamination of the manuscript sources has reinforced that insight, implying that the possibility of an instrumental finale was consistently weighed during Beethoven's creative process. One of his comments in the sketches is as follows: "Vielleicht doch den Chor Freude schöner" ("Maybe after all the chorus [on] 'Freude schöner'"), implying that Beethoven considered alternatives but decided in favor of Schiller's text. A report attributed to Carl Czerny, a trustworthy witness, conveys that Beethoven expressed doubts about the choral finale even after the first performances in 1824. Czerny reported that the composer considered replacing the choral finale with an instrumental movement without voices, for which he already had an idea in mind.

Confirmation of Beethoven's doubts is found in the *De Roda* Sketchbook, a big manuscript made up of a hodgepodge of different paper types, many of which were assembled into a book only after Beethoven wrote down the sketches. This sketchbook, which was not known to Nottebohm, contains a double leaf ruled like an orchestral score, on paper matching that used by Beethoven for some of his labors on the Ninth Symphony. At the top of one of these leaves we find the theme elsewhere labeled as "Finale instrumentale" and written in ink in D minor, the main key of the symphony. This page is shown in figure 8.1, with a transcription of the sketch in figure 8.2.

The remainder of this page is filled with sketches added later in pencil, sketches related to a different work: the String Quartet in A Minor, op. 132. Several movements of the A-minor Quartet are represented in these entries. What stands out is the sketch at the bottom of the page (fig. 8.3). This entry includes a melodic continuation of this same theme with a soaring continuation not found in versions of the theme written down earlier in connection with the symphony. The theme is now marked "Finale" and shifted into A minor, the key of the quartet. The ascent into the high register familiar from the finished Quartet in A Minor is present in this sketch.

8.1 *De Roda* Sketchbook, fol. 5r (Beethoven-Haus Bonn NE 47a).

8.2 Sketch at top of *De Roda* Sketchbook, fol. 5r, staff 1.

8.3. Sketch at bottom of *De Roda* Sketchbook, fol. 5r, staves 13–14.

This page from the *De Roda* Sketchbook documents the *trans-ference* of this passionate theme from the D-minor Symphony to the A-minor Quartet. What Beethoven considered using in his symphony but realized in his quartet involves a very different outcome, one that might even be described as an "opposite tra-jectory of the Song to Joy," or a "negative image of that transi-tion in the symphony into joyous vocality." In its character, the A-minor Quartet is one of Beethoven's most despairing composi-tions, linked as it is to his life-threatening illness from 1825. Its centerpiece is the slow middle movement, entitled "Sacred Song of Thanks to the Deity from a Convalescent in the Lydian Mode."

In the end, Beethoven remained true to his remarkable Schil-ler setting for the choral finale of the Ninth. But it is worth pon-dering how the passionate theme withheld from the symphony became the main theme of the finale of this second of the late quar-tets. Striking too is the rhythmic and motivic kinship between the main theme of the first movement of the symphony and the theme Beethoven transferred to op. 132. While absorbing the pre-existing theme into the quartet, Beethoven not only extended it melodically and changed its key, but chose to preface the finale with a piercing dramatic recitative in the first violin, a gesture audibly linked to the quartet's conflicted opening movement. The role of the recitative in the quartet reminds us once more unmis-takably of the Ninth Symphony, whose elaborate recitative pas-sages at the threshold to the finale are bound up with the recall of earlier movements.

A treasure trove of sketches relates to these recitatives. What stands out is that Beethoven tried adding words to clarify why the recall of earlier movements is rejected in favor of his choice of Schiller's idealistic poem. His Schiller setting is suggestive of folk song with universalist aspirations. Although not retained in the finished work, these words cast light on the music's expressive meaning. Conspicuous is an inscription Beethoven scrawled over the dissonant chord heard when the recall of the symphony's first movement is interrupted and rejected. He wrote: "nein diese . . . erinnern an unsere Verzweifl[ung]" ("No, this reminds us of our despair"), an inscription that underscores the tragic character of this D-minor music.

The manuscript sources thereby open up a startling perspective on these two intimately related works. What Beethoven contemplated, while composing the Ninth Symphony, was nothing less than whether the vision of Schillerian collective harmony, of joyful community, could sustain itself against the contrasting modalities of the preceding movements, especially the despairing character of the opening *Allegro* in D minor. The end of the opening movement of the Ninth sounds funereal, suggesting the burial of the heroic ideal that had sustained his art, but the choral finale resurrects that ideal. Its "effigy of the ideal" is an imaginative deed, using the inspired recitatives of the *Tempest* Sonata as a creative gateway, while showing that he still "revere[d] the dreams of early youth."

The theme Beethoven envisioned originally for an orchestral finale to the symphony but shifted to the quartet embodies a quality of somber passion. Other points of comparison exist between the D-minor Symphony and A-minor Quartet. Beethoven's handling of the recitative preface to the quartet's finale provokes reflection. A sketch for the recitative marked "Vio[lin]" on the aforementioned *De Roda* leaf absorbs a crucial rhythmic motive found in the main theme of the opening movement of the Ninth.

Commentators on the A-minor Quartet have stressed the character of suffering that infuses this composition. Conspicuous is how its fourth movement, a proud, seemingly self-confident march in A major, is ambushed by the piercing dissonant recitative leading into the last movement. Beethoven directs that the recitative be performed *attacca*, leading without a break directly from the march into the A-minor finale. The agonized recitative culminates in a crucified variant of the motive from the outset of the first movement, the figure F–G♯–A–E. The F–E semitone that closes this recitative is then absorbed into the throbbing accompaniment of the finale, the *Allegro appassionato*.

In experiencing how this A-major march is ambushed, one thinks again of the Ninth Symphony. Beethoven's "Joy" theme and the ensuing variations of the choral finale assume the character of an optimistic march in D major, a march in which gradually all parts of the orchestra and then the vocal soloists and chorus join. In the A-minor Quartet, by contrast, a march in the major mode precedes the finale; its confident mood is contradicted by the dark, impassioned recitative. In his quartet, Beethoven inverts and negates the narrative shape of the symphony. The quartet's autograph manuscript shows that Beethoven inserted the *Alla marcia* at a late compositional stage, using it as a stylized foil against which the recitative makes its mark. There is a stronger sense of critique or rejection here than in the recitative passages of the Ninth Symphony. The duple rhythm from the march is accelerated in the recitative transition. The head of the finale's theme contradicts the motive from the opening phrases of the march, as the upward thrust to the major third, C♯, is answered by an insistent descending contour stressing the minor third in the same register, C♮.

The conflict-ridden first movement of op. 132, on the other hand, juxtaposes two disparate musical ideas that prove to be closely interdependent. The initial *Assai sostenuto* unfolds in a mysterious *pianissimo* counterpoint using a four-note motto that appears in various forms in several of Beethoven's later works. The mysterious, hushed initial notes in the cello—G♯–A–F–E—embody this motive, but as the first violin climbs from E to F in a higher register we experience a shock, as the violin breaks out passionately in a chain of rapid notes. This dissonant disruption sets the tone for a radically innovative movement. Beethoven later makes reference to this disruptive gesture in his violin recitative preceding the finale.

The second movement in A major assumes a character of reminiscence. It relates to a minuet in one of Mozart's *Haydn* Quartets from the 1780s, K. 464 in A major, a work Beethoven treasured and parts of which he had copied out in score many years earlier. Beethoven had already paid homage to Mozart's A-major Quartet in composing his own earlier quartet in that key, op. 18, no. 5, completed in 1800. His backward glance does not stop there. He incorporates into the trio section of this dance movement a theme drawn from an *Allemande* for keyboard that he had written during the 1790s, before he composed his op. 18 quartets.

That brings us to the great central slow movement of op. 132, the "Sacred Song of Thanks to the Godhead in the Lydian Mode" juxtaposed with dance-like *Andante* sections in the major marked "Feeling New Strength." This unprecedented contrast has impressed many listeners. When it returns after the first *Andante* section, the austere Lydian chorale gains in rhythmic animation while expanding in register, but only in the culminating final section, after the second appearance of "Feeling New Strength," does the movement reach its unforgettable climax. Drawing on just the first phrase of the Lydian hymn, Beethoven accomplishes the seemingly impossible, generating an even greater intensity than in the music marked "Neue Kraft." What had been austere and archaically detached is imbued with almost unbearable force, with the first violin straining beyond the pattern of the hymn phrase, reaching into the musical stratosphere, as all the parts are underscored by accents.

In this climactic closing section of the *Heiliger Dankgesang* movement, Beethoven magnifies our experience of the sacred chorale through a concentrated force of introspection. Very different is his handling of the "Joy" theme in the Ninth Symphony. Yet these two themes in conjunct motion are related to one another. The "Joy" theme circles around the third of D major, rising initially from F♯. The opening phrase of the *Dankgesang* moves downward from F in a languid tempo. The opening of the *Dankgesang* is a somber inversion of the head of the "Joy" theme (fig. 8.4).

The quartet is a dark companion of the sublime Ninth, the castle's dungeon. Earlier instances of Beethoven's contrasting work-pairs had linked pieces of the same genre, one in major, one in minor. One thinks of the violin sonatas opp. 23 and 24, the *Waldstein* and *Appassionata* Sonatas, the Fifth and Sixth Symphonies, the piano trios op. 70. The connection between the Ninth Symphony and A-minor Quartet evolved from their interrelated genesis. Like Thomas Mann's fictional character Adrian Leverkühn,

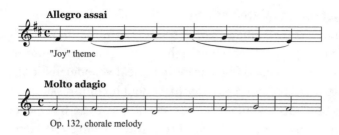

8.4 Comparison of the "Joy" theme of the Ninth Symphony with the chorale melody from Beethoven's Quartet in A Minor, op. 132/III.

Beethoven showed himself capable of regarding Schiller's "Ode to Joy" with distancing irony. In the end, however, he still affirmed the original idealistic idea, which had captured his imagination for more than three decades. The quartet offers an alternative narrative, reflecting his own grim experience of sickness and contemplation of mortality during the spring of 1825. Its narrative trajectory takes on a tragic character, especially following the despairing recitative leading into the final movement.

How then does the quartet sustain its close in the brighter A *major*? An answer to this question is bound up with our experience of the work as a totality. The lyrical, *dolce* second theme of the first movement's recapitulation had only fleetingly sustained A major. The second and fourth movements were set in this key, yet both feel like subsidiary stages in the overall musical narrative.

An analogy can be drawn here to the finale of Beethoven's penultimate Piano Sonata, op. 110 in A♭ major, another piece bound up with Beethoven's recovery from serious illness. In op. 110, Beethoven twice juxtaposes a despairing *Arioso dolente* with a spiritualized, aspiring fugue in the major. The first fugue is broken off, signaling failure, and a more pessimistic version of the lamenting *Arioso* then unfolds in G minor. When positive energies seem overwhelmed by depressive forces, at the end of the second *Arioso*, we reach an astonishing turning point, as an unexpected hushed *major* chord replaces the expected G-minor sonority. Gradually intensified repetitions of the G-major chord lead back to the exact initial position of the G-minor *Arioso* theme, its unfolding descent from G now replaced by an inversion of the fugue subject. This signals a transformation of despondency into renewed strength and vitality; Beethoven marks the ensuing passage "coming anew to life." This second fugue is more radically modernistic than the first fugue. It undergoes a rhythmic double compression that permits Beethoven to allude to the preceding scherzo-like movement, thereby absorbing a robust motive drawn from a folk song. This energy drawn from the sphere of the commonplace helps enable the lyric euphoria of the conclusion, reaching an emphatic high chord that acts as a teleological goal for the entire work.

A parallel process emerges at the end of the quartet op. 132. Following a mysterious *pianissimo* fugato passage, the main rondo theme is played high up in the cello, while the first violin attacks the theme's top pitches in a frenzy, stressing the crucial F–E semitone as the tempo accelerates to *presto*. Beethoven reinforced this passage in his autograph score, adding notes to the first violin part, and he also extended this coda through a varied repetition of a passage almost fifty measures long. The registral peak on high A from the *Heiliger Dankgesang* is twice recaptured in this coda. As in op. 110, limits are tested. At the miraculous shift into A major, the first violin prolongs its high E through six consecutive measures, yet this lofty pitch is resolved to the tonic A only 100 bars later, in the very last measure.

The coda in A major is delicately handled, and touches repeatedly on telltale features of the minor mode, especially that F♮ associated with the distressed character of the outer movements. The reality of anguish is not forgotten, but Beethoven does not after all revoke the promise of the Ninth Symphony, as did Thomas Mann's fictional character Adrian Leverkühn. One might sense an implied critique of the idealistic social vision of the Schillerian choral finale through Beethoven's rich development of his alternative "Finale instrumentale" theme, involving negation of the stylized *Alla marcia* movement in the major mode in op. 132. Yet recognition of the intertwined genesis of the symphony and quartet reminds us of how much depends in this context on the hard-won, fragile conclusion in A major. Opus 132 ends not with a public, communal vision, but with a more private artistic statement that attests to the individual confronted by adversity and mortality. As a goal for human striving, this outcome affirms unflinchingly a future-oriented potential as an alternative to skepticism and despair.

The passing of time and transience of life bring erosion and decay, but also fruition and fulfillment. In shifting attention to the impact of Beethoven's music up to the present day, we move from 1824—when he completed the Ninth at Vienna and witnessed in his deaf seclusion its premiere before an audience of hundreds—to 2012 and beyond, to the globalized world of the Sabadell flash mob, with many millions partaking in its ritual of community. Such globalization did not emerge all at once. Skepticism about the choral finale was characteristic of the initial phases in the symphony's reception history. At the London premiere of the work in 1825, a critic wrote that:

> The expense it entails for the engagement of a chorus, the necessity of repeated rehearsals, etc. etc. may perhaps forbid it ever being done again and will certainly impede both its frequent repetition or general reception.

This wildly mistaken judgment sets into relief the worldwide embrace of the work up to our own time. The onset of this development reaches back to the decade after Beethoven's death in 1827. In Paris, the reception of the Ninth Symphony was promoted by performances conducted by François Habeneck, with the piece first performed in 1831. In London and New York, the positive response to the Ninth Symphony dates from 1837, and had to do with performances led by Ignaz Moscheles. An English commentator at this time described the symphony as "a grand masonic hymn of Europe," a formulation anticipating the official role of the piece since the 1980s as a European anthem. The context of the 1837 discussion related to plans for a Beethoven statue at Bonn, an undertaking that came to fruition in 1845. The critic questioned the need for the statue, reflecting that "after all, the greatest monument Beethoven can have is the proper performance of his works: the annual repetition of the choral symphony by 1000 or 1500 persons—the grand masonic hymn of Europe upborne by 1000 voices, and supported by an orchestra of 500 instrumentalists, would be the apotheosis which even the composer would have desired for an extension of his thread of life to have witnessed."

Subsequent historical circumstances have brought breathtaking developments enabling still larger performances while bridging cultural divisions. The first rendering of Beethoven's Ninth in Asia occurred in June 1918 at the Bando prison camp in Japan, where 1,000 German prisoners were interned following their surrender after the siege of Tsingtao in 1914. The humane conditions at the camp allowed for a complete performance of the symphony with an orchestra of forty-five players and a chorus of eighty singers, participants drawn from the prison population. This set the scene for the remarkable Japanese performance tradition of Beethoven's final symphony, which is known as *daiku* or "No. 9." Since 1982, such annual performances on the first Sunday of December in Osaka have involved 10,000 participants. Beethoven has become a popular cult figure; performances of his symphony in many Japanese localities serve as a ritual occasion to honor collective achievement and the overcoming of hardships. One of these performances from 2018 with massive forces displaying conformism is depicted in figure 8.5. In no other country is the symphony performed so often with so many participants as in Japan.

At the final rally for the political campaign of Chen Shui-bian in Taiwan in 2000, on the other hand, recorded choral excerpts from Beethoven's Ninth in German resounded for an audience of 100,000 in and around the Taipei soccer stadium. As Beethoven's *Ode to Joy* was heard, the voiceover declared that "Chen Shu-bian, with the Taiwanese people, wants to create history with love and hope!" The music was featured again with whirling fireworks in Chen's 2004 reelection campaign, as he urged everyone "to vote for our democracy," but after two terms as president, Chen was charged with corruption and landed in prison. At the outcome of

8.5 Beethoven's Ninth Symphony performed by 10,000; Osaka, Japan, December 2018. Beethoven's Ninth with a Cast of 10,000 / MBS (Mainichi Broadcasting System).

the election in Taiwan in January 2020, Beethoven's music was once more conspicuous, with the finale of the Fifth Symphony as the chosen work.

Another Asian country that has embraced Beethoven's music is South Korea. One small measure of this enthusiasm is the 2008 television series *Beethoven Virus*, which distributes qualities associated with the composer to three characters bound up in a love triangle: a perfectionist conductor; a young natural musical genius; and a violinist coping with hearing loss. Since the 2000s, the rise of K-pop (Korean pop) has often absorbed elements drawn from Beethoven's music; on the other hand, in 2019, the centenary commemoration of the nationwide protest against Japan's colonial rule was marked by a performance of the *Eroica*. In 2011, a landmark cycle of all the Beethoven symphonies was performed in Seoul, with Daniel Barenboim leading the West-Eastern Divan Orchestra, an ensemble made up of musicians from Israel, the Palestinian territories, Jordan, Lebanon, Syria, and Egypt, among other countries. A driving idea of this orchestra is to help heal political divisions by bringing Arab and Israeli musicians together in concert. Founded in 1999, the 250th anniversary of Goethe's birth, its name recalls his *Westöstlicher Divan* of 1819, a poetic collection inspired by the fourteenth-century Persian poet Hafiz. Beethoven studied Goethe's *Westöstlicher Divan*, marking and commenting on passages in his own copy, which reflects his own interest in expanding his perspective beyond Europe.

What has enabled the Ninth Symphony to appeal so widely, far beyond Europe's boundaries? Part of the answer may lie in Beethoven's overall response to Schiller's "Ode to Joy." His adaptation of Schiller's poem in the choral finale is bound up with the character of the preceding orchestral movements, as indicated by the unused snippets of text he contemplated for the recitative passages, such as "No, this reminds us of our despair!" in relation to the recall of the first movement. The baritone's initial words, "O Freunde, nicht diese Töne!" ("Oh friends, not these tones!"), imply that the goal sought has not yet been achieved. Several lines in Schiller's poem disclose a notion of suffering that lies behind the striving to attain joy. It is joy, *Freude*, that redirects suffering: "Leitet sie des Dulders Bahn" ("Guideth *she* the sufferer's path"), and that idea is specified in a pair of Schiller's lines not incorporated by Beethoven into his choral finale:

Suffer on courageous millions!
Suffer for a better world!

Duldet mutig Millionen!
Duldet für die beßre Welt!

Other parts of the poem also resonate with Beethoven's message, even if they found no place in the symphony or even in Schiller's own final edited version of *An die Freude* from 1803. For the composer of *Fidelio*, the line "Rettung von Tyrannenketten" ("Rescue from the tyrant's chains"), and the entire final stanza of Schiller's original poem to which it belongs, with its message of forgiveness toward wrongdoers and disbelief in hell, will have held meaning. We know that Beethoven wrestled with Schiller's poem for many years, reaching back to his Bonn period, when he intended a setting "strophe by strophe." The larger totality of Schiller's legacy hovers over the symphony, notwithstanding Beethoven's doubts about the choral finale.

Those parts of Schiller's "Ode to Joy" foregrounded in Beethoven's music include above all the first stanza:

Freude, schöner Götterfunken,
Tochter aus Elysium,
Wir betreten feuertrunken
Himmlische, dein Heiligtum!
Deine Zauber binden wieder,
Was die Mode streng geteilt;
Alle Menschen werden Brüder,
Wo dein sanfter Flügel weilt.

Joy, lovely divine spark,
Daughter of Elysium,
Drunk with fire, we enter
your shrine, heavenly one!
Your magic brings together
What custom has roughly divided
All humans will become siblings
At the gentle touch of your wing.

What stands out are the folk-song-like character of Beethoven's tune and the elemental quality of its initial presentation, without a shred of accompaniment clothing. As in the Choral Fantasy, op. 80, which anticipates the choral finale in various ways, this music unfolds in variations with a gradually increasing participation from the orchestra. The conspicuous role of the humble bassoon in the first variation points to the principle of inclusive fraternity, to valued roles accorded all members of the ensemble. Striking is the syncopated upward leap in the melody from A to F♯ at "Alle" ("All"), which underscores the inclusiveness of the message.

The lines "Deine Zauber binden wieder / Was die Mode streng

geteilt" ("Your magic brings together / What custom has roughly divided") resonate on more than one level of meaning. What is divided may be taken to refer to class divisions, to overcoming the arbitrary barriers between members of the human community. At the same time, these lines relate to a lack of integration in human beings between the head and the heart, the rational and sensuous components of experience. A conviction about the task of art in promoting progress in social and political relations is embedded in the choral finale.

The role of the chorus in the slow sections, beginning with the text "Seid umschlungen Millionen" ("Be embraced millions"), reflects the assignment of these sections to the chorus in Schiller's poem. Here, the gaze of collective humanity is directed beyond, to the mysterious cosmic vastness of the universe. "Do you sense the Creator, world?" is a question posed to the assembled populace peering upward with awe to the canopy of stars. Since the image is naturalistic, it is unbounded; no political or religious authority is invoked. The climactic line "Above the stars must he dwell," referring to the Creator beyond the stars, is set as a musical monolith, an immovable high E♭ sonority that marks the utmost boundary of human perception, a Kantian limit evoking awe. At the original Viennese performance of the symphony on 7 May 1824, the royal box remained unoccupied, while the three movements of the *Missa solemnis* that accompanied the Ninth on the concert program had to be presented as "Grand Hymns" with German text, in order to obtain approval from the censor through an appeals process. These circumstances reflect a work that is unencumbered by the restrictions of church and state.

Three years later, the posthumous publication of Beethoven's *Heiligenstadt Testament*, with its searching melancholy and striving for "reverberations of true joy," began to influence the reception of the Ninth. As we have seen, the *Tempest* Sonata conceived at Heiligenstadt prefigures aspects of the symphony. The "Joy" theme in the Ninth corresponds to the trumpet calls in *Fidelio* in that it unveils a pivotal symbol, projecting a moment that is both "no more" and "not yet," an envisioned response to degraded conditions. The political implications of the choral finale unfold as its march-like progression contagiously infects ever more participants, dissolving boundaries, embracing millions.

In conclusion, let us illustrate the rich ongoing global reception history of the Ninth Symphony through examples drawn from various parts of the world, including Germany, Chile, the Democratic Republic of the Congo, and the People's Republic of China. Leonard Bernstein's famous rendering of the Ninth on Christmas Day of 1989 in Berlin served to dramatize a long-standing situation. The suspicion that Schiller might have wanted to foreground "Freiheit" instead of "Freude," "freedom" in place of "joy," as the key emblem of his poem had been voiced from time to time, as early as Wolfgang Griepenkerl's story *Das Musikfest* (*The Music Festival*) from 1838, but it remains unconfirmed, even perhaps improbable. By the middle of the nineteenth century, Edgar Quinet described the chorale finale as "the *Marseillaise* of humanity," anticipating the later interpretations of Romain Rolland. Bernstein's decision to change the text after the fall of the Berlin Wall sought to justify the political status of the *Ode to Joy*. Asserting that it ought to have been an *Ode to Freedom*, Bernstein made it so by changing the text, thereby linking the performance with the actual political events of 1989. In another sense, too, the words "binden wieder" or "join again together" could be understood to mark the fall of the Wall and eradication of the death strip severing Berlin and dividing East and West Germany.

As we have seen, the political import of Beethoven's music is often bound up with the idea of resistance, whether or not this enables freedom for an individual protagonist. Florestan survives, Egmont does not, yet both experience a vision of potential liberation, while the apotheosis of freedom in the *Victory Symphony* in *Egmont* is associated with real historical events subsequent to the drama. For the crowd outside the Dresden Semper Oper and the audience inside for *Fidelio* in October 1989, the Wall remained intact; by the time of Bernstein's performance in Berlin in December, it had collapsed. The use of the Ninth has responded to ever-changing situations. The disbanded all-Iranian Tehran Symphony

Orchestra was revived in 2015 with Beethoven's Ninth conducted by Ali Rahbari, with Schiller's *Ode to Joy* in the original German. Frequent commemorative performances emerged after the 9/11 attacks, as well as in response to other instances of terrorism. In May 2016, a performance of the choral finale in Brussels honored the victims of terror attacks in that city. Five years earlier, when the Occupy Wall Street movement found supportive international responses, protesters in Madrid expressed themselves through a rendition of Beethoven's *Ode to Joy*. At the protest site in New York, music students carried banners like "Juilliard Students SUPPORT Occupy Wall Street" and "Bail out Beethoven, NOT Bankers."

To be sure, the Ninth Symphony, like any cultural work, is not immune to the risks of conformism and propagandistic misuse. The Ninth was performed in celebration of Adolf Hitler's birthday; it served as the anthem of the racist regime in Rhodesia. Stanley Kubrick, in his film *A Clockwork Orange*, portrayed perverse criminality with the Ninth as its ideological container, as a trigger for evil, with the intoxicated exuberance of the music bound up with destructive transgressions. Nevertheless, examination of the symphony suggests reasons for its remarkable resilience as an untainted affirmative symbol. Joy is a precondition for the social cohesion, the vision of wholeness that sustains the choral finale. As the recitative passages and recall of earlier movements make clear, the finale's message is balanced against those contrasting modalities. Its message does not remain blind to human suffering. A joyless individual who must "steal away," in the words of Schiller's second stanza, is not thereby banished and excluded, but remains free at some later point to join the circle of joy. Certain commentators have found the work inherently exclusionary, but its reception history tells a different story. To find militant collectivity in the choral finale, invoking the counterimage of a rejected Other as "less than human," as one writer states, is questionable; Schiller's poem envisions a not-yet-achieved harmony under joy's "gentle wing"; human striving against adversity is reflected in many political contexts in which this work has played a role. A counterimage of the Other as "less than human" relates not to the Ninth Symphony or the perspective of Schiller's Marquis de Posa, for whom the world is yet "unripe for [his] ideal," but rather to the Grand Inquisitor's chilling reprimand: "humans are just numbers." By 1795, the young Beethoven recognized that achievement of a "happy outcome" of "just *humanity*" would be difficult, "even as centuries come to pass." Historical understanding can restrain reductionistic fervor: it is a pity when humanistic caution and hope are supplanted by ideological blindness, *Freude* by *Schadenfreude*. We recall that kitsch, as a system of imitation, embodies an ethical failure, if it puts forth a false pretense, a lie. Performances of the Ninth for Hitler or in Rhodesia negated its idealistic message without invalidating its positive potential.

The vulnerability of the inclusive collectivist thrust of "Alle Menschen" has been tested against dystopian images. Several conductors have juxtaposed the choral finale with Arnold Schoenberg's *A Survivor from Warsaw*, setting Auschwitz and the Holocaust against Beethoven's utopian vision. In Michael Gielen's program from 2001, *A Survivor from Warsaw* was inserted following the first three movements and preceding the finale of the Ninth. Schoenberg's *Survivor from Warsaw* brought thereby a huge intensification of the despairing "terror fanfare" marking the threshold of the symphonic finale, a confrontation paralleling some of the ways real-life situations have intersected with Beethoven's music.

During the harsh repression of the dictatorship of General Augusto Pinochet in Chile following the *coup d'état* in 1973, thousands of persons disappeared, becoming *desaparecidos* through the widespread persecution of dissidents. One survivor of imprisonment and torture was Renato Alvarado, who described the consolation and fortitude he gained through hearing the melody of Beethoven's *Ode to Joy* coming from beyond the prison walls, sung by protesting women seeking their missing relatives. Alvarado's experience paralleled the plight of Florestan in Beethoven's dungeon scene. He heard the feminine voices in the distance, promising deliverance from his ordeal, whereas Florestan imagines a dialogue with the consoling oboe melody representing his absent wife Leonore, shortly before she gains access to his cell. Alvarado described how he was held and tortured in a tower, in a room with windows blocked by iron bars. Schiller's text was adapted in Spanish roughly as follows:

> Listen brother to the Song of Joy!
> The cheerful song for those who await a new day.
> Come sing, dream as you sing, live as you dream of the new sun,
> when men will be brothers again.

Alvarado felt the melody as a "colorful butterfly in our heart. It was fantastic. It was hope." One of the women who sang, her group carrying a banner proclaiming "Unidad y Solidaridad," remembered how "the song gave us the power, like a shield, to act against the military, against the dictatorship." Another person arrested concurrently with Renato Alvarado was Michelle Bachelet, who later became the president of Chile.

A short story by the Chilean-American author Ariel Dorfman, "All I Ever Have," from 2015, focuses on music as a form of resistance assuming political meaning, showing how "the singer may die but not the song." Dorfman's musician is a trumpeter—recalling the trumpet signal in *Fidelio* that is repurposed to subvert tyranny—but his melody is the *Himno a la alegria*, the protest song against Pinochet's dictatorship. In Dorfman's tale, the trumpeter faces a firing squad, because Beethoven's *Ode to Joy*, a forbidden song, had "sallied forth from his trumpet . . . at the Presidential Palace, in front of the President and all the Ministers and all the visiting dignitaries, the song had burst forth loud and clear and clean, reaching every ear, spreading through radio and television waves, into each house of the land, above and beyond the drums and horns and tympani and the blare of the military march and anthem, the sound of his trumpet swept the square and the country and drowned out any other sound."

The Kinshasa Symphony in the Congo exemplifies the role of the Ninth in another way, as a major work taken up by the astonishing ensemble founded in 1993 by Armand Diangienda, the self-trained grandson of Congolese spiritual leader and martyr Simon Kimbangu. Kimbangu spent thirty years in prison as a determined opponent of the Belgian colonialist regime; he predicted that "the black man will become white and the white man will become black." Diangienda rallied the membership of his father's church—Simon Kimbangu Kiangani's popular Kimbanguiste Church—in creating an orchestra from scratch—the Orchestre Symphonique Kimbanguiste—that has tackled compositions including Beethoven's Ninth Symphony. Kinshasa has become the third-largest city in Africa, and the world's largest French-speaking metropolis. A 2010 documentary film by Claus Wischmann and Martin Baer drew attention to the impressive dedication and resourcefulness of the members of this orchestra. More recently, since 2016, the Dar Choral Society and Orchestra led by Hekima Raymond in Dar es Salaam, Tanzania, has performed Beethoven's Ninth while promoting tolerance in the face of racial and cultural differences, involving musicians from several African nations.

Over the past century, Beethoven reception in the world's most populous nation has undergone tumultuous changes. In 1908, the Chinese author and editor Li Shutong regarded Beethoven as a "sage of music" analogous to a kind of Confucian thinker in the world of tones. Li Shutong stressed Beethoven's lofty ethical goals, drawing the interest of Chinese intellectuals, but he also devised words for numerous school songs, including some based on Beethovenian works, such as the Ninth Symphony. The first record of Chinese participation in Beethoven performance also dates from 1908, from the Foochow Easter Monday Choral Festival, when Chinese choruses sang the hymn "Sing with All the Sons of Glory" to the music from Beethoven's *Ode to Joy*. During the 1920s, Beethoven's symphonies began to be performed in China; by 1927, the centenary of the composer's death, the founding of the National Conservatory of Music in Shanghai provided an important context for engagement with Western music. While still a student at the conservatory, the composer Xian Xinghai argued that Beethoven's importance lay in his ability to confront challenges and overcome suffering, an idea that soon assumed much importance during the war against Japan beginning in 1931. In 1939, Xian composed the *Yellow River Cantata* based on the patriotic poem by Guang Weiran, which was later adapted as a piano concerto by the pianist Yin Chengzong.

Beethovenian influence during this era was conveyed through writings of the French author Romain Rolland translated into Chinese. Rolland's *Vie de Beethoven* from 1902 was first translated by Fou Lei in 1932; an improved version appeared a decade later. As Rolland stated in his preface, his *Beethoven* was written not for the sake of factual scholarship, but to depict "a song for the wounded, suffocated heart taking breath again, one who revives to thank his Savior," a formulation echoing the composer's op. 132 quartet. Beginning in 1937, Fou Lei undertook a translation of Rolland's sprawling novel *Jean Christophe*, whose title character owes much to Beethoven. In Fou's view, as he states in his translator's preface, the life of Jean Christophe reflects the suffering and tribulations of a people facing disaster, a theme acutely pertinent to the Chinese experience during the middle decades of the twentieth century. Yet another of Rolland's books is *Mahatma Gandhi* from 1924. When Gandhi visited Rolland in Switzerland in 1931, they discussed Beethoven, whom Rolland dubbed "the European Mahatma," and the French writer played an arrangement of the slow movement of the Fifth Symphony on the piano.

The year 1941 was a pivotal one in global Beethoven reception, and a time when totalitarian regimes were widely ascendant. The Axis powers overran huge areas of Europe and Asia. Although Beethoven was a German artist who spent most of his career in Austria, the propaganda machine of the National Socialist regime was not so successful in identifying him specifically with their cause. A key scene of the film *Casablanca*, directed by the Hungarian Jew Michael Curtiz and set in 1941, reflects some of these political tensions. The Nazi contingent in Rick's café singing "Die Wacht am Rhein" ("Watch on the Rhine"), a patriotic military song, is countered and drown out by a spirited rendition of the *Marseillaise* including refugees from France and led by Victor

Laszlo, the resistance leader. Their show of resistance is seized upon by the Nazi major Heinrich Strasser to justify closing Rick's *Café Américain*. During this same year, a Belgian broadcaster on the BBC urged that the sign "V" be used to represent the victory of a liberation army, and "V for Victory" signs associated with the opening motive of Beethoven's Fifth Symphony were chalked widely in Europe. Three years later, the coded message (quoting Paul Verlaine's "Chanson d'Automne") signaling the D-Day invasion of Normandy, broadcast on *Radio Londres* on 6 June 1944, was itself musical: "The violins of autumn wound my heart with a monotonous languor," and was identified using the call sign based on the opening motive from Beethoven's Fifth.

After the end of the Sino-Japanese War in 1946, another significant translation appeared, of Robert Haven Schauffler's *Beethoven: The Man Who Freed Music* by Yaluo Peng. Her translation was a labor of love sustained through a difficult period of war and exile, and she recognized a link between the composer's identity as a liberator and the collective voice of Chinese society.

The crisis and disruption of the period of the Cultural Revolution from 1966 to 1976 strongly impacted the reception of Beethoven in China. After the rupture in Sino-Soviet relations in 1960, Beethoven became an object of criticism while the cultural relevance of his music was questioned: one commentator claimed in 1964 that "The Ninth Symphony is not a product of Beethoven's peak . . . Beethoven's ideals will never become our ideals today. His music will never be the voice of our times." Within the strict framework of Maoist revolutionary ideology, Beethoven was relegated to the category of Western bourgeois decadence and cultural imperialism, seen as a counter-revolutionary force, as "just the right thing for a handful of class enemies inside and outside the country." In 1966, the translator Fou Lei, who had been branded a "rightist" several years earlier, was badly mistreated and committed suicide. The conductor Lou Hongen went to his execution humming the *Missa solemnis*. Despite the ban on Western culture during the Cultural Revolution, performances of Beethoven still happened under exceptional circumstances, such as during the visit to China of the Philadelphia Orchestra led by Eugene Ormandy in 1973. The decision of which Beethoven symphony to play became contentious, with Ormandy's preference of No. 5 opposed by his Chinese hosts and especially Mao Zedong's wife, Jiang Qing, who preferred the *Pastoral* Symphony, No. 6.

A complete about-face in China's response to Beethoven occurred after Mao Zedong's death in 1976. A radio broadcast of the last two movements of Beethoven's Fifth by the Central Philharmonic in March 1977 signaled the end of a decade of turmoil and cruel ideological excess. The rehabilitation of Beethoven went hand-in-hand with the revival of older Chinese traditions, such as Confucianism, which had also been rejected during the Cultural Revolution in the name of class warfare. During the last half century, the growth of interest in Beethoven and Western classical music in China has been unprecedented, unmatched by any other country. A revival of Confucianism, 2,500 years after his lifetime, marches in step with the enthusiasm for Beethoven, who was born 250 years ago. Confucian *jen* or benevolence parallels *Humanität*. The destiny of Beethoven reception seems to obliterate any superficial distinction between Western and non-Western contexts.

Thirty years ago, during the student demonstrations at Tiananmen Square in Beijing, Beethoven again played a role. Starting in April, students gathered, tens of thousands by mid-May. Some began a hunger strike on 13 May; about a million persons occupied Tiananmen Square by the end of the month. In response, the government declared martial law starting on 20 May; soldiers entered the city. Before violence erupted, the students countered the official loudspeakers around the square by an improvised system of amplification using donated car batteries. The last occasion they broadcast Beethoven's Ninth Symphony was on 3 June. As one of the organizers recalled, "We used the Ninth to create an ambience of solidarity and hope for ourselves and for the people of China."

More recently, the Ninth has continued to serve in diverse circumstances as a symbol of the moral value of art. Yehudi Menuhin led a performance at Sarajevo in 1996; Simon Rattle conducted the symphony in memory of the victims of the Holocaust at the site of the Mauthausen concentration camp in 2000. Performances of *daiku* marked the response to the destructive tsunami in Japan in 2011. At the time of writing in November 2019, the symphony was performed during massive demonstrations in favor of social and economic reforms held at the Plaza Italia in Santiago, Chile. During the global coronavirus crisis, by March 2020, with the curtailment of public concerts, Beethoven's music has continued to resound through the internet: the Fifth and Sixth Symphonies in Philadelphia, led by Yannick Nézet-Séguin; the C minor Quartet played by the Dafne String Quartet in the opera house La Fenice in Venice. A "flash mob sonoro" ("sound flash mob") inviting all music lovers to perform the *Ode to Joy* together, to promote community in times of isolation, began in Italy and spread to Germany and beyond. The Chinese composer Tan Dun devised a new piece for the gongs and tamtams of Wuhan, where the pandemic began, promising that his "*Sound Pagoda: 12 Sounds of Wuhan* and Beethoven's *Ode to Joy* would be performed once the epidemic is over."

Is the Ninth Symphony then just "the vestige of an ever-more-distant world," a fading Enlightenment dream, or is this "effigy of the ideal" a seemingly indispensable assertion of human courage and potential, a futuristic beacon of hope?

We close by contemplating the statue of the composer erected at Bonn by a fellowship of musicians led by Franz Liszt in 1845. The monument miraculously withstood the devastation of dictatorship and war (fig. 8.6). Classically robed, like those French statues of *liberté* but with pencil in hand, the likeness of Beethoven has proven more enduring than many images of monarchs or despots. A century after the statue's unveiling, the composer's legacy had become a potent force against tyranny. More recently, it has served as a symbol of European unity, even as Brexiteers turn their backs on the *Ode to Joy*. At times of crisis, this music offers a focus for collective consolation, as individuals are sublimated as discrete entities within a larger whole. In distant parts of an increasingly interconnected global community, Beethoven's resilient response to conflict has inspired endurance, setting into motion a process that has gained momentum in our own time.

8.6 Beethoven statue from 1845 amid the ruins of war, Bonn, Münsterplatz, 1945.
Photo by Johnny Florea, private collection of William Kinderman.

Precarious political conditions enhance Beethoven's importance: "Where danger threatens, the forces of salvation increase too," as Friedrich Hölderlin once observed. Beethoven's life and art warn about the risks of the overtly political, of the backsliding of art into propaganda or kitsch, and remind us of the abiding value of the natural world as a vital force and source of inspiration. Works of art, in showing the highest human potential, display self-determination while curtailing ideological determination. They can unite what custom divides. For Beethoven, a most beautiful thing is the mysterious, which we contemplate rapt in awe. This quality is not merely a social construction. A self-reflective experience of freedom animates these works, from the Third Concerto to the Fifth Symphony, from *Fidelio* to the Ninth. Beethoven's humane legacy stands above the wreckage of history, defying politicians who build walls to divide peoples and enforce social inequality. As an antidote to cynicism, his forward-surging idealism and restless quest for insight into complexity are indispensable. His art harbors revolutionary potential. The "gentle breeze and rosy scent" of the luminous "kingdom in the air": does it make itself felt, or do we "shake [our] heads . . . completely indifferent, and stand there, groping in all directions"? Beethoven's "empire of the mind or spirit" is not merely abstract, and it cannot be revoked so long as we acknowledge, as the composer once expressed it, that "In the world of art, as in the whole of creation, freedom and progress are the main objectives."

Acknowledgments

This book began to take shape three years ago in Vienna, during my involvement with the development of the new Beethoven Museum in Heiligenstadt. I thank Matti Bunzl, the director of the Wien Museum, for suggesting the idea. The writing and completion of the book bridged my westward move from the University of Illinois at Urbana-Champaign to the University of California, Los Angeles. Both institutions generously supported my research; I'm thankful to Sam Young for his assistance in preparing the final typescript. Many friends and colleagues contributed to this project, as is partially reflected in the list of Sources and Documents; research is inevitably collaborative, and I apologize to all those whose contributions may not be explicitly cited. At the University of Chicago Press, the editorial staff and especially Caterina MacLean were unfailingly helpful during the production process. I am grateful to the Internationales Forschungszentrum Kulturwissenschaften (IFK) and the Musik und Kunst Universität (MUK) in Vienna, to the Wien Museum, to the Beethoven-Haus Bonn, to the Alexander von Humboldt Foundation in Bonn, and to the endowment from Leo M. and Elaine Krown Klein that supports my Chair of Performance Studies in the Herb Alpert School of Music at UCLA. This indispensable support enabled completion of the book with auspicious timing, a quarter millennium after Beethoven's birth.

W. K.
WESTWOOD, LOS ANGELES
MAY 2020

Illustrations and Examples

4.1 Portrait of Beethoven by Willibrord Mähler, 1804–1805 (Wien-Museum, Vienna).

4.2 Portrait of Julie von Vering by Willibrord Mähler (Wien-Museum, Vienna).

4.3 Allegory of the Good Government of Napoleon Bonaparte by Alexis Chataigner, entitled *Le Soutien de la France*, ca. 1801 (partial image authorized by the Bibliothèque nationale de France).

4.4 Statuette of Lucius Brutus once owned by Beethoven (Beethoven-Haus, Bonn, D-BNba, R 12).

4.5 The raising of the liberty tree on the marketplace at Bonn, October 1794; oil painting by François Rousseau. Bonn Stadtmuseum/Bonn City Museum, SMB 1992/103; Stadtmuseum (www.bonn.de/stadt-museum).

4.6 Thematic relations in the *Eroica* Symphony.

4.7 Climax of the *Eroica* Symphony/I, mm. 274–285.

5.1 Configuration of seven main characters in *Fidelio*.

5.2 Liberty statue with the guillotine, Place de la Révolution, Paris, ca. 1793. Painting by Pierre-Antoine Demachy: *Une execution capitale, Place de la Révolution*, Musée Carnavalet, Histoire de Paris. Wikimedia Commons.

5.3 *Appassionata* Sonata, op. 57: comparison of first and last movements.

5.4 Second theme of the *Appassionata* Sonata/I and the *Marseillaise*.

5.5a *Fidelio*, act 2: Florestan's vision of the angel of freedom.

5.5b *Fidelio*, act 2, melodrama with Florestan asleep.

5.6 Angel denigrating the king and glorifying Voltaire, Paris, 1791. Anonymous print *Journée du 21. Juin. Le Faux-pas. L'Homme immortel* from the series *La fuite à Varennes* referring to the royal flight to Varennes. Musée Carnavalet, Histoire de Paris G.26280. Used with permission © Musée Carnavalet/Roger-Viollet.

5.7 *Fidelio*, act 1, prisoners' chorus. Production directed by Christine Mielitz, Semper Oper, Dresden 1989 (Historisches Archiv der Sächsischen Staatstheater, photograph by Erwin Döring).

6.1 Poster with V for Victory and the beginning of Beethoven's Fifth Symphony, 1941. Wikimedia Commons.

6.2 Postcard by Paul Barbier showing Beethoven and Goethe accusing Hitler, 1939. Biblioteca Beethoveniana, Carrino Collection, Muggia (Trieste).

Note about
Abbreviations

BKh: *Ludwig van Beethovens Konversationshefte*, 11 vols. (Leipzig: VEB
Deutscher Verlag für Musik, 1968–2001).
Thayer-Forbes: *Thayer's Life of Beethoven*, ed. Elliot Forbes (Princeton,
NJ: Princeton University Press, 1964). TDR designates the German
edition of Thayer's biography edited by Deiters and Riemann (1866–
1917).

Sources and Documents

The quotations concerning "Something revolutionary" and Napoleon as "shithead" stem from Johann Doležalek as transmitted by Otto Jahn. See *Beethoven aus der Sicht seiner Zeitgenossen in Tagebüchern, Briefen, Gedichten und Erinnerungen*, ed. Klaus Martin Kopitz and Rainer Caden-bach (Munich 2009), vol. 1, 258; and TDR 5, 466. Doležalek's visit to the sick Beethoven on 12 February 1827 is confirmed by conversation book entries (BKh 11, 187–190). Schlesinger's conversation with Beethoven from 1825 is recorded in BKh 8, 103. On Franz's "dread of 'democracy,'" see Frida Knight, *Beethoven & The Age of Revolution* (New York: International, 1973), 33. On Franz's "institutionalized paranoia," see John J. Haag, in "Beethoven, the Revolution in Music and the French Revolution: Music and Politics in Austria, 1790–1815," in *Austria in the Age of the French Revolution, 1789–1815*, ed. Kinley Brauer and William E. Wright (Minneapolis: Center for Austrian Studies, 1990), 112. For an authoritative study of the enlightened emperor in the 1780s, see Derek Beales, *Joseph II*, vol. 2 (Cambridge: Cambridge University Press, 2009); for discussion of the "white revolution," see Alexander L. Ringer, "Mozart und der Jose-phinismus," in Ringer, *Musik als Geschichte* (Laaber: Laaber, 1993), 55–61. On the impact of Mozart's *Figaro*, see my study *Mozart's Piano Music* (New York: Oxford University Press, 2006), 150–151. Important docu-mentation of Beethoven's three-month stay at Vienna in 1787—correcting earlier scholarship—is offered by Dieter Haberl, "Beethovens erste Reise nach Wien—Die Datierung seiner Schülerreise zu W.A. Mozart," *Neues Musikwissenschaftliches Jahrbuch* 14 (2006): 215–255. For a lucid discus-sion of the "emancipation" of these composers, see Mark Evan Bonds,

"The Court of Public Opinion: Haydn, Mozart, Beethoven," in *Beethoven und andere Hofmusiker seiner Generation*, ed. Birgit Lodes, Elisabeth Reisinger, and John D. Wilson (Bonn: Beethoven-Haus, 2018), 7–24. Revisionist interpretations of Beethoven include Nicholas Mathew, *Political Beethoven* (Cambridge: Cambridge University Press, 2012); Stephen Rumpf, *Beethoven After Napoleon: Political Romanticism in the Late Works* (Berkeley: University of California Press, 2004); and Daniel K. L. Chua, *Beethoven & Freedom* (New York: Oxford University Press, 2017), respectively. For a discussion of aesthetic incomprehensibility in Beethoven, see Mark Evan Bonds, "Irony and Incomprehensibility: Beethoven's 'Serioso' String Quartet in F minor, Op. 95, and the Path to the Late Style," *Journal of the American Musicological Society* 70 (2017): 285–356; and "Beethoven, Friedrich Schlegel und der Begriff der Unverständlichkeit," in *Utopische Visionen und visionäre Kunst: Beethovens "Geistiges Reich" Revisited*, ed. William Kinderman (Vienna: Verlag der Apfel, 2017), 127–137. Beethoven's preference for "das geistige Reich" ("empire of the mind or spirit") as stated in an 1814 letter accords with Schiller's quest for "Symbolen des Vortrefflichen" ("symbols of perfection") in his *Aesthetic Letters*. A recent discussion of Eulogius Schneider is "'Denn Gehorsam ist die erste Pflicht freier Männer': Eulogius Schneider as a Paradigm for the Dialectic of Enlightenment" by Peter Höyng, in *The Radical Enlightenment in Germany: A Cultural Perspective*, ed. Carl Niekerk (Leiden and Boston: Brill Rodopi, 2018), 310–327. Another Bonn professor Beethoven would have known, Thaddeus Antonius Dereser, promoted Enlightenment theology in sharp conflict with Catholic orthodoxy, followed Schneider to Strasbourg, and was imprisoned during the Terror. See Sieghard Brandenburg, "Beethovens politische Erfahrungen in Bonn," *Beethoven Zwischen Revolution und Restauration*, ed. Helga Lühning and Sieghard Brandenburg (Bonn: Beethoven-Haus, 1989), 13–16. Georg Forster's German version of Kālidāsa's *Shakuntala* was based on the influential translation of the indefatigable William Jones; see in this regard the chapter "William Jones: Enlightenment Mughal, 1746–1794" in Sunil Khilnani, *Incarnations: A History of India in Fifty Lives* (New York: Farrar, Straus, and Giroux, 2016), 150–157. Khilnani describes Jones as "the greatest Orientalist of his time," adding that "Two hundred years later, Edward Said and his epigones would turn that word, *Oriental-*

ist, into a slur, but Jones produced a revolution in knowledge about language and history." The perspectives of Franz Wegeler appeared in *Biographische Notizen über Ludwig van Beethoven*, by Wegeler and Ferdinand Ries (Koblenz 1838; rpt. Hildesheim: Georg Olms Verlag, 2000). On revolutionary symbolism in *Fidelio*, see John Bokina, *Opera and Politics from Monteverdi to Henze* (New Haven, CT: Yale University Press, 1997), 65–85. Thomas Mann's comment about *Fidelio* in Nazi Germany stems from his *Briefe, 1937–1947*, vol. 2, ed. Erika Mann (Frankfurt: Fischer, 1961), 444. Insightful comments on Schiller's *Don Carlos* are offered in Lesley Sharpe, *Friedrich Schiller: Drama, Thought and Politics* (Cambridge: Cambridge University Press, 1991), 76–95. On Schiller's aesthetics and its political implications see, among other sources, Gail K. Hart, *Friedrich Schiller: Crime, Aesthetics, and the Poetics of Punishment* (Newark: University of Delaware Press, 2005); Frederick C. Beiser, *Schiller as Philosopher: A Re-examination* (Oxford: Clarendon, 2005); and the chapter on Schiller in Josef Chytry, *The Aesthetic State: A Quest in Modern German Thought* (Berkeley: University of California Press, 1989). The collection of essays on Schiller's *Aesthetic Letters* in *Text & Context. Zeitschrift für Germanistische Literaturforschung in Skandinavien* 28 (2006), ed. Klaus Bohnen and Birthe Hoffmann (Copenhagen and Munich: Fink Verlag), includes an essay on Schiller's pathbreaking post-Kantian notion of play, a contribution by Christian Benne ("Der peinliche Klassiker. Schiller und die Intellektuellen," 55–82). The initial sketch for the song "Wer, wer ist ein freier Mann?," WoO 117, was first transcribed by Gustav Nottebohm in his *Zweite Beethoveniana* (Leipzig: Peters, 1887), 36. Ernst Bloch's discussion of *Fidelio* is found in *Das Prinzip Hoffnung*, vol. 3 (Frankfurt: Suhrkamp, 1959), 1293–1297. Thomas Mann's *Tonio Kröger* dates from 1903, preceding his probing Schiller essay from 1905, *Schwere Stunde* (*A Weary Hour*).

CHAPTER II

For discussion of the "narcotic strength of the word 'freedom'" and the reaction against this "contagious plague" in the German lands, see among other sources Rolf Reichardt, "Deutsche Volksbewegungen im Zeichen des Pariser Bastillesturms. Ein Beitrag zum sozio-kulturellen

Transfer der Französischen Revolution," in *Geschichte und Gesellschaft, Sonderheft* 12 (1988): 10–27. Detailed information on Nikolaus Simrock appears in Joanna Cobb Biermann, "Nikolaus Simrock: Verleger," in *Das Haus Simrock. Beiträge zur Geschichte einer Kulturtragenden Familie des Rheinlandes*, ed. Ingrid Bosch (Bonn: Stadtmuseum Bonn, 2003), 11–56. Beethoven's letter to Heinrich von Struve is published in Julia Ronge, *"Wann wird auch der Zeitpunkt kommen wo es nur Menschen geben wird." Ein unbekannter Brief Beethovens an Heinrich von Struve* (Bonn: Beethoven-Haus, 2018). Andreas Streicher's description of his escape with Schiller in 1782 appeared posthumously as *Schiller's Flucht von Stuttgart und Aufenthalt in Mannheim von 1782 bis 1785* (Stuttgart: Cotta, 1836). Also see Christoph Öhm-Kühnle, *"Er weiß jeden Ton singen zu lassen." Der Musiker und Klavierbauer Johann Andreas Streicher (1761–1833)—kompositorisches Schaffen und kulturelles Wirken im biographischen Kontext. Quellen—Funktion—Analyse* (Munich: Strube, 2011). Streicher's claim about Beethoven's "revolution in music" appears in his letter of 6 April 1803 to Gottfried Härtel in Leipzig. See also Wilhelm Lütge, "Andreas und Nannette Streicher," in *Der Bär. Jahrbuch von Breitkopf & Härtel auf das Jahr 1927* (Leipzig: Breitkopf & Härtel, 1927), 53–69; and *Beethoven und die Wiener Klavierbauer Nannette und Andreas Streicher* (exhibition catalogue; Bonn: Beethoven-Haus Bonn, 1999). On Beethoven and Schiller, see Maynard Solomon, "Beethoven and Schiller," in Solomon, *Beethoven Essays* (Cambridge, MA: Harvard University Press, 1988), 205–215; and Geert Müller-Gerbes and Alexander Wolfshohl, "Beethoven liest Friedrich Schiller," in *Beethoven liest*, ed. Bernhard R. Appel and Julia Ronge (Bonn: Beethoven-Haus, 2016), 1–15. The affinity between Beethoven's early *Electoral* Sonata in F Minor and the *Pathétique* is weighed in on by Kevin Ngo, "Beethoven's Early Compositional Process: the Journey between Bonn and Vienna," *Beethoven Journal* 32 (2017): 62–68. On rhetorical models for the *Pathétique*, see Elaine R. Sisman, "Pathos and the *Pathétique*: Rhetorical Stance in Beethoven's C-Minor Sonata, Op. 13," *Beethoven Forum* 3 (1994): 81–105. Concerning Beethoven and Franz Hoffmeister, see Maynard Solomon's chapter on "Beethoven's 'Magazin der Kunst'" in his *Beethoven Essays*, 193–204. An assessment of the Shakespearean influence in Beethoven's first quartet is found in Stephen Whiting, "Beethoven Translating Shakespeare: Dra-

matic Models for the Slow Movement of the String Quartet Op. 18, No. 1,"
Journal of the American Musicological Society 71 (2018): 795–838; see also
my essay "Transformational Processes in Beethoven's Op. 18 Quartets," in
Kinderman, ed., *The String Quartets of Beethoven* (Urbana: University
of Illinois Press, 2006), 24–26. On Beethoven as "Jean Paul of music," see
Martin Geck, *Beethoven's Symphonies*, trans. Stewart Spencer (Chicago:
University of Chicago Press, 2017), 30–31. Nannette Streicher's comment
about Beethoven's laughter was recorded by Vincent Novello (*Beethoven
aus der Sicht seiner Zeitgenossen*, vol. 2, 952, 964); for Czerny's report of
his mocking laughter, see *Beethoven: Impressions of His Contemporaries*,
ed. O. G. Sonneck (New York: Schirmer, 1926), 31. The extended quotation from Jean Paul comes from the section on "humoristic totality" in
his *Vorschule der Ästhetik* (*Jean Paul Werke*, vol. 9, ed. Norbert Miller,
Hanser Verlag), 125. Comparison between Beethoven's op. 2, no. 3, with
Sterne's *Tristram Shandy* is made in my essay "Beethoven's High Comic
Style in Piano Sonatas of the 1790s, or Beethoven, Uncle Toby, and the
'Muckcart-driver,'" *Beethoven Forum* 5 (1996): 121–126. Heinrich Christoph Koch compared the concerto to Greek tragedy in his *Versuch einer
Anleitung zur Composition*, vol. 3 (Leipzig, 1793; reprinted Hildesheim,
1969), 331. The quotations about Mozart's K. 491 come from Charles
Rosen, *The Classical Style: Haydn, Mozart, Beethoven* (New York: Norton, 1997), 249; and Eva Badura-Skoda, *Wolfgang Amadeus Mozart, Kla-
vierkonzert C Moll KV 491* (Munich: Wilhelm Fink, 1972), 3, respectively.
Beethoven's use of contredance-style finale themes in concertos reaches
back to his earliest Concerto in E♭ Major, WoO 4, from 1784. For consideration of the concerto genre as a dynamic forcefield with socially encoded
meanings, see Susan McClary, "A Musical Dialectic from the Enlightenment: Mozart's *Piano Concerto in G Major, K. 453*, Movement 2," *Cultural Critique* 4 (1996): 129–169; Joseph Kerman, *Concerto Conversations*
(Cambridge, MA: Harvard University Press, 1999); and the closing chapter of my study *Mozart's Piano Music* (New York: Oxford University Press,
2006). Beethoven's C-minor Concerto underwent an extended genesis; it
was apparently played for the first time in April 1803, with Beethoven as
soloist, but aspects of the conception predated its completion by several
years. The Schiller quotation about "divined instinct" and "creative force"
stems from the ninth of his *Aesthetic Letters*. On musical processes in

Beethoven with potential external significance as actions, see Robert Hatten, "Staging Subjectivity as Spiritual Freedom: Beethoven's 'Emergent' Themes," in *Utopian Visions and Visionary Art: Beethoven's "Empire of the Mind"—Revisited*, ed. William Kinderman (Vienna: Verlag Der Apfel, 2017), 75–88; and *A Theory of Virtual Agency for Western Music* (Bloomington: Indiana University Press, 2018). On the possible connection of Beethoven's Variations on "See, the conqu'ring hero comes" to Napoleon Bonaparte, see John Clubbe, *Beethoven: The Relentless Revolutionary* (New York: Norton, 2019), 155–158; I am grateful to Clubbe for making his book available to me in advance of its publication. Beethoven wrote to Bernadotte, the king of Sweden and Norway, on 1 March 1823, recalling their meetings in 1798. The report of Bernadotte's alleged role in encouraging Beethoven to write a symphony connected to Napoleon stems from Anton Schindler, who is often an untrustworthy witness.

CHAPTER III

In November 2017, Vienna's first Beethoven Museum opened in Heiligenstadt, where the composer spent his pivotal half year in seclusion during 1802. I served as co-curator with Lisa Noggler-Gürtler and Peter Karlhuber. My edited bilingual book *Utopische Visionen und visionäre Kunst: Beethovens "Geistiges Reich" Revisited* (*Utopian Visions and Visionary Art: Beethoven's "Empire of the Mind" Revisited*) marked the advent of the museum (Vienna: Verlag Der Apfel, 2017); the *Beethoven Journal* 32 (2017) features articles about it. The original manuscript of Beethoven's *Heiligenstadt Testament* is held in the Staats- und Universitätsbibliothek in Hamburg; a facsimile edition with translations of the text into several languages was issued by the Beethoven-Haus Bonn in 1999 as *Heiligenstädter Testament*, ed. Sieghard Brandenburg. The *Heiligenstadt Testament* was first published in the *Allgemeine musikalische Zeitung* 19 (1827). For a recent personal response to Beethoven's deafness, see Robin Wallace, *Hearing Beethoven: A Story of Musical Loss & Discovery* (Chicago: University of Chicago Press, 2018). The catalogue of Beethoven's sketchbooks is *The Beethoven Sketchbooks: History, Reconstruction, Inventory* by Douglas Johnson, Alan Tyson, and Robert Winter (Berkeley: University of California Press, 1985). Beethoven's sketches for the ballet music

The Creatures of Prometheus are found in the Landsberg 7 sketchbook, an edition of which was published in 1927, ed. Karl Lothar Mikulicz (rpt. Hildesheim/New York: G. Olms, 1972). The *Kessler* Sketchbook has been published by the Beethoven-Haus, ed. Sieghard Brandenburg (facsimile 1976; transcription 1978). An edition of the *Wielhorsky* Sketchbook was published by Nathan Fishman (*Kniga eskizov Beethoven za 1802–1803 gody*, 3 vols. [Moscow, 1962]). On the chronology of Beethoven's two drafts for the first movement of the *Tempest* Sonata, see Barry Cooper's chapter on the sonata in his book *Beethoven and the Creative Process* (Oxford: Clarendon, 1990); on Beethoven's work on the Variations op. 35 using the *Kessler* and *Wielhorsky* Sketchbooks, see Christopher Reynolds, "Beethoven's Sketches for the Variations in E-flat, Op. 35," in *Beethoven Studies* 3, ed. Alan Tyson (Cambridge: Cambridge University Press, 1982), 47–84. Also see my essays "The First Movement of Beethoven's *Tempest* Sonata: Genesis, Form, and Dramatic Meaning," in *Beethoven's "Tempest" Sonata: Perspectives of Analysis and Performance*, ed. Pieter Bergé (Peeters: Leuven, 2009), 213–234; and "Beethoven at Heiligenstadt in 1802: Deconstruction, Integration, and Creativity," in *The New Beethoven: Evolution, Analysis, Interpretation*, ed. Jeremy Yudkin (Rochester: Boydell & Brewer, 2020), 148–160. Tovey's comment about Shakespeare's Miranda is found in *A Companion to Beethoven's Pianoforte Sonatas* (London: Royal Schools of Music, 1931), 121. For Czerny's reference to the rider on horseback, see his *On the Proper Performance of All Beethoven's Works for the Piano*, ed. Paul Badura-Skoda (Vienna: Universal, 1970), 44, 54. On Prospero's developing political awareness in Shakespeare's *Tempest*, with discussion of parallels to Plato's *Republic* and to Machiavelli, see Lauren Arnold, *Rule in* The Tempest: *The Political Teachings of Shakespeare's Last Play* (Ashbrook Statesmanship Thesis): https://ashbrook.org/wp-content/uploads/2012/06/2009-Arnold.pdf. Concerning the genesis of the *Eroica* Symphony, see *Beethoven's "Eroica" Sketchbook: A Critical Edition*, transcribed, edited, and with a commentary by Lewis Lockwood and Alan Gosman, 2 vols. (Urbana and Chicago: University of Illinois Press, 2013). On the chronology of this source, see Katherine Syer, "A Peculiar Hybrid: The Structure and Chronology of the 'Eroica' Sketchbook (Landsberg 6)," *Bonner Beethoven-Studien* 5 (2006): 159–181.

Thayer's interview with Mähler appears in Thayer-Forbes, 336–337. In 1815, Mähler made a second portrait of Beethoven, now held at the Gesellschaft der Musikfreunde in Vienna. Beethoven's letter to Macco dates from 2 November 1803. Owen Jander compared the hand gesture in Mähler's portrait to the depiction of the right hand of Beethoven's grandfather Ludwig van Beethoven (1712–1773) in a portrait by Leopold Radoux, a painting the composer possessed, which is now held at the Beethoven-Haus in Bonn (Jander, "Self-Portraiture and the Third Movement of the C-Minor Symphony," *Beethoven Forum* 8 [2000]: 25–70). For Mähler's comment about Beethoven's hand gesture, see Thayer-Forbes, 337. The age-old gesture of pointing as part of a visual-manual language is a focus of the 1800 study by Joseph-Marie de Gérando, *Considération sur les diverses méthodes à suivre dans l'observation des peuples sauvages*, trans. by F. C. T. Moore as *The Observation of Savage Peoples* (London: Routledge, 1969; reprinted Berkeley: University of California Press, 2021). Fletcher's discussion of "symbolic action" appears in his *Allegory: The Theory of a Symbolic Mode* (Princeton, NJ, and Oxford: Princeton University Press, 2012), 151–152. The references to Beethoven's dress and hair are found in *Beethoven: Impressions By His Contemporaries*, ed. Oscar G. Sonneck (New York: 1967; first published 1926), 21, 26. Two letters from fall 1803 from Beethoven's student Ferdinand Ries to Nikolaus Simrock in Bonn refer to his intended move to Paris. Ries confessed that "Beethoven will remain here at the most 1½ years. Then he will go to Paris, which makes me extremely sorry," and "Beethoven is to receive the libretto for his opera soon. After that he plans to leave." The letters are cited in Erich H. Müller, "Beethoven und Simrock," *N. Simrock Jahrbuch* 2 (1929): 23–24, 27. Thomas Jefferson's comment about the "tree of liberty" comes from his letter to William Stephens Smith from 13 November 1787. For more detailed discussion of Mähler's portrait, see my essay "Beethoven and Freedom in the Age of Napoleon: Willibrord Joseph Mähler's Allegorical Portrait," in *Beethoven 7: Studien und Interpretationen*, ed. Magdalena Chrenkoff (Krakow: Akademia Muzyczna w Krakowie, 2018), 429–444. In this context, one thinks as well of the anonymous depiction of *Bonaparte Showing the Apollo Belvedere to His Deputies* (Bibliothèque

Nationale, ca. 1800); this etching shows Napoleon pointing to the famous Apollo statue, which had been brought to Paris after his Italian campaign. On the "intense dash of red," see Clubb's essay "The 'Eroica' in its artistic context: Willibrord Joseph Mähler's Portrait of Beethoven," in *Nature, Politics, and the Arts. Essays on Romantic Culture for Carl Woodring*, ed. Hermione de Almeida (Newark: University of Delaware Press, 2015), 7–36; and Clubbe, *Beethoven: The Relentless Revolutionary*, 245–246. In the German context, persons could be identified metaphorically as trees, as in Wolfram von Eschenbach's addressing assembled guests in the Wartburg as "ein stolzer Eichwald" ("a proud forest of oaks") in act 2 of Wagner's *Tannhäuser*. Jakob Haibel became Mozart's posthumous brother-in-law in 1807 when he married Sophie Weber. In his correspondence related to the allegorical ballet, Beethoven makes reference to the Italian title, *Prometeo*. His disappointment with the ballet master Viganò is expressed in a letter to Franz Anton Hoffmeister from 22 April 1801. For discussion of the playbill of the ballet, see Thomas Sipe, *Beethoven: Eroica Symphony* (Cambridge: Cambridge University Press, 1998), esp. 13. The fundamental source on the genesis of the *Eroica* Symphony is *Beethoven's "Eroica" Sketchbook: A Critical Edition*, transcribed, edited, and with a commentary by Lewis Lockwood and Alan Gosman, 2 vols. (Urbana and Chicago: University of Illinois Press, 2013). On the role of the *Wielhorsky* Sketchbook in the genesis of the *Eroica*, see Lockwood's essays in his *Beethoven: Studies of the Creative Process* (Cambridge, MA: Harvard University Press, 1992), esp. 142–143. The Promethean dimension of the *Eroica* receives attention in Paul Bertagnolli, *Prometheus in Music: Representations of the Myth in the Romantic Era* (Aldershot: Ashgate, 2007); and Constantin Floros, *Beethoven's Eroica: Thematic Studies*, trans. Ernest Bernhardt-Kabisch (Frankfurt: Peter Lang, 2013). On Napoleon's consolidation of power and use of propaganda in 1804, see Adam Zamoyski, *Napoleon: The Man Behind the Myth* (London: HarperCollins, 2019), 353–370. The 2003 BBC/Opus Arte film *Eroica: The Day That Changed Music Forever* recreates the first rehearsal of the symphony, and includes a performance conducted by John Eliot Gardiner. On the reception history of the *Eroica*, see among other sources Scott Burnham, *Beethoven Hero* (Princeton, NJ: Princeton University Press, 1995). Lack of understanding of the Prometheus symbolism has often diminished appreciation of the last two movements and the symphony as a whole. George Grove, in *Beethoven and His Nine Symphonies* (London: Oxford University Press, 1896, 80), reported that "the Finale has often been a puzzle" and cited the description of a performance in 1827 that "most properly ended with the Funeral March, omitting the other parts [meaning the Scherzo and Finale], which are entirely inconsistent with the avowed design of the composition." Beethoven's comment about keeping "the whole in view" appears in a letter to Georg Friedrich Treitschke from March 1814. The affinity of Beethoven's scherzo to the folk song is reported in Adolf Bernhard Marx, *Beethoven: Leben und Schaffen*, vol. 1 (Berlin, 1859; rpt. Hildesheim: Georg Olms, 1979), 273.

CHAPTER V

The memoirs of Jean-Nicolas Bouilly are found in *Mes recapitulations* (Paris: Louis Janet, 1837). Valuable are the studies by David Galliver, "Jean-Nicolas Bouilly (1763–1842), Successor of Sedaine," *Studies in Music* 13 (1979): 16–33; and *"Fidelio*—Fact or Fantasy?," *Studies in Music* 15 (1981): 82–92. Information on Eulogius Schneider is offered in Thayer's biography of Beethoven; documentation of Schneider's activities in Strasbourg during the Terror is preserved in the so-called "Blue Book" discussed in Erich Hartmann, *Das Blaue Buch und Sein Verfasser. Ein Beitrag zur Geschichte der Französischen Revolution in Strassburg* (Strassburg: Universitäts-Buchdruckerei von J. H. Ed. Heitz, 1911). When he left the Franciscan religious order in 1789, Eulogius Schneider became a "secular priest" with papal permission. A positive perspective on Schneider's revolutionary activities stems from Jewish tradesman Moshua Salomon, who reported that "If he had not held his hand protectively above us and defended our newly-acquired civil rights again and again, I and my Jewish co-citizens would have fared quite badly in the time of terror." Schneider's German translation of the *Marseillaise* as *Kriegs-Lied der Marseiller* appeared at Strasbourg in 1792. Also see Peter Höyng, "'Denn Gehorsam ist die erste Pflicht freier Männer': Eulogius Schneider as a Paradigm for the Dialectic of Enlightenment," in *The Radical Enlightenment in Germany: A Cultural Perspective*, ed. Carl Niekerk (Leiden and Boston: Brill Rodopi, 2018), 310–327. Regarding the *Marseillaise*, see Esteban Buch, *Beethoven's Ninth: A Political History*, trans. Richard Miller (Chicago: University of Chicago Press, 2003), 26–44. On *Fidelio* as a response to Mozart, see Edward W. Said, *On Late Style: Music and Literature against the Grain* (New York: Pantheon, 2006); and *Music at the Limits* (New York: Columbia University Press, 2008), 228–249. On the cultural context of the opera, also see Philip Gossett, "The Arias of Marzelline: Beethoven as a Composer of Opera," *Beethoven-Jahrbuch* 10 (1978/1981): 141–83; and Paul Robinson's edited volume *Ludwig van Beethoven: Fidelio* (Cambridge: Cambridge University Press, 1996). On the genesis of Beethoven's Sonata in F Minor, op. 57, see Martha Frohlich, *Beethoven's "Appassionata" Sonata* (New York: Oxford University Press, 1991). Simon Schama describes victims defiantly singing the *Marseillaise* while being taken to the guillotine in *Citizens: A Chronicle of the French Revolution* (New York: Alfred A. Knopf, 1989), 804. Johann Gottfried Seume's *Spaziergang nach Syrakus im Jahre 1802* first appeared in 1803 (rpt. Munich: Deutscher Taschenbuch Verlag, 1994). Bismarck's comment on the *Appassionata* is cited in Rudolf Huch, *Die Tragödie Bismarck: Otto von Bismarck—Sein Leben, Seine Persönlichkeit, Seine Kämpfe. Biographie* (Herrsching/Leipzig/Vienna: Deutscher Hort Verlag, 1938; rpt. Einbeck: Militaris, 2018), 32. On Lenin and Beethoven, see Frederick W. Skinner, "Lenin and Beethoven: Beyond the 'Appassionata' Affair," *Beethoven Journal* 18 (2003): 62–65. On Beethoven's revolutionary reputation in the Soviet Union around the time of the anniversary year 1927, see especially the chapter entitled "The Music of 1927: Commemorating the Tenth Anniversary of the Revolution and the Centennial of Beethoven's Death" in Amy Nelson, *Music for the Revolution: Musicians and Power in Early Soviet Russia* (University Park, PA: Pennsylvania State University Press, 2004), 185–206. On the genesis and orchestration of Florestan's vision of Leonore in the dungeon, see Michael C. Tusa, "A Little-Known Sketchbook from the Year 1814: The *Fidelio* Sketches in *Landsberg 9*, pp. 17–68," in *Von der Leonore zum Fidelio*, ed. Helga Lühning and Wolfram Steinbeck (Frankfurt: Peter Lang, 2000), 186–187, and sources cited therein. The radical print "1791" celebrating Voltaire is discussed in Joan B. Landes, *Visualizing the Nation: Gender, Representation and Revolution in Eighteenth-Century France* (Ithaca, NY: Cornell University Press, 2003), 86–88. Images of anal trumpets appear in illuminated medieval manuscripts, as in the *Mirror of History* (*Speculum historiale*) from Vincent of Beavais, and in later artworks by Hieronymous Bosch and Pieter Bruegel. In an unused version of the opening titles of the 1975 comic film *Monty Python and the Holy Grail*, the mock majesty of royal trumpets is juxtaposed with a host of anal trumpets, whose dissonant drone bears comparison to those plastic trumpets (vuvuzelas) heard in South African stadiums beginning in the 1990s. On political meanings of *Fidelio* in the context of the tradition of rescue opera, see Stephen Meyer, "Terror and Transcendence in the Operatic Prison, 1790–1815," *Journal of the American Musicological Society* 55 (2002): 477–523, esp. 513–518. Thomas Mann's comment about *Fidelio* in Nazi Germany stems from his *Briefe, 1937–1947*, vol. 2, ed. Erika Mann (Frankfurt: Fischer, 1961), 444.

CHAPTER VI

For a discussion of Beethoven's interaction with Prince Carl Lichnowsky from the beginning of his residence in Vienna, see Tia DeNora, *Beethoven and the Construction of Genius: Musical Politics in Vienna, 1792–1803* (Berkeley: University of California Press, 1995). Concerning Carl Lichnowsky in his familial context, see Leonore Gräfin Lichnowsky, "Aus der Geschichte unserer Familie," *Das Beethoven-Bildnis des Isidor Neugaß und die Familie Lichnowsky*, ed. Martin Staehelin (Bonn: Beethoven-Haus, 1983), 41–50. Lichnowsky's string quartet, which continued as the "Schuppanzigh Quartet" in later years, is discussed in Oldrich Pulkert, "Das Knabenquartett des Fürsten Lichnowsky," in *Ludwig van Beethoven im Herzen Europas*, ed. Oldrich Pulkert and Hans-Werner Küthen (Prague: České lupkové závody A.G., 2000), 452–458; the same volume contains a detailed, illustrated essay on "Beethoven und das Adelsgeschlecht Lichnowsky" by Karel Boženek based on materials from Jaroslav Čeleda (120–170); also see my edited volume *The String Quartets of Beethoven* (Urbana and Chicago: University of Illinois Press, 2006), 2, 11. Lichnowsky's generosity had limits: he sued Mozart for nonpayment of a debt related to their journey together to Berlin in 1789. Theodor von Frimmel dates Beethoven's departure from Grätz as probably late October 1806 in his article "Eine Überlieferung aus dem Jahre 1806," in *BeethovenJah-*

rbuch 1, ed. Frimmel (Munich and Leipzig: Georg Müller, 1908): 67. Eichendorff's report about Troppau is cited in Hermann Anders Krüger, *Der junge Eichendorff. Ein Beitrag zu Geschichte der Romantik* (Oppeln: Verlag von Georg Raschke, 1896): 75. Eichendorff's diary entry for 30 October 1806 (*Lubowitzer Tagebuchblätter Joseph von Eichendorffs*, ed. Alfons Nowack [Groß Stehlitz: Verlag von A. Wilpert, 1907: 48] describes their return to Lubowitz as follows: "... im Regen nach Hause, wo uns die Nachricht von Halles traurigem Schicksal wahrhaft erschütterte. Schwarze Bangigkeit" ("... in the rain going home, where the report about the sad fate of Halle truly shattered us. Black anguish"). The water stains on the autograph manuscript of Beethoven's op. 57 can be seen in *Ludwig van Beethoven: Klaviersonate "Appassionata" f moll op. 57* (Laaber: Laaber, 2011). On the rise of anti-French sentiment starting around 1806, see Karen Hagemann, "Francophobia and Patriotism: Anti-French Images and Sentiments in Prussia and Northern Germany During the Anti-Napoleonic Wars," *French History* 18 (2004): 404–425. An informative volume about Reichardt, including his contact with Immanuel Kant in his native Königsberg, is *Johann Friedrich Reichardt: Autobiographische Schriften*, ed. Günter Hartung (Halle: Mitteldeutscher Verlag, 2002). On Beethoven's December 1808 concert, see John Clubbe, "Beethoven *contra* Napoleon? The *Akademie* of December 22, 1808, and Its Aftermath," *Bonner Beethoven-Studien* 10 (2012): 33–62. An attempt at a Nazi interpretation of Beethoven's Fifth was made by Arnold Schering, who found in it a "fight for existence waged by a Volk that looks for its Führer and finally finds it." See David B. Dennis, *Beethoven in German Politics, 1870–1989* (New Haven, CT: Yale University Press, 1996), 151, 233. Perverse was the Nazi code name for their devastating bombing raid on Coventry on 14 November 1940: "Moonlight Sonata." Beethoven's sketchleaf with its notation of Martini's romance and Dalberg's *Die Aeolsharfe. Ein Allegorischer Traum* is discussed in Hans-Werner Küthen, "Ein Unbekanntes Notierungsblatt Beethovens zur 'Mondscheinsonate,'" in the aforementioned volume *Ludwig van Beethoven im Herzen Europas*, ed. Pulkert and Küthen, 438–450. A view of "Scene by the Brook" as an "imperiled paradise" stems from Raymond Knapp, "A Tale of Two Symphonies: Converging Narratives of Divine Reconciliation in Beethoven's Fifth and Sixth," *Journal of the American Musicological Society* 53 (2000): 291–343, quo-

tation on 341. Also see Sylvia Bowden, "The Theming Magpie: the Influence of Birdsong on Beethoven Motifs," *Musical Times* 149 (2008): 17–35.
The possible influence of the call of the *Goldammer* bird on the opening
of the Fifth should not be dismissed. Concerning the Beethoven Pastoral
Project as a global initiative against climate change, see the website
https://www.dw.com/en/more-than-just-a-walk-in-the-park-the-forces-
of-nature-in-beethovens-pastoral-symphony/a-41413450. Beethoven's
original annotated copy of Sturm's *Betrachtungen* is held in Berlin at the
Staatsbibliothek zu Berlin preußischer Kulturbesitz, Musikabteilung. On
Humboldt's indebtedness to Schelling and Goethe and their rejection of
any "chasm" between the Self and nature, see Andrea Wulf, *The Invention
of Nature: Alexander von Humboldt's New World* (New York: Alfred A.
Knopf, 2015), 126–130. Increased awareness of the interconnected web
of life stems from studies of fossilized microorganisms from early in the
earth's history as well as from studies of present ecosystems, such as Peter
Wohlleben, in *The Hidden Life of Trees: What They Feel, How They Communicate* (London: William Collins, 2017; first published in German,
2015), which recognizes in old-growth forests an interactive organic network. Arnold Schmitz drew attention to the relation of Beethoven's Fifth
Symphony to French Revolutionary currents in *Das romantische
Beethovenbild: Darstellung und Kritik* (Berlin and Bonn: Dümmler, 1927;
repr. 1978). Also see Peter Gülke, *Zur Neuausgabe der Sinfonie Nr. 5 von
Ludwig van Beethoven, Werk und Edition* (Leipzig: Peters, 1978), 52–53;
Rhys Jones, "Beethoven and the Sound of Revolution in Vienna, 1792–
1814," *Historical Journal* 57 (2014): 947–971; and the 2016 BBC documentary film *The Secret of Beethoven's Fifth Symphony* produced by Guy
Evans, featuring John Eliot Gardiner and the *Orchestre Révolutionnaire
et Romantique*. David Cairns writes about the symphony when performed
at Paris in 1828 that "the French were hearing their own music of the
Revolutionary period transfigured and universalized" (Cairns, *Berlioz*,
vol. 1: *The Making of an Artist* [Berkeley: University of California Press,
2000; first published 1989], 265). The connection of Beethoven's Fifth to
his deafness is weighed in Matthew Guerrieri, *The First Four Notes:
Beethoven's Fifth and the Human Imagination* (New York: Knopf, 2012),
8–12; and Owen Jander, "'Let Your Deafness No Longer Be a Secret—Even
in Art': Self-Portraiture and the Third Movement of the C-Minor Sym-

phony," *Beethoven Journal* 8 (2000): 25–70. My own more detailed discussion of the Fifth and Sixth is in *Beethoven* (Oxford: Oxford University Press, 2009), 146–153. Beethoven's complaints about "cabals and low tricks" are found in his letter to Breitkopf & Härtel dated 7 January 1809; on his conducting of the *Eroica*, see Thayer-Forbes, 410–471. August Kühles's painting "Beethoven op. 81" (referring to op. 81a) dates from around 1900. To this day, the logo of the German postal service is a *Posthorn*. Concerning irony in Beethoven's F-minor Quartet, see Mark Evan Bonds, "Irony and Incomprehensibility: Beethoven's 'Serioso' String Quartet in F minor op. 95 and the Path to the Late Style," *Journal of the American Musicological Society* 70 (2017): 285–356; and Kurt von Fischer, "'Never to Be Performed in Public': Zu Beethovens Streichquartett Op. 95," *Beethoven-Jahrbuch* 9 (1973/1977): 87–96. For more detailed discussion of the "Flea Song," see my essay "Flea Circus on the Keyboard, or Beethoven in Auerbach's Cellar: Political Satire in Beethoven," in *Blumenlese für Bernhard R. Appel* (Bonn, 2015), 55–66. Anna Pessiak-Schmerling's report appears in *Ludwig van Beethovens Leben von Alexander Wheelock Thayer*, vol. 4, ed. Hermann Deiters and Hugo Riemann (Leipzig: Breitkopf & Härtel, 1917), appendix 2, 518. For Beethoven's confession to Gleichenstein, see Thayer-Forbes, 488; regarding his encounters with Goethe, Thayer-Forbes, 537. In his memoirs, Metternich related how his antipathy to the Revolution arose from his experiences as a student in Strasbourg around 1790, just before Eulogius Schneider moved to that city. Metternich described how "from the beginning of the French Revolution I was its close observer, and subsequently became its adversary; and so I have ever remained, without having been once drawn into its whirlpool" (*Memoirs of Prince Metternich* (chapter 1: Apprenticeship), trans. Mrs. Alexander Napier (London: Bentley, 1880)). Franz Janschikh's comments about Napoleon and the "iron convictions" of "children of the Revolution" are found in BKh 1, 209–210. The quoted aphorism known as "German Greatness" ("Deutsche Größe") appears in *Schiller's Werke*, 1, ed. Robert Borberger (Berlin: G. Grote'sche Verlagsbuchhandung, 1901), 481. This aphorism was not published during Schiller's lifetime, and received no title from the poet. The nationalistic title stems from Bernhard Suphan in 1902. The history and reception of this text is discussed by Maike Oergel in "The German Identity, the German *Querelle* and the Ideal State: A

Fresh Look at Schiller's Fragment *Deutsche Größe*," in *Schiller: National Poet—Poet of Nations*, ed. Nicholas Martin (Amsterdam and New York: Rodopi, 2006), 241–255.

CHAPTER VII

The restaurant *Zum schwarzen Kameel* still exists in its historical location in the Bognergasse in Vienna's first district; its name stems from Johann Baptist Cameel, who founded the establishment in 1619. The restaurant's logo showing a black camel stems from Ferdinand Georg Waldmüller, an artist who also painted a portrait of Beethoven. The motto "To the black camel" may call to mind the Turkish siege of the city in 1683, when the Turks brought camels with their army. Bernard's entries of quotations from Schiller's *Votivtafeln* and Goethe's *Faust* are found in Bkh 1, 134. The original publication of "An die Musen" is in Schiller's edited volume *Musen-Almanach für das Jahr 1797* (Tübingen: Cotta, 1797), 156, where the entry appears in the *Tabulae votivae* as a collaboration of Goethe and Schiller. Gelinek's complaint against Beethoven is recorded in BKh 1, 339; the same conversation book from March 1820 contains Beethoven's entry of "Die Welt ist ein König" (326) and Blöchlinger's complaints about Austrian politics (346); Weber's verse about Gelinek, and Gelinek's "amusing nonsense" about Beethoven's working method as related by Tomaschek, appear in Thayer-Forbes, 139, 248–249. Curiously, "Joseph Gelinek" was used as a pseudonym cloaking the identity of the Spanish author of the murder-mystery thriller *Die 10. Symphonie Thriller*, a novel centered on Beethoven's legendary Tenth Symphony that appeared in several languages in 2009. Hermann Broch's writings on kitsch are "Notes on the Problem of Kitsch," in *Kitsch: the World of Bad Taste*, ed. Gillo Dorfles (New York: Bell), 49–76; and two essays in his *Schriften zur Literatur 2: Theorie*, ed. Paul Michael Lützeler (Frankfurt am Main: Suhrkamp, 1975). The quotations from Wolfgang Welsch stem from his *Ästhetisches Denken* (Stuttgart: Reclam, 1990), 10, 11. For Tomaschek's comments on *Wellington's Victory* and related material, see Thayer-Forbes, 565. Ludwig Misch considered the work a "masterpiece of its own genre" in his *Beethoven Studien* (Berlin: Walter de Gruyter, 1950), 153–162. For Alfred Einstein's assessment of *Wellington's Victory*, see his "Beethoven's Military Style," in his *Essays on Music* (New York: Norton, 1956), 244. Another, little-known patriotic setting by Beethoven that remained a sketch is "Österreich über alles" from 1809, a draft of which is transcribed in Leon Plantinga, "Beethoven, Napoleon, and Political Romanticism," in *The Oxford Handbook of the New Cultural History of Music*, ed. Jane F. Fulcher (New York: Oxford University Press, 2011), 488. Winkler's comments on the Congress of Vienna appear in his *Germany: The Long Road West*, vol. 1 (Oxford, 2006; first published Munich, 2000), 48, 64. Regarding Beethoven's comments to Treitschke about the "small tiny ones" (*KleinWinzigen*) and related sources, see especially Maria Rößner-Richarz, "Beethoven und der Wiener Kongress aus der Perspektive von Beethovens Briefen und Dokumenten," in *Beethoven und der Wiener Kongress (1814/15)*, ed. Berhard R. Appel, Joanna Cobb Biermann, William Kinderman, and Julia Ronge (Bonn: Beethoven-Haus, 2016), 79–118, esp. 110. "Democracy as the failure of ceremony" is an expression from Alain Badiou, *Five Lessons on Wagner* (London: Verso, 2010), 157. The police report wrongly identifies the composer as "von Beethoven" instead of "van Beethoven"; see August Fournier, *Die Geheimpolizei auf dem Wiener Kongress* (Norderstedt: Vero, 2013; first published 1913), 289; and the discussion of related issues in my essay "Beethoven and Napoleon: A Reassessment" in *Beethoven und der Wiener Kongress (1814/15)*, ed. Bernhard R. Appel, Joanna Cobb Biermann, William Kinderman and Julia Ronge (Bonn: Beethoven-Haus, 2016), 23–46. Beethoven's comment that "my kingdom is in the air" ("mein Reich is in der Luft") appears in a letter to Franz von Brunswick dated 13 February 1814. *Meine Reise zum Congress* by Weissenbach appeared in 1816 with J. B. Wallishausser in Vienna; the cited quotation about Beethoven is on 234. On the Tambora eruption and its consequences, see Gillen D'arcy Wood, *Tambora: The Eruption That Changed the World* (Princeton, NJ: Princeton University Press, 2014). Beethoven's incomplete Piano Trio in F Minor is discussed in my book *The Creative Process in Music from Mozart to Kurtág* (Urbana and Chicago: University of Illinois Press, 2012), 42–76. On Beethoven's Diabelli Variations, see my book *Beethoven's Diabelli Variations* (Oxford: Clarendon, 1987), and my essay "The Evolution of Beethoven's Diabelli Variations" in the facsimile edition of the autograph score (*Ludwig van Beethoven: 33 Variations in C Major on a waltz by Anton*

Diabelli for piano op. 120, vol. 2 [Bonn: Beethoven-Haus, 2010], 46–72). The successful Broadway play *33 Variations* by Moisés Kaufman is centered on the Diabelli Variations. For an interpretation of Diabelli's waltz as "the earthly stuff out of which the celestial is spun," see chapters 1 and 8 of Maynard Solomon, *Late Beethoven: Music, Thought, Imagination* (Berkeley: University of California Press, 2003); Solomon reflects on a "surplus of constantly renewable energy" in artistic masterpieces in his *Beethoven* (New York: Schirmer, 1977), 315. On Mauricio Kagel's "Homage from Beethoven," see Nikolaos Stavlas, "Reconstructing Beethoven: Mauricio Kagel's *Ludwig van*" (doctoral thesis, Goldsmiths, University of London, 2012), http://research.gold.ac.uk/7151/. Leonard Shlain's comments on Manet's *A Bar at the Folies-Bergère* from 1882 are found in his book *Art & Physics: Parallel Visions in Space, Time & Light* (New York: William Morrow, 1991), 435–437. More detailed discussion of the Sonata op. 111 is offered in my study *Beethoven* (New York: Oxford University Press, 2009), 251–265. Beethoven drew the Egyptian inscription from Schiller's essay "Die Sendung Moses"; Schiller took it in turn from Carl Leonhard Reinhold. See in this regard *Beethovens Glaubensbekenntnis: Drei Denksprüche aus Friedrich Schillers Aufsatz "Die Sendung Moses,"* ed. Friederike Grigat (Bonn: Beethoven-Haus, 2008); and Carl Leonhard Reinhold, *Die Hebräischen Mysterien oder die älteste religiöse Freymaurerey*, ed. Jan Assmann (Neckargemünd: Mnemosyne, 2001). On Schelling, see my study *Beethoven* (New York: Oxford University Press, 2009), 7–9, 299; and Josef Chytry, *The Aesthetic State* (Berkeley: University of California Press, 1989), 109–110, 135–147.

CHAPTER VIII

The YouTube flash-mob presentation of Beethoven's *Ode to Joy* was organized by the Banco Sabadell: https://www.youtube.com/watch?v= GBaHPND2QJg. On Beethoven's "Joy" theme as anthem of the European Union, see Caryl Clark, "Forging Identity: Beethoven's 'Ode' as European Anthem," *Critical Inquiry* 23 (1997): 789–807. Thomas Mann's reference to the "taking back" of Beethoven's Ninth appears in *Doktor Faustus: Das Leben des deutschen Tonsetzers Adrian Leverkühn, erzählt von einem Freunde* (Stockholm: Bermann-Fischer Verlag, 1948), 743; English translation by Helen Tracy Lowe-Porter (New York: Knopf, 1948), 470. Earlier studies of the sketches for the Ninth Symphony include Gustav Nottebohm, "Skizzen zur neunten Symphonie," in his *Zweite Beethoveniana: nachgelassene Aufsätze* (Leipzig: Peters, 1887), 157–192; and Sieghard Brandenburg, "Die Skizzen zur Neunten Symphonie," in *Zu Beethoven: Aufsätze und Dokumente*, 2, ed. Harry Goldschmidt (Berlin: Verlag Neue Musik, 1984), 88–129. Beethoven's spelling of the designation in his manuscript is "finale instromentale." The *De Roda* Sketchbook is held in the Beethoven-Haus Bonn and can be viewed in their digital archives: https://da.beethoven.de/sixcms/detail.php?id=15324&template=dokseite_digitales_archiv_en&_eid=&_ug=De%20Roda&_dokid=wm104&_mid=Werke%20Beethovens&suchparameter=&_seite=1–61. The despairing character of the A-minor Quartet is discussed in Joseph Kerman, *The Beethoven Quartets* (New York: Knopf, 1967); also see my essay "Beethoven's Last Quartets: Threshold to a Fourth Creative Period?," in Kinderman, ed., *The String Quartets of Beethoven* (Urbana and Chicago: University of Illinois Press, 2006), esp. 282–294. On the Sonata op. 110, see my article "Integration and Narrative Design in Beethoven's Piano Sonata in A♭ Major, Opus 110," *Beethoven Forum* 1 (1992): 111–145. The complexities of German Beethoven reception are discussed in David B. Dennis, *Beethoven in German Politics, 1870–1989* (New Haven, CT: Yale University Press, 1996). The extensive literature on the Ninth Symphony includes among other sources Heinrich Schenker, *Beethoven's Ninth Symphony: A Portrayal of Its Musical Content, with Running Commentary on Performance and Literature*, trans. John Rothgeb (New Haven, CT: Yale University Press, 1992); Nicholas Cook, *Beethoven: Symphony No. 9* (Cambridge: Cambridge University Press, 1993); David Levy, *Beethoven: The Ninth Symphony* (New York: Schirmer, 1995); Dieter Hildebrandt, *Die Neunte: Schiller, Beethoven und die Geschichte eines musikalischen Welterfolgs* (Munich and Vienna: Hanser, 2005); Alexander Rehding, *Beethoven's Symphony No. 9* (New York: Oxford University Press, 2018); Harvey Sachs, *The Ninth: Beethoven and the World in 1824* (New York: Random House, 2010); Maynard Solomon, "Beethoven's Ninth Symphony: A Search for Order," in *Beethoven Essays* (Cambridge, MA: Harvard University Press, 1988), 3–32; and notably Esteban Buch, *Beethoven's Ninth: A Political History*, trans. Richard Miller (Chicago: University of

Chicago Press, 2003). The London critic from 1825 is cited in Andreas Eichhorn, *Beethovens Neunte Symphonie. Die Geschichte ihrer Aufführung und Rezeption* (Kassel: Bärenreiter, 1993), 37. Extensive discussion of the Ninth is offered in my study *Beethoven* (New York: Oxford University Press, 2009), 289–307. Beethoven's shaping of the "Joy" theme is charted in Robert Winter, "The Sketches for the *Ode to Joy* in *Beethoven, Performers, and Critics*, ed. Winter and Bruce Carr (Detroit: Wayne State University Press, 1980), 176–214. Regarding Beethoven's Ninth in Japan, see Eddy Y. L. Yang, "The *daiku* Phenomenon: Social and Cultural Influences of Beethoven's Ninth Symphony in Japan," *Asia Europe Journal* 5 (2007): 93–114. On Beethoven and Soka Gakkai Buddhism in Japan, see Levi McLaughlin, "Faith and Practice: Bringing Religion, Music and Beethoven to Life in Soka Gakkai," *Social Science Japan Journal* 6 (2003), 161–179. The rally of the Democratic Progressive Party (DPP) in Taipei 2000 is shown in the following video, with Beethoven's "Joy" theme heard starting around 8:50: https://www.youtube.com/watch?v= bKQwOhlK5Mo. On the "Song of V" during World War II, see the website "Music and the Holocaust": http://holocaustmusic.ort.org/resistance-and-exile/french-resistance/beethovens-5th-symphony/. German conductor Wilhelm Furtwängler's dilemma in performing at Nazi ceremonies is documented in *Furtwängler: A Film* by Bradleigh Stockwell, narrated by Martin Bookspan (Wilhelm Furtwängler Society of America, 2010); also see Roger Allen, *Wilhelm Furtwängler: Art and the Politics of the Unpolitical* (Woodbridge: Boydell, 2018). Peter Tregear discusses "The Ninth after 9/11" in *Beethoven Forum* 10 (2002): 221–232. Concerning the Belgian producer Victor de Laveleye's role in using the sign "V" in 1941, see Michael Stenton, *Radio London and Resistance in Occupied Europe: British Political Warfare 1939–1943* (New York: Oxford University Press, 2000), 99. For analysis of the aesthetics of violence in Kubrick's film, taking into account Anthony Burgess's dystopian novel *A Clockwork Orange* and Schiller's text, see Peter Höyng, "Ambiguities of Violence in Beethoven's Ninth through the Eyes of Stanley Kubrick's 'A Clockwork Orange,'" *German Quarterly* 84 (2011), 159–76. For the soundtrack of Kubrick's 1971 film, Wendy Carlos (born Walter Carlos) electronically adapted and warped Beethoven's Ninth using a Moog synthesizer. Regarding "phantom causes" in revolutionary politics, see Adam Zamoyski, *Holy*

Madness: Romantics, Patriots and Revolutionaries, 1776–1871 (London: Weidenfeld & Nicolson, 1999). Recent discussion of the allegedly exclusionary second strophe of Schiller's poem is offered in James Parsons, "Beethoven, the Choral Finale, and Schiller's 'Exclusionary' Second Strophe," paper presented at the Eighth New Beethoven Research conference, Boston, October 2019; also see Parsons, "'Deine Zauber binden wieder': Beethoven, Schiller, and the Joyous Reconciliation of Opposites," *Beethoven Forum* 9 (2002): 1–53. In *Citizens: A Chronicle of the French Revolution* (New York: Alfred A. Knopf, 1989), 492–493, Simon Schama identifies anticitizens as "required outsiders" who helped shape the self-identity of the French revolutionary collective. Such exclusion is not presupposed by the envisioned community in the Ninth Symphony, despite Daniel Chua's claim that "the humanism it champions treats its Other as less than human" ("Beethoven's Other Humanism," *Journal of the American Musicological Society* 62 [2009]: 585). On the symphony's worldview as "Weltanschauungsmusik" and its performances with Schoenberg's *A Survivor of Warsaw*, see Hermann Danuser, *Weltanschauungsmusik* (Schliengen: Edition Argus, 2009), 58–91. Regarding reductionist claims based on "social construction," see Peter Kivy, *The Possessor and the Possessed: Handel, Mozart, Beethoven, and the Idea of Musical Genius* (New Haven, CT: Yale University Press, 2001), esp. 216–217. The broad popular appeal of Beethoven's "Joy" theme in Latin America was connected to its use as a *Himno a la alegria* in the 1969 hit song by Miguel Rios, arranged by Waldo de los Rios. Ariel Dorfman's short story, sketched in 1966 but completed and published in 2015, appeared in "Sounds of Solidarity," *Index on Censorship: The Global Voice of Free Expression* 44 (2015): 100–108; quotation on 107. The 2010 documentary film *Kinshasa Symphony* was directed by Martin Baer and Claus Wischmann. The performances of Beethoven's Ninth in Dar es Salaam are reported in "Beethoven comes alive in Swahili" in *The East African* (June 18, 2016), https://www.theeastafrican.co.ke/magazine/Beethoven-comes-alive-in-Swahili--/434746-3254932-10ve5boz/index.html. On Beethoven in China, see among other sources Liu Xiaolong, "From a Sage to a Musician: Beethoven in China," in *Beethoven in Context*, ed. Glenn Stanley and John Wilson (Cambridge: Cambridge University Press, 2021); Edmond Tsang Yik Man, "Beethoven in China: The Reception of Beethoven's Music and Its Political Implications, 1949–1959" (master's thesis, University of Hong Kong, 2003); Mingyuan Hu, *Fou Lei: An Insistence on Truth* (Leiden: Brill, 2017); and Banban Wu, "Beethoven's Shifting Reception in China, 1910s–1970s" (master's thesis, Duke University, 2016). In a letter first published in *The Nation* in 1931, Romain Rolland reported about Gandhi's visit that "on the last evening, after the prayers, Gandhi asked me to play him a little of Beethoven . . . I played him the Andante of the Fifth Symphony." Rolland's role as an apologist for Joseph Stalin attracted critique from the writer André Gide among others; in Gide's 1919 novella *La symphonie pastorale* (referring to Beethoven's *Pastoral* Symphony), the "blindness" of the pastor figure invites comparison to the failing Gide recognized in Rolland. Regarding events at Tiananmen Square and elsewhere, see Jindong Cai and Sheila Melvin, *Beethoven in China: How the Great Composers Became an Icon in the People's Republic* (New York: Penguin Random House, 2015); and Kerry Candaele and Greg Mitchell, *Journeys with Beethoven, and Beyond* (Sinclair Books, 2012), as well as Candaele's documentary film *Following the Ninth: In the Footsteps of Beethoven's Final Symphony*. Concerning Tan Dun's composition first performed in February 2020 in Antwerp, Belgium, in which twelve large gongs symbolize a harmonious coexistence between nature and humanity, and the affinity of the Wuhan gongs to Beethoven's *Ode to Joy*, see "Special Wuhan composition makes European debut": http://en.chinaculture.org/2020-02/24/content_1475969_2.htm. For a discussion of the Ninth as the "vestige of an ever-more-distant world," see Esteban Buch, *Beethoven's Ninth: A Political History*, 263–267. The ongoing reception history of Beethoven's Ninth as part of a new global culture reminds us that "globalization did not dissolve everything solid into the circulation of commodities," as Harry Liebersohn observes in *Music and the New Global Culture from the Great Exhibitions to the Jazz Age* (Chicago: University of Chicago Press, 2019), 261. The Hölderlin quotation, "Nah ist / und schwer zu fassen der Gott / Wo aber Gefahr ist, wächst / Das Rettende auch," stems from his hymn *Patmos* from 1803. Beethoven's statement about "freedom and progress" in "art, as in the whole of creation," appears in his letter to Archduke Rudolph from 29 July 1819.

Index